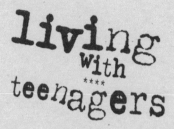

living
with
****
teenagers

Until June 2008 Anonymous was the author of the 'Living with Teenagers' column for *The Guardian*. She is the mother of three teenagers whom she loves very much. She lives with her family in London.

living
with
****
teenagers

One hell of
a bumpy ride.

headline
review

First published in 2008
by HEADLINE REVIEW
An imprint of HEADLINE PUBLISHING GROUP

First published in paperback in 2009
by HEADLINE REVIEW

2

Cataloguing in Publication Data is available from the British Library

978 0 7553 1755 4

Typeset in Aldine401 BT by Palimpsest Book Production Limited,
Grangemouth, Stirlingshire

Printed in the UK by
CPI Mackays, Chatham ME5 8TD

Headline's policy is to use papers that are natural, renewable and recyclable
products and made from wood grown in sustainable forests. The logging
and manufacturing processes are expected to conform to the environmental
regulations of the country of origin.

HEADLINE PUBLISHING GROUP
An Hachette Livre UK Company
338 Euston Road
London NW1 3BH

www.headline.co.uk
www.hachettelivre.co.uk

Acknowledgements

These columns would never have existed if Sally Weale at *The Guardian* hadn't been such an inspired and trusting (and trustworthy) editor, convincing me that it was finally time someone told the truth about life with teenagers. A big thank you to her, as well as Becky Gardiner and Steve Chamberlain on *The Guardian* family pages, who went to such great lengths to conceal our family's identity.

And I would never have dared make all of this into a book without the infinite wisdom and protection of a wonderfully secret agent who took me on out of nowhere, and her ruthlessly discreet assistant who has never blabbed. Thank you so much to them, as well as that cabal of best friends who have always known the truth and kept it to themselves. And to my darling husband, whose idea and fault all of this was. I mean the kids, not the book.

A Letter to My Teenage Children

Dear Eddie, Becca and Jack,

If, one day when you're no longer teenagers, you ever bother or dare to read this book, there are some things you should know.

I always wanted children. Maybe because I loved being a child myself, I don't know. But all my motherly instincts always seemed to be there, ready and waiting. I can't remember a time when I didn't want to take care of things, feed and stroke them, make them safe, make them happy, make them feel loved.

So I had pets (far too many). Some of them settled in and joined the family and some of them died and when they died I grieved for them, passionately. I loved my dolls, too. I'd dress and undress them and line them up on the lawn in the sunshine and bathe them in a bright-red washing-up bowl – Sindy, Sarah, Suzette and Claire. They were my babies, my earliest memory of happiness. You'll laugh because none of you, not even Becca (especially not Becca!), ever played with dolls, but to me those children were absolutely real. I remember the huge wave of responsibility and love I felt at night when I fell asleep pressing my hot seven-year-old cheek against Sindy's shiny plastic hair.

I was lucky. In my twenties, life was smooth and happy and things seemed to work out for me. I had a job I really liked and then I met your father and began to love him at a time when I was still young enough not to have to worry at all about when – or even if – my real babies would come along. Looking back, this was more of a luxury than I realised. There seemed to be so much time then – enough time for everything. I never doubted I would be a mother one day.

We didn't have much money and our jobs were constantly changing, but we were perfectly happy. So it felt absolutely right when, after being married for a couple of years, we were talking about babies and your father shrugged and said, 'What are we waiting for?' One of the things I love about your father is that he never sits around waiting for real life to start. He doesn't hesitate or make excuses. He just gets on and lives.

So you were very much wanted, all three of you. And as soon as we knew I was expecting Eddie, the first, we did all the things that all careful, excited parents-to-be do. We went to the classes, we read all the books. Your father teased me about how hard I revised, how I could have sat an advanced exam in pregnancy. Every night in bed I lay there, flicking backwards and forwards, frowning, reading all about which trimester I was in, how to breathe, how to walk, what to eat and what not to eat, trying to reconcile the strange, cold diagrams on the page with what was happening inside me.

That was you, Eddie. You were slowly taking shape inside me, cell by cell, limb by miraculous limb. The first time I felt you moving – butterfly wings snaffling in my belly – I burst into tears. Because already I knew I loved you and suddenly I realised how very much there was at stake, how much there was to lose.

I look back and think how touchingly optimistic we were, how much we trusted in our bodies, our love, luck, life. I don't remember ever being scared, or even apprehensive, about this monumental journey we were setting out on, this thing from which there was no turning back. We thought we knew exactly what we were doing and we never for one moment imagined anything could or would go wrong. But we were very young then – not a lot older than you are now, Eddie. I think if I had done all this in middle age I would have been so much more cautious, so much more afraid.

Your three births were the best moments of my life. Yes, they were messy and painful, but still in my memory they shine out as bright and uncomplicated – the kind of moments when everything suddenly comes clear. I remember a feeling of utter well-being. I was so alert and awake and alive. I remember seeing each of your faces for the first time and experiencing that full-on flood of recognition which is love.

We really liked being parents. We liked the romance of it. I think we imagined that as long as we tried to do things right – as long as we fed you good food, kept you warm and safe, held your hands, took special care of you – it would all turn out fine. So I breastfed you all for as long as I could and then researched exactly what teat and bottle to use. We washed, we sterilised, we made up formula milk in exactly the right proportions, rejected shop-bought baby food for the freshest home-cooked. Your father boiled and puréed carrots and parsnips with a look of intense satisfaction on his face. He was quite proud that, by blending it with peas and potato, he could get spinach down you. Especially you, Jack.

As you grew older, we encouraged you to take care of your teeth, bought you the right width-fitting shoes and taught you all to kick a ball and to swim (hoping to cure Becca's long-held terror of hair-washing). We got you all doing sport, delayed the purchase of a Playstation for as long as we could take the moaning, and agonised over how much TV you should watch each day. We got as many expert opinions as we could about whether Eddie should have his tonsils out, reassured Becca that it was great that she was the only girl in the basketball team, worried about how to break it to Jack that his beloved stick insects were not 'standing still' but dead.

We checked you all regularly for nits and worms and when

you had them we treated you with the least harmful, most organic and natural formula. We washed you, dried you, dealt with nappy rash, chickenpox, ear infections, projectile vomiting, nightmares and homework.

It didn't stop there. We read you books, told you stories and jokes, we watched your endless, hilariously shambolic home-rehearsed plays. We bought you Lego and Duplo and (second-hand) Brio and covered the kitchen table in newspaper so you could paint. We helped you make necklaces out of pasta and castles out of cardboard and your father endlessly changed batteries in all your various gadgets, while I sat up late making Ninja Turtle outfits out of old curtains, always with a matching one for Becca's teddy.

We tried hard to treat your growing minds with care and respect. We tried to talk openly with you about life and death and how babies are made. Working on the basis that information is always empowering, we tried to tell you honestly what the world was like, to answer your questions without either frightening you or giving you more than you could cope with. When our (elderly) dog fell down dead, we let you see and touch the body, and took it as a good sign that you immediately got bored and asked for burgers.

We took great care of you, but not (we hoped) too much care. We wanted you to be safe, but we also believed that children need to be allowed to take risks. So we vetted each space for possible danger – we knew where the ponds and biting dogs and strangers were – but still we tried hard to give you freedom and time. I knew that my own imagination had been nourished by long childhood afternoons left unsupervised in the open fields, so we tried to give you that, too, the essence of a good growing-up – the chance to explore, to make your own way, your own mistakes, to get dirty, exhilarated, straightforwardly exhausted.

We did the things, in other words, that all loving parents do. And do you know, we enjoyed every single moment. That's the eerie hypnotic spell of parenthood: that you find yourself just lapping it up – the good, the wonderful, the scary and the plain old middle-of-the-night awful. If all this sounds a little smug, then maybe it's meant to. I think we were very smug, your father and I. I think back then we thought we'd got it mostly right and at the same time managed to enjoy it too. Family life was great. You were bright, happy, delicious, naughty, funny children and we adored you. Could any parent ask for more?

And then, one by zombie one, you turned into teenagers.

How could we not have seen it coming? When you have babies, toddlers, people warn you that It All Goes By So Fast. You laugh and say I Know What You Mean. But you don't. You have no idea. You don't realise till it's too late. And it happens in a jolt, a burst, an instant. It happens on a dull October night when you're innocently chopping tomatoes for supper, wiping the counter, boiling the kettle, while your back is turned. There's no warning, no sign or clue to alert you to the fact that life is about to change completely.

One day Jack was still climbing into our bed for a morning cuddle (warm and pissy pyjamas, bliss of curly, honey-blond hair) and the next moment there he is, towering four inches above me in an open doorway, spotty and hooded and growling. One day Becca was crouched on the floor in white vest and knickers, chewing the long dark end of her plait and asking me what colour crayon she should use for the princess's hat; the next she's staring at me with narrowed, sooty eyes and asking me if I realise how much everyone hates me.

And Eddie, our calm, serious, frank, open Eddie. I still don't know where that boy went. The boy who was kind to animals, who tried hard to be good at cricket, who used to pat my hand and ask me brightly how my day had been. My first baby, my darling.

'One day he'll tell you to fuck off,' his father had joked when we brought him home from the hospital in his Moses basket and the fuzzy black curve of the top of his tiny head nearly broke my heart. I laughed. We both laughed. And then one day, of course, he did.

Sometimes I feel that the harder we try as parents, the more we are destined to get it wrong. Some days I feel that we probably did get it all wrong – that we knew nothing in those days of brown bread and carrots and Start-rite.

Sometimes, weeping at the latest insanity in our family, I can begin to think it's all pretty hopeless.

But then suddenly it's another day and it'll only take the smallest thing – a sliver of the old Ed showing through, or Becca caught looking at me with soft eyes, or Jack struggling so hard to be reasonable that he practically implodes with the effort. And your heart lifts and you think yes, it's true what people say. It does go fast, you do lose them . . . but you also get them back. Leave the nursery window open and they fly back in eventually.

So one day, instead of fuming about whatever expletive had most recently been flung at me, I sat down and wrote about it. Writing it calmed me down. It also made me laugh. It made me see how absurd some of my expectations are, how ludicrously selfishly teenagers behave, and how much I still love and enjoy them despite all this. And it made me realise – with a sinking heart – that I know nothing. The longer I am a parent, the less I seem to know. I used to think experience counted for something, but I'm not so sure any more. As parents we are programmed (thank you, God) to forget. So each day is a new day. Into the battle. Your only reliable weapons are consistency, forgiveness and love. Out of this feeling a newspaper article, and then a column, and now this book, were born.

I've insisted on anonymity for all of us throughout. It's not because I'd mind you reading it all one day if you want to. I stand by every single word that is written here and it's all true, all done (I hope) with warmth and love. But I know that teenage life is tough enough, excruciating enough, and I don't think you need this – the attention and glare of it. It would be too embarrassing, and just by existing (I know you'd all rush to agree) I've embarrassed you enough already.

One more thing I need to tell you.

Having babies is the most transforming thing. It changes everything – every idea, every person, every shape or colour. Everything is different from that moment on, and you never get your old self back. The funny thing is, you don't even want to. All you can think of is making things OK for your child. And holding your breath and keeping all your fingers crossed and shutting your eyes and hoping things will turn out all right.

You three have frightened me, amazed me, delighted me, upset me, driven me to seriously low and high places – despair but also, definitely, ecstasy. You've been my best and worst times, you've made me laugh till I cried, and sometimes you've just made me cry. But still somehow – simply by existing – you fill me with hope. Even when we've screamed and shouted at each other in the morning, when I hear the sound of your key in the door, your gloomy little sigh as your school rucksack hits the ground, my heart jumps.

And that's it, that's all that matters. My life has been a million times bigger, better, richer and more special for having you three. You're such a gift, such a blessing, my biggest and best adventure. Nothing has made me feel so alive as being your mother, and I cannot thank you enough for this.

I love you. That's the big thing, the only unchanged thing, the big, definite unchangeable. I love you and I'll always love you – steadily, crazily, hopefully. That's the deal your father and I made when you came out of us and there's no getting out of it. To keep on loving you whatever happens, however surprising or sad or worrying or uncontrollable life turns out to be.

I know nothing at all about being a parent, except how good it feels to love you.

Eddie's Parts

Remember those long-ago days of dealing with toddlers? Guileless, smiley darlings one moment, venom-spitting monsters the next? Remember how an entirely innocent action on your part – the inadvertent suggestion of the wrong dungarees, the Weetabix milk straight from the fridge – could provoke unquenchable two-year-old fury and, in one quick second, transform a sunny morning into the black den of hell?

Well, what they never tell you is that a dozen or more years on you'll find yourself right back there in that same dark place. Except that this time there's a crucial difference: they're taller than you. And cleverer. And considerably more ruthless – only this time they can't be strapped into a pushchair or bodily carted to their rooms. This time you'll be the one sobbing helplessly, banging your head against the glass wall of their impenetrable selfishness.

When our Eddie was two and a half he was a happy boy.

But if you produced the wrong-coloured bib in the morning, his lip would wobble and, like an insufficiently electrocuted cat, he'd stiffen, throw his head right back and attempt to slide off the high chair. So either you gave in and got him the red one (it was all about fire engines) or you stuck with the lilac and fastened your safety belt. No prizes for guessing which option was favourite.

Now, a decade and a half on, here he is, seventeen furious years old, over six foot, skinny rock 'n' roll arms, hair straggling onto his shoulders. January, 7 a.m. Deepest winter. It's the first day of term and he stands on the stairs, towel round his waist, yowling.

'What's the matter, darling?' I am all motherly zen calm.

'It's this fucking bollocks, for fuck's sake, I'm so fucking sick of it. I can't go on like this.'

'Like what, sweetheart?'

'With no fucking clean underwear, that's what. Where the fuck is all my clean underwear?'

'Have you looked in your drawers?'

'Of course I fucking well have, you fucking moron. What do you take me for?'

'Well, the laundry basket is empty so are you sure there are no dirty pants on the floor of your room?'

'Oh, fuck off!'

He thumps back upstairs and I stand for a moment in the hall. It's a wintry morning, dawn struggling to squeeze itself

12

between the trees. He just told me to Fuck Off. I sprint upstairs two at a time, passing a white-faced Rebecca (fifteen) on her way down. She raises two dramatic hands in front of her face and flinches as though I'm about to assault her.

'There's food on the table,' I say, ignoring the histrionics.

I push open Eddie's door without knocking. His cat sits hunched on his bed, watching the wall as if it's TV. 'Don't you dare tell me to fuck off just because you and you alone have failed to put your underpants in the wash,' I tell him. I bend and gather no fewer than three dirty pairs off the floor.

He stares at me as though I'm a serial killer. 'I – have – no – underwear,' he says slowly.

'What do you call these?' I shake them at him.

In addition to the underwear, his floor currently boasts a light sprinkling of Rizla papers, three encrusted bowls (mustard? banana? worse?) and fifty Minidiscs. Maybe a hundred.

He continues to assess me with cool, glittery eyes. 'I really think you should calm down, you know. Listen to yourself. Are you in therapy? You should be.'

I want to slap him. I want to cry. Instead, I turn and leave the room.

His younger brother, Jack (fourteen), stumbles onto the landing in a haze of deodorant and with the punched-in-the-eyes look of someone who's formed too intense a relationship with his computer. Jack has promised he will turn over a new leaf this term and get all his school stuff ready the night before.

'What's up?' he says, seeing I look tearful. He has his mud-scuffed school bag in one hand and battered art folder in the other. I silently pray that his pen, travel pass and house keys are also in there somewhere.

'Just please go and eat some breakfast,' I tell him.

He gazes at me. 'You're scary.'

'Scary? Why?'

'I don't know. You just are.'

Downstairs I sink into a kitchen chair.

Jack sniffs the milk carton. 'You don't get it, do you?' he says.

'Get what?'

'Oh, never mind.'

When they were little, we had three pale beech chairs from Scandinavia – I'd read they were good for posture. We used to line them up in these little chairs – Eddie, Becca, Jack – and feed them vegetables, wholemeal toast, mashed fruit. When they'd finished, we lifted them down, one by one, wiped them with a clean, damp cloth we kept by the sink. Then I'd brush their teeth with special expensive paste that didn't contain fluoride. We thought we were so very clever, so loving, so in control.

I don't feel in control any more. Sometimes I feel it would be good to disappear, to walk away without stopping, drop off the edge of the world.

'Please,' I ask Jack as quietly as I can. 'I cooked you an egg. I am literally begging you to eat it.'

Jack looks down at his plate. The dog pads over with a hopeful look.

'Would you pay me?' says Jack.

I shut my eyes.

'Jack,' I say, 'all I want is for you to go to school with something inside you. All I want is for you to be well nourished.'

Rebecca, immobile and hunched in front of a piece of bread, glares at me. 'You talk like that and you expect us to be well adjusted. No wonder Ed needs to get out of his head all the time on drugs.'

My heart flips exactly as she intends it to.

Cruel and Neglectful Parenting

One time, when Eddie was about ten months old, we were in Asda, cruising the flickering fluorescent aisles. Suddenly I realised that the trail of wet I'd vaguely become aware of on the floor was coming from us. From Eddie, to be precise.

It was a hot June day and, like any sensible mother, I'd brought him out wearing just nappy and vest. But the nappy was now soaked and – for once – I'd forgotten to bring a changing bag or indeed a clean nappy. Even if I bought a pack right now, I could hardly change him on the supermarket floor. I remember the (then) excruciating choice: abandon the exhaustive trolley and take wet baby straight home. Or finish shopping as quickly as possible while pretending not to notice the incessant dripping.

In the end, since Eddie was perfectly happy, I went for the latter. And it was all OK until I came to the checkout.

''Scuse me,' said an old lady behind me as Eddie gummed a banana, blissfully unaware of his sodden state. 'Don't you know your baby needs changing?'

I blushed, laughed apologetically and said we were on our way home.

She gave me a look of keen disgust. 'That child's wet, he is, sitting there in his own filth. Call yourself a good mother?' She raised a disdainful chin and swapped queues.

Eddie is as unlikely to wet himself these days as he is to accompany me to the supermarket, but how he would leap with joy to hear such a reaction from a member of the public now. Because these days, at a vengeful seventeen, he believes himself to be the undeserved victim of outrageously cruel and neglectful parenting.

He believes it to be unforgivable of us, his parents, to want to try to get him to bed by a decent time on a school night, when All His Friends get to crash 'whenever'. He sees it as nothing short of sick and perverted that we harbour this sadistic desire to have him eat three square meals a day and refrain from ingesting a clutch of illegal and habit-forming substances. None of His Friends' Parents ever make a fuss about food, or even think of suggesting their offspring might fancy unloading the dishwasher or indeed doing anything whatsoever to lend a hand with the family chores. Not only that, but all His Friends' Parents manage to be pleasantly and unjudgementally stoned most evenings, while (amazingly) holding down responsible jobs, making sure there is plenty of fast food and Diet Coke in the fridge and being nice to their kids.

'Nice', of course, means giving those same kids money. Lots of it. Because in the end, what it boils down to is this: how can we be so downright evil as to deny him the regular, unconditional cash handouts that he sees as his basic human right? Even though he refuses to take up any of the many neighbourhood offers to earn a gobsmacking seven pounds per hour babysitting, still he is appalled at our miserliness. He says it's all very well for us to go on about earning money, because we're lucre-grabbing capitalists who measure our karmic worth in pound signs. He, on the other hand, is an Artist. He has Things To Do. Sometimes he writes poetry, sometimes he sketches. Sometimes he just walks the streets and lets his mind . . . well, drift. But how can he be expected to do it without a decent pair of Onitsuka trainers on his feet?

Interestingly, maybe even ironically, Eddie's best friend breaks all these rules. Adam – whom he's known since primary school – is polite, good-looking, well mannered and works hard at school. Adam doesn't seem to be swimming in cash; in fact, Adam did a paper round a year or so ago and sometimes goes so far as to do decorating work for his father in the holidays. Inconveniently for Eddie, Adam often seems to spend at least part of the weekend willingly doing things with his parents, and in the summer he goes away on holiday with them, apparently without having to be forced. Eddie really likes Adam and spends a great deal of time with him. But because he knows Adam is a hopeless advertisement for his cause, he's taken to rolling his eyes at the mere mention of his friend's name, giving the vague impression that he's either a lost cause or a moron, or both.

The way Adam is – polite, thoughtful, intelligent – that's how I used to think Eddie would turn out. OK, not 'think'. I was certain. When our Eddie was about two and a half, we went away for a weekend with some friends with a similar-aged child. At bedtime, Eddie had his bath and his story and went down in his cot without a murmur, only calling me back for one more kiss. (I remember that kiss – the clean warmth of bedtime Eddie, stiff-washed pyjamas, baby spit and honey hair.)

The Other Baby stayed up and sat grizzling on the sofa while his parents cooked supper. He was so tired his face kept on crumpling into angry, confused tears. But every time he was asked if he wanted to go to bed, he shouted 'No!'

(like, duhhh!) until, at eleven o'clock (yes, eleven!) he was finally carted, half wailing, half manic, to his cot.

Eddie's father and I looked at each other, shocked, happy, smug. Call that parenting? Who exactly was in charge here? Didn't kids need boundaries and lots of them? We would never let that happen to us.

Now Eddie stays up till two, three, four on a school night, phone in one hand, computer mouse in the other. Some nights he falls asleep only half undressed, teeth uncleaned, and it devastates me to discover him in the morning, in a tangle of crumb-strewn bed linen, one arm round his cat, face still lit by the blueish light from the monitor.

Yes, of course we try to get him to sleep. We beg and plead and threaten and cajole him. We talk to him like a baby and we talk to him like a man. No words have yet been coined which will make him turn his light off earlier and get some sleep. And yes, it pains me to realise that The Other Baby is probably now asleep by eleven, working hard at school, apple of his parents' eye. We don't dare ask.

Eddie says we stress him out, that we're his only problem. He says that if we really loved him, we'd give him enough money to lead his Own Life and never have to talk to us at all. 'Call yourselves parents?' he scowls. 'You should be fucking well ashamed of the way you're bringing up your kids.'

Oh, old lady in Asda, I should have listened to you.

19

Sensitive Souls

The thing you have to remember about teenagers today is they're sensitive, poetic, tortured – nothing like the dull, bourgeois losers we were at their age.

Thursday, 6.45 a.m. I push open Rebecca's door to reveal a room strewn with Kotex (thankfully unused) and crumpled copies of *Cosmopolitan* (read, re-read and re-re-read).

She moans loudly. 'Go-away-leave-me-alone-don't-touch-me-get-your-hands-off-me,' while dragging her long, dark hair across her face like a molten hijab.

'I'm not coming near you,' I assure her, gathering up the sanitary towels like so many pieces of Kingsmill. 'Please don't go back to sleep. And you shouldn't have these all over the floor. Have you got a period?'

'No! Have you?' She rolls out of bed, stands swaying for a second like a newborn colt, then collapses lavishly. Something about the way she flings her arms out among the glossies – expertly epileptic – stills all my feelings of sympathy. I notice that her toenails are painted black.

'Do you have a pain?' I ask her calmly.

'How can you be so fucking cruel?' she explodes in reply, clutching herself.

I tell her to get dressed and eat breakfast then see how she feels.

Downstairs, Eddie, canvas rucksack dangling from a

shoulder, is spreading Marmite on toast. He arranges the toast with the fastidiousness of a Ritz waiter, then takes a clean tea towel and wipes it carefully round the edge of his plate.

'I don't like shit on the plate,' he says when he sees me watching. He sniffs and drops the tea towel on the floor. 'The thing is, Mum,' he says, detaching each crust from the toast and flicking it vaguely towards the bin, 'what am I meant to do about Gran's birthday?'

'How do you mean "do"?'

'I mean,' he says, turning up the volume, 'how in fuck's name am I meant to get cash to get her something?'

'Well, let me see,' I say. 'You could rob a bank. Or you could start a multi-million-pound corporation. Or . . . you could just do a paper round like everyone else your age.'

During this speech, Rebecca staggers into the room and collapses face-down on the floor. We both ignore her.

'Do you want me to die?' she mutters. And then, when this elicits no response, 'He spent his pocket money on Guinness.'

'Fuck off,' says Ed.

'When I was your age,' I begin, 'I had a Saturday job—'

'But it was different then,' he says. 'You had no social life. And anyway how am I meant to have some time to myself to chill and do my drawings?' (Eddie plans to be the new Robert Crumb.)

Jack, who throughout this exchange has been wiping every square millimetre of his trainers clean with saliva-drenched kitchen towel, says, 'It is different, Mum. You have to admit you were quite a boring person at his age.'

'I'm sorry?'

'Well, you didn't have any friends. You were happy to work in a shop because you had no social life.'

Their father comes in ready for work. 'Swimming starts today, yes?' he asks me, referring to Becca and Jack's team sessions which he normally chauffeurs.

'No, it's next week.'

Becca sits up quickly. 'Really? Not today?'

She gets up, opens the fridge door. Her whole body has relaxed, smoothed, lengthened.

I'm in the middle of making a mental note to probe this anxiety source as soon as she's in a better mood, when she switches into attack mode. 'The thing is, Mum,' she says, swigging milk from the carton, 'Ed's right. You can't possibly compare you as a teenager with us now. It's like the way you don't know how to listen to music.'

'Yeah,' says Jack. 'Basically there's a bit more to it than just letting it go into your head and out again.'

'While trying to think up something clever to say about it,' adds Becca.

'But,' Jack says, lacing his trainers, 'it's not your fault. It's the way you are.'

'It's like a disability, I guess,' Rebecca says, with a happy smile.

'Who wants a lift to the bus stop?' asks their retreating father.

'Is he disabled, too?' I ask.

They hesitate. 'Well, he has shit taste in music but he has an iPod at least.'

After they've all gone, I start to load the dishwasher but find myself frozen in the mid-1970s. I think of the chilly bus into the centre of Leeds on a Saturday morning to my dull job at Dolcis. The lunch hours spent buying David Cassidy singles. ('You lived through Punk and you listened to *him*?!') Yes, there were long afternoons of stacking shoeboxes and measuring feet, but I did go to parties and I also wrote poetry. On the other hand, I'm pretty sure I was polite to my parents and I certainly bought everyone a birthday present.

Like they said, I was a very boring person at their age.

Jack's Underarms

'By the way,' says Jack as we settle down together to watch a recorded episode of *Morse* (a strange new craze), 'I'm getting hairs under my arms.'

'Are you, honey?'

Jack is my baby. He was born on a winter's lunchtime – a birth so exhilaratingly easy that I got up straightaway afterwards and walked around with him still moist in my arms. I'd never seen such a gloriously feral-looking baby, covered in the monkey fur they call lanugo all down his back. Adorable, dark-eyed: I could tell he was going to be nice to know.

'Yeah, just three hairs. All under one arm, actually.'

'Well, don't worry, I'm sure you'll get some under the other one soon.'

'I'm not worried. And anyway I already got pubes.'

'Pubes?'

'You know. Down there.'

I'm about to explain that it's all, in fact, called pubic hair, when the sitting-room door bangs so hard against the wall that plaster showers onto the carpet. Becca – furious-faced, kohl eyeliner halfway down her face – lurches into the room. I can't help noticing she's wearing two of my socks. Not a pair but two odd ones. Has she pinched both pairs? I decide this isn't the moment to ask.

The dog moves swiftly out of her way as she places herself in front of the TV ('Hey, fuck off,' says Jack) and turns her demon gaze on me.

'Can you please tell Him, your sweet dear little angel, not to take my portable DVD player – in fact not to *ever* go in my fucking room at all without my specific fucking permission or else I will cut off his fucking balls.'

I sigh and press PAUSE. Everyone in Oxford freezes.

'Did you do that?' I ask Jack.

He shrugs and does his blank-eyed, yob-mafia face.

'Well, did you?'

He gazes stonily ahead. Then: 'Isn't it between me and her?'

I make the mistake of considering this possibility for one nano-second too many.

Becca throws herself to the ground and seems to bite the carpet. 'I can't believe it. I simply cannot believe you're doing this!'

'Doing what?'

'Letting him get away with it! I saved up for that. For years!'

I'm trying to begin to tell her that I haven't yet even made a judgement, when real, gusty, liquid sobs issue from deep inside her.

'Becs, for goodness sake, what is it?'

Jack grabs the zapper and unpauses John Thaw. I grab it back, refreeze him.

'My God,' Becca sobs, 'can't you see how out of control he is? Call yourself a parent! You have the IQ of a fucking hamster. No wonder he's so fucking . . . remedial. Look at you both, snuggled up together. Christ.'

That's it. I stand up and switch the TV off properly. The dog also stands up. I turn to Becca.

'I am not snuggled up with him, I am not on his side and I am trying – if you will let me – to sort this out. How can I make myself any clearer?'

Becca flinches against the wall and covers her head with her hands. 'That's right, go on, hit me.'

'I'm not going to hit you, you silly girl. Why on earth would I want to hit you?' (This is a lie. Against all my better judgement, right now I would love to.)

But Becca's lying in such a strange scrunched-up position that something black and shiny is protruding from her Levis back pocket. I recognise it immediately as the Chanel lipstick I mislaid last week.

'Becca, is it true you're wearing my socks?'

'Shut up.'

'And have my best Chanel lipstick in your pocket?'

'That's right, very clever, change the subject!'

'It's just I can't see how you can accuse Jack of going into your room and taking your things if you're perfectly happy to swipe my stuff.'

Becca springs up to her full height, which is only a little less than mine. Her eyes are steady and as her hair swings I catch the rancid-sweet smell of smoke in it.

'And please tell me you haven't been smoking?' I add – a calm if reckless afterthought. That does the trick. She backs out of the room slowly as if I were on fire.

Jack puts the TV back on. 'I think that's the murderer.' He grunts happily.

'I handled that very badly,' I tell him.

'Hey, don't cry,' he says.

'I'm not crying.' I wipe my eyes on the back of my hand. 'Anyway, she's a mangy cunt.'

'Jack! I never, ever want to hear you say that again.'

'OK, OK. But . . . can I ask you something, Mum? About sex?'

I relax. 'Of course you can, sweetheart. Fire away.'

'Well, it's just . . . I heard this thing at school, right? That a woman was having sex with this guy, right? And she had this huge epileptic fit so her you-know went all tight, yeah? And they had to amputate the man's penis to get it out. I mean, otherwise he was going to die of suffocation or something and . . . and . . . I mean, could that really ever possibly happen, do you think?'

breakfast

Remember the furious toddler days, when you had to allow at least an hour to get them out of the house? Potty, wash hands, wipe faces, socks, find coats. Then – pushchair unfolded – there'd be a sudden explosion: which shoes? The red ones! No, the blue! No, the red! In less than three seconds you're in meltdown and you're sitting on the hall floor, keys in lap, as a pair of chubby legs drums a skirting board in fury.

But one day, we thought, we'll be calm middle-aged people and our kids will be teenagers and, well, life will swing by.

Now I shall relate what happened here in this house this very April morning. You can trust me that every single word is true. I wouldn't make it up. I don't need to.

27

6.50 a.m. Nice Mother stumbles along corridor to re-wake three teenagers for school. Two growl at her like coyotes parted from their carcass. One says something that sounds too much like 'Fuck off.'

6.55 a.m. Nice Mother goes downstairs and starts toasting bagels and frying eggs.

7.05 a.m. Eggs are cooked and on the table. Nice Mother yawns and stares at them.

7.10 a.m. Eggs are chilling. Nice Mother goes to stairs and calls (in a loud but uncombative voice), 'Breakfast!'

Two replies are heard. One (Ed) is definitely 'Fuck off.' The other (Becca) is simply a long, gothic scream. Nothing from Jack. Nice Mother knows this means they're coming.

7.15 a.m. Eggs have now been cooked for twelve minutes. Jack comes in and starts eating his. Without any hesitation or complaint for once. Nice Mother, stupidly encouraged, makes mistake of asking him how he slept.

7.17 a.m. Becca enters in school shirt and knickers, takes one look at egg and says: 'Don't – eat – eggs.'

Nice Mother takes a breath. 'OK,' she says. 'Have some juice, then.'

Becca folds her arms. 'You have to make me something solid.'

'Poached?'

''Nother thing with bagel. Not egg.'

'Help yourself,' says Nice Mother and (frantically pleased

28

with herself for staying calm) she walks steadily from the room.

7.31 a.m. Nice Mother dares to come back into kitchen. All children gone, getting ready for lift to school with Reasonable Father. She looks at dog. Dog looks at her. She puts egg plate on floor.

7.32 a.m. Dog happy. Another scream from Becca upstairs.

7.34 a.m. Eddie staring into the fridge.

The lift is due to leave at 7.40. Father stands in hall and rattles keys. 'Six minutes,' he says very pleasantly to Eddie.

'No need to shout,' says Ed.

Reasonable Father opens his mouth, then shuts it.

7.36 a.m. Jack runs through hall. 'Where the fuck are my gloves? Black gloves? And my blazer?' (Yes, Jack wears black woollen gloves even in late April.)

7.39 a.m. Eddie is standing in front of open fridge door and eating a fromage frais.

'OK,' says Reasonable Father, 'I'm going.'

'He's going!' Jack yells up the stairs. Becca responds with a Carrie-like screech.

'I'm not ready,' says Eddie, calmly licking his spoon.

Becca appears at the foot of the stairs, face flushed with fury. 'How dare you! I really don't have my shoes!'

'Where are my gloves, for fuck's sake?' says Jack.

Nice Mother ought to scuttle for gloves and shoes. But today something snaps in her heart. Instead she looks out of the kitchen window and notices that, even though it's only 7.40, there's sun in the garden and one tree is on the edge of bursting into blossom. Her heart lifts. She wonders what time of year you're supposed to plant potatoes.

7.41 a.m. Reasonable Father has started the car, with only Jack in it.

'Such a wanker,' says Eddie. 'Why can't he hang on for two lousy seconds?'

Becca is screaming, only drawing breath to lace her shoes.

It all happens very quickly then: Eddie opens the door and the dog, seeing his chance, runs off up the road. Nice Mother rushes – not dressed for shelf display – onto the path to call him back. Becca runs past and sees Ruthless Father's car disappearing. She gives the most chilling scream of the morning so far, throws school bag and duffle on the pavement, closely followed by self. Black hair fans over asphalt. 'No, no, no!' she cries in anguish.

Eddie walks off.

'Goodness, Becca, calm down,' says Nice Mother, because several passers-by are probably already speed-dialling Childline on their mobiles.

Then Nice Mother realises that one thing and one thing only is enabling this scene to continue: the Nice Mother. She steps inside and shuts the door. She listens with beating heart on the other side. Noise stops all but instantly. When she opens the door a minute later, the pavement is empty: Becca either abducted by aliens or gone to school. Dog re-enters house.

When, years ago, I dreamed of how life would be with teenagers, I saw myself standing in sunshine with a tall Eddie or willowy Becca or artistic Jack (little Jack!). They might be spotty or long-haired but, well, they'd be calm. And vertical. I wouldn't have to lift them or wipe them or find their clothes. It was possible, I tenderly supposed, that they'd be a tad monosyllabic. But whatever else it was, life with my grown children would involve normal people standing eye-to-eye and talking. Wouldn't it?

Eddie's Cat

When Eddie was six a neighbour's cat had kittens. We went round to visit them, a fatal thing to do.

'Look, Mummy, it really loves me,' he breathed as the small, grey, fluffy thing lay on its back in the crook of his arm and purred. Eddie's face was bright with happiness. It was the first time he'd ever sensed undiluted affection emanating from something that wasn't a parent.

That kitten – yes, of course he kept it; how on earth could we refuse him the first intense relationship of his life? – is now a rather cross, elderly cat called Nellie (named in honour of the elephant from his then-favourite but now long-forgotten Early Learning Centre song tape).

Nell sits dozing on Eddie's shoulders on weekend mornings when he's too blurry and hung-over to get up. Or hunkers down among the alarming rubbish on his bedroom floor and waits, frowning, for him to come home from school. Or – saddest of all – pads up and down, baffled and bereft, on the more and more frequent nights when he stays out later than an ageing cat can stay up.

It breaks my heart to see her on those nights. I know that emptiness all too well – the not knowing what to do with your body, your heart, your mind, until you know your boy is safely back home.

Eddie was a particularly affectionate child – compassionate, spontaneous, loving – but he doesn't seem to care very much about anyone these days. Is this normal for his age? Will it pass? Will he one day emerge from his chrysalis of cold self-absorption, a kind and loving butterfly-man? I really hope so, but the truth is I don't know.

He did have a girlfriend, briefly, last year – a leggy, blue-eyed cellist called Lulu. But I never heard him speak very nicely to her and it wasn't much of a surprise when she stopped coming round.

'He likes girls, but he can't be bothered with a girlfriend right now,' explains Becca, who, when she's not spitting in his face, is his closest confidante. 'He says it's all too much effort.'

'Effort in what sense?' I say, remembering Lulu's hennaed hair and oh-so-cool Converse sneakers.

'Well, he doesn't want to have to ring someone up all the time. He says if they want to see him, they should do the running around.'

There are a lot of things I could say to this, but instead I tell Becca I'm quite sad that he stopped seeing Lulu because I liked her.

'Oh, he still sees her,' Becca says, 'but only for sex. They're just not going out any more.'

This time I can't stop myself: 'But that's horrible!'

Becca pulls her hair down over her eyes and squints at me. 'Why?'

'He's using her. It's so . . . cold.'

'It's her choice.'

'I think it's wrong.'

'Why?'

'Because it's not a relationship.'

Becca rolls her eyes. 'Re-lay-shun-ship! Mum, get real, for fuck's sake. He has needs.'

'But . . . I'm thinking of Lulu.'

Becca laughs. 'Maybe she has needs, too.'

Just as kids – rightly – don't want to contemplate the possibility of their parents having sex, so the reverse is true. It's not that you don't want your child to have a fulfilling sexual relationship one day, but you need to think of it as exactly that: a relationship, with all the warmth and context that word implies. And though yes, of course I know that Eddie will probably sometimes want simple sex-for-sex's-sake, still I'd rather not go there.

'Anyway,' says Becca, 'I think Jack's going to have a proper girlfriend before Ed does.'

'Really? But,' I say, thinking of the box of Lego that still languishes on his bedroom floor, 'has he ever . . . kissed a girl?'

'Well, let me see,' says Becca, who's enjoying this now. 'He's snogged, yes, and he's pulled, and the other day he topped one.'

'What on earth does that mean?'

'Felt under her top, what d'you think? He reckons he's going to have sex pretty soon. Do you think he's too young?'

'At fourteen? Yes, I do,' I say, making a mental note that I need to talk to Jack.

I said Eddie doesn't care much for anyone these days. Well, it's not quite true. He does, I think, care very much about Nellie.

When she was missing the other day, he actually got out of bed before nine on a weekend to look for her. And he still holds and kisses and caresses her the way he did on that first morning long ago.

When she dies – and it can't be long now – he's going to be heartbroken. But then again maybe that's exactly what he needs: a shattered heart. Maybe it doesn't matter who does it to him first, cat or girl; he needs to experience the raw desolation that is loss. Is that a strange thing for a mother to wish on her child?

Jack's Revision

Thursday night, about eight o'clock. Jack is standing at the foot of the stairs with his hands clasped behind his back, grinning like a diplomat at a cocktail party.

'Um . . . could I possibly have a quick word with you, Mum?'

I look up from the key I'm fruitlessly trying to disentangle from its fob. I've ripped a nail. I put my finger in my mouth.

'Are you all right?' asks Jack. His face still has the full-on appeal of childhood – large eyes, wide cheekbones, small nose – but any day now it will mix itself exactly as his elder brother's did. It will turn strange and unlikely and lycanthropic. Then just as suddenly it will reshuffle itself, grow bristles and become handsome; a face to make women's hearts crash.

'I've broken my nail,' I say.

'Oh dear. Can I do anything?' The little frown, the concerned lean forwards.

'OK,' I laugh, 'what is it? What do you want?'

Jack takes a breath. He didn't want his unaccustomed sympathy spotted. 'Well, plans for this weekend, OK?'

'Hold on a moment. You've got exams starting Monday, right?'

35

'They're only small ones.'

'Small exams?'

'What I mean is . . . they're not incredibly important.'

I put down my keys and sigh. Jack's school career has always been peppered with this perky, lazy optimism. Ask him if he's been set any homework and he'll tell you yes, but only a bit, and the teacher stressed that it should take no more than half an hour. If it's art, he'll insist it's just supposed to be a sketch – 'They said we'd be doing the real work next week.'

Of course, in Jack City next week never comes. The mental space Jack inhabits is a bright and relentlessly sunny place, unclouded by homework, exams or future responsibility.

'Look,' I begin, 'I thought we talked about this. Remember: after last year, you said you'd revise properly?'

'What I was thinking' – Jack sits down on the bottom stair and gives me an earnest look – 'is I'd get up really early on Saturday, say elevenish, have my breakfast, then do a good two hours' revision . . .' He hesitates. 'Then I'll stop for lunch to watch the match—'

'What time does the match start?'

'Well, kick-off's at one.'

'And when does it end?'

'Well . . . um . . . about 3.45.'

'OK, so that's nearly three hours off. Then what?'

Jack widens his eyes. 'Then of course I'll do some more revision. Till about maybe five—'

'Just one more hour, in other words.'

Suddenly the new polite Jack shudders and morphs back into normal Jack. His shoulders collapse, his long legs crumble and tears spring to his eyes. 'What do you want from me?' he cries. 'I mean it. How much bloody revising can a normal person do?'

He springs up, dignity marred only by his jeans which, as usual, are belted so far down his thighs that his boxers are totally (and deliberately) visible – mystifying pleats of elasticised cotton puffing out of the top.

At precisely the moment when we least need him, elder brother scuffs his way down the stairs.

'Don't listen to her,' he tells Jack. 'She's a fucking capitalist maniac who only rates people by their earning power. Not everyone wants to be a Surrey accountant or City stockbroker.'

I don't remind him that he just had a birthday and all he wanted was cash.

'All I want,' I sigh, 'is for him to pass his Maths and French.'

'There's more to life than money, for fuck's sake,' sniffs Eddie, who, having finished his own exams, gets up at 4 p.m., makes coffee, spills half of it on the floor, where it joins his discarded towel and underpants, then demands ten pounds from me so he can 'Go and have some fun, for Christ's sake.'

Next, Becca's pale face is glimpsed through the banisters. 'She's been brainwashed by Him,' she says, meaning their father. 'She herself is as brainless as a ferret, but she does everything He tells her. She's His fucking parrot, don't you see?'

'Parrot or ferret? I can't be both,' I point out wearily.

'We don't all think that, Mum,' says Jack kindly.

I try to say thank you, but I can feel my nose stinging with unshed tears, so I walk away. Outside the garden is still blazing hot. At least the washing will be dry.

'Where the fuck are you going?' says Ed. 'We're talking to you.'

'Yeah,' Becca says. 'That's pretty cowardly, to walk away as soon as you're in the wrong.'

Outside the birds are calling and the sky is the colour of dust. I unpeg the washing, wonder why I feel so ganged-up-on. It's not as if these are my exams. I took mine. I drew up careful revision charts and revised even the subjects I had never understood (and duly failed them). And I'm still that same person at heart – a good girl who worries and is frightened, not of failing but of not trying. I think my children sense that and laugh at me.

A Night Out

Saturday night and Jack is at a sleepover so we offer to take Ed and Becca to a film. Maybe we'll get a Chinese afterwards. There's always something unexpectedly nice about being with just two out of your three children. Two don't outnumber you. Two remind you of how it used to feel before you got unrealistic and made another one.

Last time the grown-ups chose the film and it was *Pierrepoint*. But Ed pointed out that films about hanging weren't a bundle of laughs on a Saturday night, so this time they get to choose and it's *Down in the Valley*. The poster has a cowboy on it. 'It's supposed to be really good,' says Becca, who has put violet kohl around her eyes and is wearing one of my newer T-shirts.

As the film starts, my heart sinks. It looks like it's going to be a teen movie, all about leggy, doped-up kids going to the beach to get more doped-up. The young girl meets a guy at the gas station and they kiss in the bath. He's a bit too good to be true. Can I really take two hours of this?

Then it changes – totally. It turns into a film about a delusional young man – expertly played by Edward Norton – and his increasingly uneasy hold over this beautiful but reckless teenager who is rebelling against her dad, her life, everything. It turns out Norton was indeed too good to be true – in fact, he's a fantasist and believes (queasily, dangerously) that he's a cowboy hero straight out of the movies. And he's a little too fond of guns.

The scene where he shoots her in the stomach – in a sudden childish fit of pique because he can't get what he wants when he wants it: *pow!* – is rightly shocking and moves the film into a different key. We thought we were watching *Romeo and Juliet* and it turns out to be *Taxi Driver*. Norton's character is charismatic but ultimately terrifying and the film is a deft examination of the point where harmless eccentricity flips into madness.

That's how we see it, anyway. But, sitting in the Red Dragon afterwards, it turns out our two denim-clad babies have an entirely different take.

'He didn't mean to shoot her,' Becca says slowly, as if explaining to a five-year-old. 'He just got a bit worked up and lost his temper.'

'You can't go blaming him for one moment of losing his cool,' says Ed. 'What the dad did was much worse.'

My mouth falls open. The dad in the film is a man with a mild anger problem, definitely flawed, definitely not straight out of the good-parenting handbook (actually, one of the strengths of the film). But he loves his daughter, wants her to be safe, and sees the fantasist for what he is long before we do.

'Excuse me,' I say. 'The dad is just an ordinary man doing his best. He's far from perfect but—'

'He hit her and forced her to hide in her room,' points out Becca with a look of disgust on her face.

'There's no doubt,' says their own dad, who has been known to lose his temper on occasion, 'that he has an anger problem. But the key thing, surely, is that he shows remorse. He loses his cool and then he is sorry.'

Ed and Becca look at each other. 'Oh, come on,' says Ed. 'I think the Ed Norton character is a bit sorry to have shot her.'

'But not sorry enough to call an ambulance. He runs away.'

'He picks up the phone!' says Becca, 'There's a moment when he's about to dial.'

'And then doesn't. He legs it, happy to let her bleed to death.'

Ed shrugs. He's not worried.

Becca is pleating her napkin and frowning. 'OK, but the dad, he's really violent.'

Her father gulps. 'And shooting someone in the stomach isn't violent?'

Ed sighs and lays his hands on the table. 'That guy, what's really complex about him is, he's just a rebel. He doesn't fit in with the world the way people want him to. Is that so wrong?'

I feel the heat go to my cheeks. 'When you hurt people, yes, it is: very wrong. I'm sorry, Ed, but that guy has a world view so warped you'd have to call it madness. He's mentally unstable. He needs help. And if you can't see that, I'm actually quite worried.'

Ed swigs his Coke, unmoved. 'You see it that way, I see it another way.'

'There are no two ways of seeing it,' their father says. 'The director clearly set out to make a film about the attractiveness of a dangerously deluded person.'

41

'The thing about you guys that is so fucking annoying,' says Becca, 'is that unless people fit in with your exact idea of things, they must be insane.'

'But,' I say weakly, 'that character *was* insane.'

Becca cackles and looks at Ed, then back at me. 'You see?' she says.

And with triumph spilling out of her voice, she orders noodles with king prawns and black-bean sauce.

Inset Day

Wednesday. An inset day, so no one's at school. I slept badly because it's so hot and I'm tense because I have to go to hospital later for a scan – nothing all that scary, not really, but I hate scans, I hate hospitals and I hate gynaecological explorations.

I used not to be like this. Back when I was young and elastic and always pregnant, I thought nothing of pulling off my knickers and letting any old person take a look. Midwives, doctors, junior doctors, students – they could all go right ahead. I was so mightily proud of the way my belly swelled and curved till my navel popped out, then shrank back down again. I was scared of nothing and was pretty much in love with the whole palaver, the mysterious, magical romance of baby-hatching.

But that was then. Now the three babies are rude and

thoroughly credible hulks who feel nothing for the poor womb that rocked and nurtured them. Now I'm always tired and the periods – useless and inconvenient floods – are always heavy. Now the uterus, their sometime home, needs a scan; and could they care less?

There are peach skins and strawberry tops and grape stalks all over the kitchen counters (and floor). 'Is this you?' I ask Ed, who has recently taken to making himself a smoothie and sipping it in the sun with the latest *NME* on mornings when he doesn't have to go to school first thing.

Eddie puts his feet up on the table and yawns. 'Dunno. Maybe. I dunno.'

'Well, could you clean it up, please?'

'I've got to get on. Me and Adam might be doing something later. I might have to get to Marble Arch.'

'How does doing something with Adam, who has probably already unpacked the dishwasher for his mother this morning, prevent you from clearing up your mess?'

'Actually, Mum,' says Eddie, without moving a muscle in the direction of the hoover, 'I have a bone to pick with you.'

'Oh yes?'

'Well, yeah. You see, every evening I make sure there's enough fruit for the next day. And then you go and use it on your yoghurt. How bloody selfish is that?'

I sit down. Every corner of me seems to ache. 'Does it

ever cross your mind that you could go and buy some fruit, perhaps? Like I do.'

'Oh, I can't spend my whole life doing things for other people,' says Ed without a trace of irony.

I'd laugh but I'm too tired. 'But . . . you do nothing for other people. Not one thing. Not ever.'

Ed neatly changes tack. 'By the way,' he says, 'when're you going to get the grill fixed?'

'You mean the grill that's been broken ever since you and Becca left it on all night?'

'Yeah. It's ridiculous not to be able to make cheese on toast. Nothing works in this house. I mean, all my friends have working grills.'

I take a breath and lay my head on my hands.

'What's wrong with you?' says Becca, who has walked in, still in T-shirt and knickers. She is opening and closing the breadbin as if something might appear in it if, like Tommy Cooper's bottles and glasses, she repeats the action often enough.

'Nothing,' I say. 'I'm just tired. I've got to go to the hospital later.'

The word 'hospital' falls into the abyss, has no effect on either of them.

'Why is there never any fucking bread?' asks Becca, piling her hair on her head and glancing sideways at herself in the mirror.

'She says she won't even get the grill fixed,' says Ed.

'Nothing fucking works in this house,' mutters Becca.

'By the way,' says Jack, who has been magnetically drawn to the mother-baiting arena, 'when do I get the fiver you promised me for tidying my room?'

'Have you tidied your room?'

'Not yet. I'm doing it this afternoon, but I wondered if you could advance me?'

I want to scream, but I don't. I stand up and take a little breath. 'OK, here we go. Jack, you don't get money till you do the job. Becca, if you want bread, put on some clothes and go and buy some. Ed, if you don't clean up that fruit mess right now that blender's going straight to the charity shop. Who the bloody hell do you think you all are?!'

I go and open the window and breathe in the summer morning air. I feel my head and wonder if I need a Nurofen. The children stand in silence for two seconds.

'What's up with her?' says Becca.

'Menopause,' says Ed.

'I'm too young for the menopause,' I growl at him. 'Sadly.'

'You're never,' pipes up Becca with the chirpy confidence of the newly fertile. 'It can easily start by your age. We did it in PSHE.'

'Mum, what is the matter?' says Jack who actually does sound as if he cares. 'You look all white in the face.'

'I'm OK,' I sigh. 'I just didn't sleep very well, that's all, and I have to go to the hospital later.'

Now Eddie looks interested. 'Which hospital? I mean, what direction are you going in? Is it anywhere near Marble Arch? Could you give me a lift?'

Eating Out

Because Becca has been marginally less rude for the past week – well, OK, six days – and because she kept her cool when Jack chucked a glass of water in her face last night, I say I'll take her out to lunch.

'I haven't eaten out in months,' she sighs, fanning through her split ends. 'It's like I've been in prison or something.'

My daughter has always been keen on new food. When she was four or five, if you asked her what she wanted for lunch she'd say, 'Legs. With minty sauce.' (This when the boys were, as they still drearily are, fixated on pasta, pasta, pizza, pasta, pasta.) Now if you ask the same question, the answer is: 'Sushi. In the place with a conveyor belt.'

She'll add this last bit with slightly narrowed eyes. As if the sucker who is offering to spend hard-earned cash on feeding her might actually try to trick her into somewhere without a rotating food dispenser. Which would be tragic, because Becca's definition of heaven is endless small tasty dishes floating perpetually past her eyes/mouth/nose.

'It makes such a difference to Dad and me when you behave maturely,' I tell her, as we wait for the crispy seaweed to loop round. 'You know when I came down the other morning and you were clearly tired but you didn't say anything nasty?'

She keeps her eyes on the conveyor belt. 'Uh-huh.'

'That was really nice. And then when Jack threw the water—'

'Fucking bastard.'

'Well, you did the right thing by not rising to it. For once.'

Becca rolls her eyes. 'I wanted to bite his face off.'

I decide to ignore the underlying psychopathy. 'But you didn't, and that's what's important. So you see, you made him look worse.'

Our noodles arrive and Becca's wordless for a moment. She unwraps her chopsticks and sniffs them reverently.

'The thing about Jack,' she says with her first mouthful, 'is he's a really horrible person.' I start to speak but she points a chopstick at me. 'Unless you and Dad get off your arses and do some parenting, you're going to wind up with a problem kid on your hands.'

Only one? I think as she pauses to ladle more noodles into her mouth, stare still fixed on the conveyor belt.

'Well, we're taking quite a tough line with him,' I begin, but Becca laughs so loudly that heads turn.

'A tough line? That's what you call it? That child is totally spoilt. He does whatever he wants.'

'It's really difficult,' I say, 'to discuss the parenting of one child with another one. Don't you see that you all feel the same way? You all think the other two are spoiled and you're the only one who gets the discipline?'

She blinks at me over her chopsticks and I can tell she doesn't buy it. I ask her instead what she wants for her birthday, which is in two weeks' time, and she says the best present of all would be to have a lock put on her door so she didn't have to deal with Jack.

'Or you could send him away,' she adds with a glitter in her eye.

'Send him away where?'

She shrugs. 'I don't know. Boarding school or something.'

'Your father and I will talk about the lock,' I assure her.

Four hours later, Jack comes out to help me shop, but first I buy him tea at Pret A Manger. He has a chicken salad wrap, some crisps, a bar of chocolate and lemonade. It seems a lot.

'You absolutely swear,' I say, 'that if I buy you all this now, you'll still eat supper?'

He widens his eyes, then offers to put back the lemonade and have tap water. 'To save you money.'

'It's OK,' I say, watching him unwrap the wrap very slowly as if it were about to detonate. He extracts a length of cucumber and places it to one side. Does the same with a sliver of red pepper. Wipes fingers on jeans.

'We need to talk,' I begin sternly, 'about what you did to Becca.'

He gives me a level look. 'She interrupted me.'

'For goodness sake, Jack. Chucking water in her face was an entirely aggressive act.'

'What am I meant to do?' He takes a bite of the wrap and immediately sticks a finger in his mouth, roots around, extracts another piece of cucumber.

'That's a chicken salad wrap,' I point out. 'You freely chose it. Why are you now taking all the salad out?'

'Look, Mum,' he says, 'I think you don't understand. If someone is interrupting me when I need to speak, then I gotta take some action, right?'

'Now you're sounding like a character out of the bloody *Sopranos*.'

'Language, Mum.'

'I'm telling you now. If you do that kind of thing again, you'll be grounded.'

Jack smiles.

'Don't smile. I'm serious. It's unacceptable.'

'No,' he says, 'I wasn't smiling about that. I was thinking about something I saw in a pet shop. The loveliest thing. A baby white rat. And I was wondering, if I promise not to chuck water at Becca again and if I keep it in my room and do all the clearing up of the shit and stuff, could I possibly get one?'

I shut my eyes and tell Jack that a rat is the last thing I need in my life at the moment.

He tells me I'm selfish, that I put my own needs first, that if it was Becca who'd asked for a rat, she'd be given one just like that. I reply that this is so untrue and that no child of mine is having a rat right now. He calls me a liar. I say he's horribly spoilt. He says that if he is, it's all my fault. I tell him that's probably true. We drive home in silence. And no, of course he doesn't eat his bloody supper.

Getting Home

It is 4.50 p.m. I am upstairs working and making a difficult phone call when I hear the front door slam. Something about the slam – all right, the way it makes the whole house shudder – tells me it's my Becca, home from school. I decide I didn't hear it and continue on the phone.

But after about fifteen seconds, I hear a strange bleating noise coming from the hall, as if a lamb were caught in an illegal snare. I ignore it and continue my call. Ten seconds after that comes a bleaty screech – lamb attacked by hyena? Then the sound of a body slumping – lamb carcass on floor? Then Becca's voice screaming at desperate, tearful, screaming pitch, 'Anyone heeeeeeeere?!!'

'I'm really sorry,' I apologise to the very important person at the other end of the phone, 'I'm going to have to call you back.'

When my children were very small, I loved picking them

up from school. There was something about that first sight of them emerging through the bright-blue door – grubby, dishevelled, forlorn with hunger – that stung my heart. I'd sweep them up and get them home, dish out milk and biscuits, let them unload their days. Then we'd watch some TV together. Lots of cuddling, sitting on laps. *Zaap!* and *The Sooty Show* were favourites.

There was a brief year towards the end of primary school when this routine faded. Suddenly they weren't as tired and life was exciting. There was hockey club, or pottery club, or tea at friends' houses.

But once they were all at secondary school, I reinstated it. In fact, if anything, it seemed all the more vital now they had to make their way home, weighed down by rucksacks, on the sweaty Jubilee Line. So I did what my own mum did when I was that age. I made sure I always got home from work by four o'clock. I had healthy snacks – hummus and wholemeal bread, milk, cake, fruit – at the ready and I watched with pleasure as they wolfed it down. We'd talk a bit, then back to work – me to my study, they to homework. I felt smug. It was good being a mum.

But then – when? – it drifted. Some days I couldn't get home in time. And they no longer seemed to come home all together but one by one and in different states of moodiness. Jack might say he was starving, then refuse to eat anything at all because the bananas were 'too spotty' or the bread was the 'wrong type'. Becca might march straight into the sitting room and slump, strangely and non-specifically furious, and grab the TV zapper. If I pointed out that her rucksack was still strapped to her back, she'd tell me to mind my own business and leave her alone.

Sometimes Eddie didn't come home for hours. 'We like to linger on the way home,' he said, when I asked him where he'd been.

'Linger where?'

He shrugged. 'We sit on the wall outside the newsagents and talk.'

'He means smoke,' said Becca quickly.

'Drop dead,' said Ed.

There followed a period of compulsory breath checks as they entered the house. The smell of mint was all-pervasive and worrying. I was torn between thinking a little smoking after school was probably par for the course (I never did it, but then I was a ridiculously good girl) and, well, longing for the days of hummus and plums.

Meanwhile, Becca is still screaming. To the uninitiated it sounds like someone in serious pain. You'd think she needs a doctor, quite possibly an amputation. But I know my Becca.

So I open my study door. 'Hi, darling. How's things?' I call as breezily as I can.

'It's—*aaargh!*'

'Yes?'

'Just . . . Where are you? Why the fuck is no one ever here when I get home?' This last punctuated with a single sob.

I take a breath and walk slowly downstairs. Becca is sitting awkwardly, legs akimbo, on the hall carpet as if she fell there, which she probably did. Her school tie is askew, her skirt flumped and eyes smudgy with crying.

I look at her. She looks at me.

'Well?' she glares.

'Well what?'

'What the fuck is it?' she says. 'Whaddya you want now?'

We had our children fairly young and many of my friends' kids are only just beginning to hit secondary transfer. One woman whose eldest starts in September tells me she's going to copy my routine of stopping work at four – she's self-employed – and making sure there's food on the table as soon as they get home. She says she read an article somewhere which said teenagers' growing brains are weirdly and biologically different from ours – that's why their behaviour is so skewed – and nutrition is absolutely key.

She reckons this is the key to a happy adolescence. But then so, a few years ago, did I.

Warm-weather Clothes

Becca wants to go to Camden Lock. The trouble is, it's three o'clock on Sunday, she had breakfast an hour ago, and she's been off school half the week with a strange non-specific virus.

Her father says she's perfectly fit, that she misses way too much school, that if she's physically well enough for a shopping trip, she should go upstairs and catch up on the days she bunked off.

I'm not so sure. Some of those mornings when she croaks (admittedly somewhat melodramatically), 'I feel i-i-i-i-ll. I've definitely got a temperature – feel me!' she does look very white and pasty and her forehead is either scalding hot or eerily clammy.

'Sorry to intrude with dreary old facts but it has been exceptionally hot recently,' her father points out.

Still, ever since she was a baby, Becca's been quick to get a fever. It was always Becca who crested 100°F on the thermometer, whom we had to dunk in a bath of cool water, who once got so delirious she fought a whole herd of bison off her bunk bed ('They're galloping up my legs – get them off me!'). At least in those days I could make her rest. Five-year-olds don't hassle to go to Camden at weekends.

'Are you sure you're up to it?' I ask her now from my chair in the cool shade of the garden. 'You've got to get better, get back to school. You've got your birthday cinema thing on Friday. I'm not sure you should go anywhere today, darling.'

'You don't understand,' says Becca, who stands frowning in bright sunlight. 'I'm so hot I'm burning up!'

'But, sweet-pea, it's touching thirty degrees and you're wearing tight skinny black jeans and socks and a synthetic shirt with a long-sleeved T-shirt underneath.'

She gawps at me as if I should be sectioned. 'These? They're the thinnest clothes I've got. What the fuck else am I supposed to wear?'

'Maybe take off the socks? A skirt?' her father suggests in his best sardonic public-schoolboy voice.

She stamps her foot. 'I need the socks to keep my feet from sweating, you moron!'

I decide to attack on another front. 'OK, what are you going to eat for lunch? You can't go out on an empty stomach. There's some salad from yesterday in the fridge.'

'I don't eat leftovers,' she mutters, stomping back into the house.

'I insist you eat something!' I call after her.

Five seconds later, Jack appears. He's wearing jeans, two T-shirts layered one on top of the other and a black hoodie zipped up to the chin. 'Me and Becca are going to Camden.'

I look at him. At least he's attended school all week, though he swears there's no homework.

'I tidied my room,' he says, reading my mind.

'Are you going to have some lunch before you go?'

He blinks. 'I ate a banana.'

'That's not enough.'

'I'll eat another one, then.'

'Something a bit more substantial, please.' I get up slowly from my nice comfy chair, because I need to see what Becca's doing.

'Mu-um,' says Jack. 'Calm down. We need to get going.'

In the kitchen, there's good news: Becca has decided to eat. The bad news is that she's sighing, sweating and chopping onions. A pan is coming to a dramatic boil on the stove.

'What on earth are you making?' I ask her.

'What does it look like?' she snaps at me.

'I don't know. That could be why I'm asking.'

She tips rice into the pan, scrapes the onions in to sizzle and reaches for the mince.

'You really want to cook a full hot meal now?' I ask her.

There's a moment's stillness and then she gives a wail and flumps to the floor.

'I don't know!' she cries. 'I'm too hot to think.'

I turn off the pans. 'Becca,' I say, 'you're not well. You can't possibly go out feeling like this.'

'Oh, great,' says Jack, as he sees his trip to Camden going up the spout.

Becca pounces to her feet and tosses her hair. 'I'm fine,' she says through gritted teeth. 'Getting out of this hell-house will cool me down.'

We let them go. They refuse their father's offer of a sandwich and catch the 274 into Camden, empty-stomached and wrapped for arctic conditions. I decide I am a bad mother, but what else can I do? We return to our seats in the shade.

They come home in time for supper, both in a considerably better mood.

'I'm sorry I shouted at you,' says Becca, clearing some cups from the table.

As they go to watch TV, their father puts down his wine glass and gives me a steady look. 'OK, a fiver that she'll be sick in the morning.'

'She wouldn't dare,' I tell him. 'Not after being out all afternoon.'

But then the wonderful thing about our Becca is that she's daring. She's very daring.

Holidays

For weeks they've been longing to have a chance to do nothing, begging to be left in bed, left alone, left to their own devices. And now, precisely sixty-eight hours into the school holidays, I hear Jack's voice in the hall.

'Fuck. Oh, fuck. Fuck, fuck, fuck.'

'What is it, Jacko?'

His lanky shape appears in the doorway. He blows his fringe out of his eyes.

'There's nothing to fucking do, that's all.'

I look at him. 'You mean now?'

He stares at me like a zombie. 'Yeah. I'm at such a fucking loose end!'

'Fancy unloading the dishwasher for me?'

'No.'

He moves quickly next door into the sitting room. I hear him throw himself on the sofa, trainered feet hitting the floor. I hear the yowl of Eddie's cat being pushed out of a perfectly good sleeping place (note: cats are never stuck for something to do).

'For heaven's sake,' I say, following him, 'let's think of something for you to do.'

'There's nothing,' he says, and he folds his arms and shuts his eyes.

'OK, would you and Becca like to go and see a film?' I say, weighing the cost against the potential number of hours' peace and deciding it's a bargain.

'There's nothing on,' says Jack, 'and anyway I'm not spending a single second with that warped person.'

I get a sudden flash of summer holidays in the old days – trips to the Natural History Museum, Jack still in a pushchair, Becca running up and down the long corridors in her red Start-rites. Ed would go off on his own for half an hour to explore. We'd synchronise watches: meet me under the dinosaur's tail at half past. He was always there. He had always discovered something interesting to show me.

'What?' says Jack. 'What're you thinking now?'

'Just remembering the good old days when we used to do stuff like go to the Natural History Museum.'

Jack raises himself to a sitting position, blinks at me. 'Can we go there now?'

I laugh. 'Sweetheart, that was years ago. And last time I tried to take you, when you were about twelve, you said it was boring. Well, actually you used a less nice word.'

'But,' Jack wisely points out, 'I'm older now.'

'OK,' I try. 'Why don't you and Becca go there together?'

Jack slumps down again. 'Don't want to go with her. Want to go with you.'

Becca comes in. She's carrying a large jar of Nutella, with the lid all askew, and a wooden spoon.

'Where? Go where?'

We tell her.

'I'll go,' she says, 'but only if we can have those chicken dinosaur shapes for lunch.'

'Yeah,' says Jack without a trace of irony. 'The shapes. Plus hoops on the side.'

'You think they still do them?' asks Becca.

'They must do. For all the other kids who came along after us,' says Jack forlornly, sounding for all the world like a Lost Boy who has just been catapulted out of his pram.

I take the Nutella from Becca and screw the lid back on firmly.

'Look, guys,' I say, 'if you seriously want me to take you

59

to see the dinosaurs, I will, of course I will, but it can't be today. I'm working from home today and have a report to write. If you are nice, quiet, well-behaved teenagers, maybe we can go tomorrow.'

'Yay!' shout Jack and Becca in unison.

Ed comes in (further note: not from upstairs but from the front door, having been out all night).

'Yay what?'

'Mum's taking us to the Natural History! Tomorrow! But not you,' Becca adds.

'You're way too old,' says Jack. 'You're eighteen.'

Ed stares at us all as if we're off our rockers. 'I am not too old,' he says stiffly. 'What a fucking stupid thing to say.'

'You want to come?' I ask him, amazed.

'Of course I do. Why wouldn't I? Hey, d'you think they still do dinosaur shapes for lunch?'

'Now,' says Becca, 'since we have tomorrow sorted out, I thought I'd organise today. Who would like to bake a cake with me?'

Jack raises a docile hand.

'Me,' he goes. 'I mean yes. Please. I would.'

'I can help for a bit,' says Ed, 'but I have to go at twelve.'

So they go into the kitchen, my three teenagers, my three strange children who mostly hate each other, frequently hit each other, but sometimes, even these days, startle me all over again.

60

They start blending butter and sugar, adding cocoa, lighting the oven, while chatting earnestly about Do You Remember The Earthquake? And the Volcano Section? And Will the Scariest Dinosaur Still Be There?

And I need to go and do my work but I don't – I can't. Instead I sit for a moment, baffled, the energy knocked right out of me. It makes no sense, and I don't know quite what happened just now, but it feels as if something which normally goes wrong, went right. Scary.

Sleepovers

Even as a small baby, Ed was mystifyingly promiscuous. At nine months, he would happily sleep over at any old person's house, gurgling with delight as he saw his travel-cot being set up. Anywhere and everywhere: his nan's, a friend's, a hotel – the stranger and further from home the better. People marvelled at what a versatile, secure baby we had.

But the versatile infant turned into a manically, obsessively sociable nine-, ten-, eleven-year-old. We were glad he had friends, but why did every single visit have to end in a sleepover? Why did every single friend who came to tea arrive (clearly instructed by Ed) clutching pyjamas and toothbrush?

Well, in the same way that alcoholism will skip a generation, so this mad sociability seems to have skipped a child in our household. Our middle child, Becca, is (to date) a home-loving girl whose idea of a fun Friday night is an evening in front of *The O.C.* She sees her many friends in normal ways and for normal lengths of time – cinema or a party, then home to sleep in her own bed.

But not Jack. If anything, he is even worse than his brother. Or maybe it's that, whereas Ed invited them one at a time, Jack likes to block-book.

'Is it OK if Angus and Ferdie come over on Friday?' he asks me while he's (bizarrely, diplomatically) unloading the dishwasher.

'You mean to stay?'

He shrugs. 'They'll just kind of doss down wherever.'

'So you do mean to stay?'

'Um . . . there might be Tasha and my friend Sophie, too.'

'Girls?'

'I think those are girls' names, yes.'

I ignore the ill-judged sarcasm. 'But, sweetheart, where will you all sleep?'

'We'll put some mattresses down in my room,' says Jack, whose room is the size of a matchbox.

'Five of you will never fit in there.'

'Tash might have to have Little John with her.'

'Little John?'

'Yeah. You know, her brother, the one that doesn't have any friends.'

I sit down. 'Now hold on a moment. You're saying you

want to have . . . let's see, one, two, three, four, maybe five people to stay here for the night on Friday?'

Jack inserts his fingers into a hole in his jeans and carefully rips to enlarge it.

'Don't tear your jeans.'

'They're already torn. Look, Mum, we'll all go to bed late anyway so we'll hardly sleep—'

'So you'll therefore be exhausted for cricket practice on Saturday.'

He realises his mistake. 'What I mean is, of course we'll sleep in the sense of "sleep". But, well, I mean, there's not going to be an orgy or anything.'

'Who's having an orgy?' asks his father (a little too hopefully) as he walks in.

I sigh. 'Jack seems to want to have about half a dozen people to sleep over on Friday,' I tell him.

Hot indignation crosses Jack's face. 'Not half a dozen! Five! Can't you fucking well count?'

'OK, OK.' I try to calm him.

'Though I did say Sophie might be able to bring Anna if she has nowhere else to go that night.'

'Nowhere else to go!' My voice has risen to a squeak. 'Who are these kids with nowhere to sleep?'

'They've got somewhere to sleep,' his dad points out. 'They just like sleeping together.'

'Not sex or anything,' Jack quickly adds.

'I should hope not,' I say.

'They're not coming anywhere near me,' says Becca, who has quietly slunk in. 'They smell.'

'They do not,' says Jack.

'They do. They make his room reek of food and sweat and farts.'

'Fuck you,' says Jack and moves as if to karate-chop his sister in half. She screams and throws a trainer at him.

'We've nothing against sleepovers,' their father tells them, 'except you never do any clearing up and it generates far too much work for us.'

'Last time you came asking for sheets at midnight,' I remind him.

In the middle of all of this, the set is completed: Ed comes downstairs. Jacket on, bag slung over shoulder. 'I'll see you guys,' he says.

'Where are you going?'

'Out.'

'What time will you be back?'

'Not tonight, probably.'

'But . . . where are you staying?'

'Dunno. I'll find somewhere.'

I remind Ed that he's spent the last three nights away from home and as he's hoping to go to Edinburgh next week he ought perhaps to consider spending some time at home.

'I'll think about it,' he says, without missing a beat. The front door slams.

'You want him to stay the night here but not my friends?' Jack queries.

'Well, be fair,' says his father. 'Your mother did give birth to him. And he's lived here ever since.'

Jack seems to think about this, then brightens. 'If Ed's going to Edinburgh, yeah? Well, that means his room is free. So how about I get, say, three of my closest friends to move in for a week?'

For once, even Becca bursts out laughing.

beside the sea

It's the middle of August. The cottage we've rented has white-painted floorboards, pale stripy curtains, chintzy loose-covered furniture and is within spitting distance of the sea. You can lie in bed and (just about) hear the clonking of spinnakers in the harbour. Seagulls wheel and shriek above us. You can smell salt and seaweed. London seems a million miles away. It's heaven.

But Eddie, Becca and Jack encounter something entirely different. They see a small, uncarpeted hovel in the middle of a needlessly smelly place with too many 'bloody noisy' birds. They see two weeks of enforced separation from friends, Gamestation, Camden Lock, Star Café and hanging around with nothing much to do on their adored grimy North London streets. London is a million miles away, and they think it's hell.

Our first truly panicky moment comes as we arrive and unpack the car. Becca – who has managed to carry in just one small bag before collapsing on the sofa with a pain in her arm – suddenly springs to her feet and starts caroming around the cottage. She runs in and out of every room, opening and shutting doors. She seems to be having difficulty breathing and her face is very, very white.

'What is it, sweetie? Are you OK?' I ask her.

'I am asking you for the eighth time to come help unload this car,' calls her father from outside.

But Becca's looking so seriously unwell that I tell him to hold off for a moment.

'I – just – don't – believe – it,' she says in a shaky voice.

'Don't believe what?'

'How could you do this to me?'

'Do what?'

She sinks down to the floor with her head in her hands. 'There's no fucking TV!'

I can't remember what the rental catalogue said about television. It never occurred to me to check.

'Hey, does that really matter so much?' I ask her brightly, even though I know the answer. Oh my God, do I know the answer.

She narrows her eyes and stares at me. 'I can't believe you don't care. Such a bitchy thing to do to us.'

'Look,' I say, 'we're on holiday. We'll find other stuff to do.'

But Becca's backing away from me as if I've suggested she spend a fortnight without oxygen.

'Are you completely mad?' She punches the door. 'I mean it. Have you gone out of your mind?'

'Can I please have some help unloading this car?' comes her father's semi-desperate, semi-explosive voice.

Suddenly Jack shouts from the little room at the end of the passage: 'It's OK, Becs, it's in here. Some weirdo's put it in the cupboard. There's an aerial and everything.'

All the colour comes back into Becca's face. 'Is there cable?' she asks weakly, in her can't-blame-a-girl-for-trying voice.

Ed puts a hand on her arm. 'Not sure, but there's definitely TV, I promise. OK?'

Jack is back in the room: 'I found it for her.'

Becca smiles sweetly at her brothers. It's a once-in-a-lifetime moment. Sibling solidarity. Only the possible loss of electronic stimulus could engineer this.

An hour later, we've unpacked and made a cup of tea. The three teenagers have done a full survey.

'What's that horrible smell?' (Jack, wrinkling his nose as I open the window and the salt air rushes in.)

'How the hell am I going to wash my hair?' (Becca,

surveying the Victorian claw-footed bath with no shower attachment.)

'There's no pier!' (Jack, as they troop back in from a recce of the village.)

'Isn't that nice?' I say – the tea has buoyed me up and made me feel somehow rebellious.

'Don't you realise that means there's nothing to do? Get that? N–o–t–h–i–n–g.'

His father puts his loafered feet up on the table. 'Don't worry, I'm sure you'll find something pointless to spend your money on,' he says jauntily.

They stare at us, this pale-faced, black-hooded trio like a clutch of rejects from *Lord of the Rings*. Their father and I exchange glances – we're thinking the same evil thing: they're trapped.

'Have some cake,' I say, smiling. 'Try removing your hoodies. Chill out, why don't you?'

I push the Victoria sponge towards them and pick up the paper. And I don't look at them again. Slowly Becca removes her jacket and sits down. Jack keeps his on but reaches for a slice of cake. Ed yawns and slumps on the sofa. Becca passes him cake. He takes it, thrusts it in.

I pretend to read the paper but steal a sideways glance at them. They're exhausted. No one speaks. They all eat cake and, as they chew, some of the sad, urban tightness in their faces starts to loosen.

I reckon this holiday will do them a world of good.

To be continued ...

beside the sea 2

The story so far:

Of all the tortures parents can inflict on their teenagers, the most pleasurable surely has to be the annual August ritual of keeping them out of London. Normal people might call it a welcome break from the city, from the stifling heat, from urban routine. They might even go so far as to call it a holiday. But for Eddie, Becca and Jack, two weeks trapped in an idyllic Cornish fishing village is something to be endured without grace or happiness.

That's not quite true. In the nine days we've been here, they've actually had some fun. They've hired bikes and spent hours cycling along the coastal paths. They've swum, eaten fish and chips, rented DVDs from the anarchic selection at the newsagent down the road (and expressed delight and wonder at the fact that they only cost a pound a shot).

Not only that, but there have been whole days when Jack has forgotten to wear a hoodie in the stifling heat, days when Becca has actually left her bed and ventured out into the sunshine before midday. There was even a rainy day when we came into the room to find all three of them poring over a jigsaw – and crept away quickly before the spell was broken.

There have been times when they've seemed almost relieved to have the stressful choices of urban living taken away from them.

They would rather die than admit any of this.

'It's not that I'm having such a terrible time here,' Jack generously admits as he stands shovelling tinned pasta into his mouth. 'It's just that I have stuff I need to do in London.'

I look at him. His face is tanned, the shadows are gone from under his eyes, his appetite has more or less doubled. I wonder what the 'stuff' can possibly be. I wonder if it involves Rizlas, Breezers or spray paint.

'You don't mean "need",' his father points out. 'What you mean is you have stuff you'd like to do.'

'What stuff is this, anyway?' I ask. 'You were going on about being bored when we were still in London.'

Jack paces up and down the little sitting room of our rented cottage like a much-misunderstood panther.

'Look' – he turns back to his father, exasperated – 'I need a couple of days there, that's all. That would do it. To stop me being so bloody fucking pissed off about being here.'

We tell him that using language like that only diminishes his case. And anyway there's no way we're letting him go back alone on the train to London.

'Not alone. I never said alone. I mean with Ed.'

Ah. With Ed. The issue has been further confused by the

70

fact that his older brother is about to catch a train to London en route to Edinburgh.

'Ed's going to Edinburgh,' we tell him. 'He's only changing trains in London. He's not even there for a night.'

'So I'll just go home for one night, then catch a train back here.'

'You can't possibly stay at home alone. You're fourteen years old.'

Jack rolls his eyes. 'This is pathetic. I mean, what's gonna happen? Why can't you guys trust me?'

I point out that it might have something to do with the fact that only a few days before we came on holiday, he left the bathroom tap running with the plug in. I didn't know about it until the water dripped onto my head through our bedroom ceiling.

Becca, still in her nightie, has been sitting in silence on the sofa throughout this discussion. Outside, the sun is shining and seagulls are crying.

'What you guys don't seem to understand—' she begins.

'Can't those birds ever fucking shut up?' interrupts Jack.

'One more swear word from you and I'm deducting from your allowance,' his father says.

Becca gives Jack a dark look. 'OK,' she says to Jack. 'I was going to defend you, actually. But fine, forget it.'

'I don't need to be defended by someone as moronic as you,' says Jack.

'I'm cut to the quick,' Becca says.

It's taken me a long time to learn it, but sometimes teenagers are only horrible to each other because you, the nice, loving parent, are there. Leave the room and it is all magically defused.

As living proof of this, when we get back from taking Ed to the station, Jack has a gleeful announcement: 'Guess what? We've bought some marshmallows and we're going to make a bonfire and toast them on the beach.'

'Is it OK if we take that lemonade in the fridge?' Becca asks sweetly.

'And do you have a torch?' Jack says.

'What do you need a torch for?'

'In case we have an adventure.'

We watch them go, bubbling over with excitement.

'They don't know whether they're the Osbournes or the Famous Fucking Five, do they?' observes their father.

I say he should watch his language if he wants his full allowance.

Eddie's Jeans

Eddie's clothes are not like other people's clothes.

You and I wear something, it gets dirty, we put it in the laundry basket, we wash it, maybe iron it, and – hey presto! – it's ready to wear again. Simple, yes?

Not so with our Eddie. Eddie's clothes can appear, clean

or dirty, any time, absolutely anywhere. His underpants still, after all these months, go to extraordinary lengths to evade him. They've been known to emerge from the dog's basket, the back seat of the car, have even been found stuffed behind radiators, caked in fluff and rejected, spat-out toffees.

'Mum, where the fuck have you gone and put my jeans?' he says, standing in the kitchen in T-shirt and underpants.

'Well, hello, poppet, nice to see you, too,' I say, adding that it would be hard for me to have put his jeans anywhere, since I've only just this second walked through the door.

We've been back from holiday about three minutes, but he returned from Edinburgh three days ago. Three days of Eddie alone in the house. The depressing thing is we had more confidence leaving him in charge here a couple of years ago than we have now. At fifteen or sixteen, he might have had a party, but he'd have done everything possible to clean it up, cover it up. Now he just lets the chaos unfold around him. He calls it living in the moment. I call it being scarily selfish. His father uses stronger words.

I do a brief tour to inspect the damage. The odour of sour milk is to be expected; the smell of my basil and lime room-spray is more worrying.

'You haven't been smoking in here, have you?' I ask.

'How can you even ask me that?' he says, and something about the toddler solemnity of his face makes me so want to believe him.

We continue the tour. He follows me, scratching his naked legs. His cat follows us both, mewing loudly.

'You might've at least bothered to feed your own cat,' I tell him as she gobbles the food I put down. He mutters something about her not seeming hungry.

We reach the back door. 'How long has this been like this?' I ask him.

'Like what?'

'With the key still in.'

'It's locked.'

'Yes, but the key is just sitting there. Anyone could smash the glass and get in.'

Eddie yawns. 'For fuck's sake, Mum. Anyway, the front windows don't close properly. You have to admit that's pretty insecure for a start.'

For a stupid second I almost allow myself to be seduced by this logic. Meanwhile, Eddie plays for time.

'They're my one and only pair of jeans,' he says bleakly, 'If they're gone, then it's all over. I mean it. I've quite seriously got nothing else to wear.'

'What exactly do you mean by "it's all over"?'

His sister, who's sitting on the kitchen table, using a bread knife to scratch her mosquito bites, answers for him. 'He means he'll have to go back to bed. Which is cool because it's what he's going to do anyway.'

'Becca,' I say, 'you're going to cut yourself.'

'I'm so sick of people taking my clothes,' says Eddie miserably.

'Yeah, right, like we rush back from holiday in order to jack your Levis,' says Becca, who has given up on the blade and started slapping her legs with the flat of the knife.

'Becca,' I say, 'step away from the knife.'

'Maybe,' Ed says slowly, 'I left them in Edinburgh.'

'That would mean you got on a train in your underpants,' I point out. 'If they really are your only pair.'

'What are you doing now?' he says as I open the door of the broom cupboard, the dishwasher, the downstairs loo.

'Looking for your jeans.'

'They won't be there.'

He's half right. My next stop is the sitting room, where, sure enough, a denim leg is sticking out from behind a sofa cushion. I hand the jeans to Ed.

'Who the fuck had them?' he growls.

'The sofa. The sofa had them. Naughty sofa. And by the way,' I say, 'there's a clean and ironed T-shirt of yours on the chair in the hall. It's been there since before we went on holiday. Can you please take it up to your room now – and I mean Right Now, not in three days' time.'

'Great,' he says, and I watch as he pulls off the dirty one and puts on the clean one, dropping the dirty one exactly where the clean one was. Before I can say anything, there's a howl from the kitchen.

'Mum, help!' Becca yells. 'I cut my finger!'

I stand for a moment, look at the dirty T-shirt, listen to my daughter's piercing cries. I decide I've helped enough. 'Never mind. There's an old T-shirt here you can use as a tourniquet,' I say. And I go upstairs to run a bath.

Jack's Watch

A few days before the beginning of the autumn term. It's a sweltering early September afternoon and we're in Jack's room going through his clothes to see what he needs for school. The Arctic Monkeys, the pre-McLaren England XI and most of the cast of The O.C. are watching us.

'What about your trousers?' I say. 'You've grown like mad over the summer.'

'The old ones are fine,' he says, mainly because he's much more interested in the idea of the promised new watch, rucksack and pencil case (all crucial status symbols) than in boring pale-grey Vilene trousers.

'Put them on,' I order him.

He yawns. 'Don't need to.' He holds them against his thigh area. 'They're fine, look.'

I reply that we can only know if he puts them on properly.

He yawns again. 'Oh, Mum, I can't be bothered.'

'OK, no shopping trip.'

With trance-like slowness he pulls off his jeans and puts on the school trousers.

'See?' I exclaim. 'Way too short!' I feel oddly happy. It's not so much that I have an insane desire to purchase new school uniform, more that there is something ineluctably satisfying about seeing your kids get longer and stronger.

But my younger son – taller by the second, although today sporting an unattractively ripe pimple on his left cheek – coughs and quickly jerks the outgrown trousers down. It means they fit him at the bottom but no longer reach at the top.

'This is how I wear them,' he tells me firmly.

'Like that? But you can see your underpants.'

'So?'

I sigh. 'I know you wear your Levis like that, but . . . your school trousers?'

'It's the look, man.'

A year ago I might have put my foot down. But now? Please believe me when I say that the level at which Jack chooses to wear his trousers is the least of my worries.

Two hours later we are in Brent Cross looking at watches. In the shadowy depths of my stupid, motherly heart I know this is a futile, evil assignation. Because Jack loses all watches. Always has. Always will. But parenting is an act of blind optimism, is it not?

So when we talked about watches, it went something like this.

77

'What happened to your last one?'

'It's somewhere. It keeps itching me – that rubber's really yuck. I have to keep taking it off all the time and then I can't remember where I've left it.'

Now I know how he broke the family record for lateness last term.

'All right,' I said. 'We'll have a look at watches. And you'll give me the rubber one so we can get a new strap for that and keep it as spare, OK?'

'We should just get me a cheap one,' he said with winning solemnity, 'because of my awful record with watches.'

We select an olive-green Nike watch. Thirty pounds. Not too expensive but way too expensive to lose.

His face softens as the lady gets it off the display. 'One like that, I'd never lose it.'

'You swear?'

'Mum' – he looks at the watch as tenderly as if it's made of live puppy dogs – 'I've really, really changed.'

I hand over my card, punch in my pin. Jack gets the bag and I get the receipt. I fold it over twice. Jack thanks me from the bottom of his heart; my own heart wobbles. The devil laughs loudly.

Back home we show our purchases. New socks, new shoes, pencils, a watch. I kind of swallow that last bit, but nothing gets past Jack's father.

'A *what*?!'

'He needed one.'

'But what about the other one?'

'And the one before and the one before and the one before that?' adds Becca.

'He'll give it back to you,' I say, before Jack can chime in with some ill-advised rude comment. 'We have to get a new strap for it.'

'But I thought you said you lost it?' Becca says as loudly as she can.

'He hasn't lost it.' I turn to Jack. 'You'll get it now, won't you?'

He shrugs. His face worries me. 'I didn't say I knew where it was.'

'You said . . .' I try desperately to run through the conversation we had. 'You said you did—'

'No. I said it was "somewhere". "Somewhere", OK? Somewhere could be anywhere.'

'But . . . in our house, yes? It's in your room?'

'Not necessarily,' says my darling younger son. 'It could be at that party or where we were playing football or . . . um . . . I just don't know, OK?'

Silence. His father looks at me. Becca looks at me and mouths the word 'lost'. I look at Jack. Jack looks at his new watch.

And maybe this is a family moment, OK? Maybe his father and I need to talk. Because even teenagers can change, yes?

So maybe I'll just get back to you in a month, or a couple of weeks, or, all right, this time next week, and we'll see if he still has it. Deal?

On the bus

Eddie, Jack, the dog and I are on the number 11. It's rush hour and there are barely any seats, but somehow our Eddie manages to get one. He plonks his denimed self down and proceeds to fiddle with his iPod. I'm on the verge of ordering him to get up for me – apart from all the other more obvious considerations, I am struggling with serious period pains – but then I see a woman at least a couple of decades older who is also standing.

I attempt to point her out to Eddie, but it's a lost cause. He's remorselessly plugged into Lily Allen. Eventually he sees me, frowns, removes the earpiece for about three seconds, looks around, then puts it back in and shuts his eyes.

'What is it, Mum?' asks Jack, who is holding most of the dog's lead as well as the shopping (and who, by the way, has not, as we go to print, yet lost his new watch).

'What's the matter with him?' I mutter. 'He needs to let that lady sit down.'

Jack shrugs. 'He won't.'

'What do you mean? Why won't he?'

'Eddie doesn't believe in giving up his seat on buses.'

80

I look at my eldest baby who is slumped against the window, ingesting the beat.

'Oh,' I say.

Jack bites his lip. 'Well, he would I think, for a really decrepit person. I mean a person who could hardly even stand,' he guesses thoughtfully. 'I'm not the same,' he adds hastily. 'I give my seat up to old people all the time. Even if they don't look that old. I like the feeling of when they're grateful to me.'

'Too right,' I say, keeping my eyes on his charmless brother. 'It's called putting others first.'

And without wasting any more time I lean over and yank the iPod out of his ear.

'Eddie,' I say in a loud whisper, 'there's someone who needs to sit down.' As he slowly shuffles to his feet, I tap the old lady on the arm, indicating the seat. She looks surprised, but thanks me and sits.

Eddie glares. 'What makes you think she even wanted to sit down?' he asks me.

I give him a scathing look.

'Look, Mum' – my darling firstborn tries another tack – 'she's not even that old.'

'I don't believe it. What are you saying? You need to see a birth certificate?'

For a moment Ed looks as if he might say yes. 'I just don't get it,' he says. 'I mean, I have as much right to sit down as anyone else, don't I?'

'No,' I reply. 'You're young, you're fit, you're strong.'

'OK,' he says, 'what about fat people? I mean really obese people. Should I give up my seat for them? I mean because their legs are about to give out because they've gorged themselves on fast food?'

'You eat fast food,' Jack points out quickly.

'OK, then,' Eddie goes. 'OK, then . . . smokers?'

'You smoke,' his brother says. It's too easy.

'But I'm not fat,' Eddie says.

I glance around, embarrassed. At least half the people on this bus are probably over their optimum weight. Right in front of us, in fact, is a young, extremely fat man, baseball cap pulled down over eyes.

But my boy's not letting go. 'I seriously want to know who I'm supposed to give up my seat for?' he says. 'OK, forget smokers. What about murderers? Got an answer for that?' And so saying, Eddie flops into a suddenly vacated seat.

I am bewildered. When Ed was little, he had the biggest heart. He shared his last biscuit with the new boy at school because he didn't want him to feel lonely. He cried at the end of *Snow White*. If someone in the street had the same hairdo as Grandma, he'd run up to them, arms flung wide.

Suddenly, his brother – who, let's face it doesn't often get the upper hand in this life and who (yes) has lost more watches than we can count – steadies the shopping between his legs and draws himself up to his full height.

82

'How about,' he says loudly, 'people who've actually paid? Do you think you should give your seat up for them?'

It's a great moment. Ed – who is never at a loss – is blushing.

'What do you think?' Jack, who is on a roll, continues. 'If a person is fat but has bothered to pay for a ticket, do they deserve a seat more than a thin boy who goes out of his way to cheat on London Transport as often as he can?'

'What you morons don't understand is the whole system is fucking crap,' Ed mutters. 'Someone has to stand up to it.' And, still bright red, he gets to his feet. But only because our stop has come.

Eddie's Teeth

Eddie's first toothbrush was a bright-red Thomas the Tank Engine one. He had MacLean's Baby toothpaste, which came in a shiny, white plastic tube with orange and pink writing. He always wanted to be the one to squeeze it and I always let him. Right from the start, I wanted to teach him to take responsibility for his body, his health and I suppose, in some way, his happiness. Ten months old didn't seem too young to start.

I remember – burningly, the way mothers do – exactly how it felt to scrub those two tiny, slightly serrated, bottom teeth of his. A pea-sized blob of toothpaste, a gentle circular motion.

Now spit. Now wipe your mouth on the towel. Good boy, kiss on the head, well done.

All through their childhood, Eddie, Becca and Jack had regular dental check-ups, saw hygienists, had electric tooth-brushes, had the advised fluoride treatment on their back molars. They liked the smelly fruit stickers that the dentist gave them. They knew that fizzy drinks and sweets caused decay and they mostly managed to avoid the former. We only had chocolate on Saturdays and all three of them were remark-ably good about this. 'I'm saving it for Saturday,' Jack would say when given Maltesers or Twixes at the end of a children's party or at school.

Ed got away without a single filling until he was about thirteen – and then just the one. I felt secretly sad, but it wasn't the end of the world, just the end of those perfect, unblemished teeth. He promised to brush better and for a while I really do think he did.

Eddie, just eighteen and with a whole life of smiles ahead of him, is sitting in front of me now and his front teeth are brown. I mean brown. I cannot tell you how it hurts me to say this. He says he doesn't know whether it's from nicotine or coffee. I feel it's more likely to be as a result of that even more corrosive teenage vice: not taking any physical care of yourself whatsoever. Thinking you're immortal. Getting a physical high out of abusing your lungs, your teeth, your life.

'Oh, for fuck's sake, Mum,' he says, as he sits there picking the *pain* from around a *pain au chocolat*. 'I do clean my teeth. Just not every day, that's all.'

'Not every day! You should clean them at least twice a day. I do mine three times and I never miss a day of flossing.'

I know how I sound. But my mouth was full of fillings by the time I was Eddie's age. The dental drill was a perpetual feature of my childhood. I was determined this would not be the case for these three.

Eddie sighs. 'There's no point in cleaning them in the morning because I don't eat breakfast.'

'But do you want your breath to smell? Do you want to be unkissable? Everyone has stale breath in the morning.'

Eddie shrugs. He has missed over a year of dental appointments. And last time he deigned to turn up, he got away without any fillings – I was relieved, amazed, annoyed. Maybe he is lucky, maybe he has super-strong teeth, maybe the fluoride paid off, or maybe he is indeed immortal. Either way, he came home complacent – can you blame him? – and continued not to brush very much.

I inform Eddie and Jack that I've made appointments for them both at the hygienist.

Jack shudders. 'I'll see her,' he says, 'But I don't want a check-up. I don't want that dentist anywhere near me.'

'Why on earth not?'

'Because I haven't been cleaning my teeth recently and I don't want a filling.'

I take a breath. I try to explain to my younger son that fillings aren't a thing you elect either to have or not to have. 'If you have a cavity,' I say, 'you'll need a filling.'

'What I'm saying is I probably do have a cavity and I don't want a filling.'

'OK, fine. You'll end up in agonising pain, then.'

Jack shrugs. He doesn't believe me. So what am I to do when I take him to the dentist next week – hope I'm proved right, or wrong?

OK, I admit it, I'm feeling kind of heartbroken about this. I can't shake the memory of that little red Thomas the Tank Engine brush, you see, the blob of toothpaste, the passionate sense that I was doing everything right for my kids. Or trying to.

The trouble with making babies is that it turns you into a deluded fantasist. From the ecstatic seriousness of those first birth classes, through to those first steps, and the day those baby teeth come through, you are seduced into believing life can, after all, be perfect. That it might just be possible to create a delectably unblemished person if you throw enough love, passion, energy and time at it. And then teenagers come along to prove that whatever you do, it's not, you can't, you won't: it's quite simply out of your hands.

Losing Stuff

Five o'clock and the doorbell goes. I run downstairs and Jack is standing there. He doesn't say, 'Sorry' or 'Thank you' or 'Hello. How are you, Mum?' He just walks in.

'Hey,' I catch hold of his blazer as he passes. 'Where's your key?'

He shrugs me off. 'In my room somewhere, I think.'

'You haven't lost it?'

He gives me a look. 'Please leave me alone. I've had a shit day.'

'Well,' I tell him, 'please apologise when you get me running all the way downstairs. I'm not a doorman. I have better things to do than—'

The doorbell rings. This time I don't even have to move. I open it and there's Becca. Hot and sweaty and cross-looking, her satchel dragging her shirt off her shoulder.

She pushes past me. 'Need the loo – out of my way, please.'

'Where's your key?' I shout after her as she drops her bag and runs upstairs.

'Don't know,' she says. 'For God's sake, Mum.'

'Not you, too!' I shout a bit louder than I mean to. 'I seriously need to know where your key is.'

Becca's face appears through the banisters. 'I can search

for the key now and pee all over the stairs, or else I can go to the loo and look later. Which do you want?'

I sit down on the stairs. 'That's two lost keys,' I say crossly to Jack. 'It's a security risk. I want them found. I mean it. Today.'

Jack puts his rucksack down. 'I never said I'd lost it.'

'Where is it, then?'

'I just don't have it, OK?'

I look at my son and feel a sudden snatch of pity. 'Why did you have such a bad day?' I ask him.

'Well, first off I've got to do a detention tomorrow – said I couldn't do it today. And second off I lost my lunch card so I hardly ate anything. And third off—'

'Hold on. Why the detention?'

'I didn't have my PE shorts.'

'Why not?'

'I don't know. I thought I had them but—'

'You've lost them, too? PE shorts and lunch card? And your key? Oh, Jack!'

'I know they're somewhere,' he says gloomily.

Somewhere. Everything my children have ever possessed is in a place called Somewhere. The original Oyster card that Jack lost before he got the temporary one that he lost while we were waiting for the permanent replacement (which is now – at least temporarily – lost) to come. The key that Ed swore he'd left at a friend's house, explaining that the friend's bedroom was way too untidy for it to be worth anyone looking for it. The school tracksuit bottoms that disappear on a regular basis. The little crystal necklace that I stupidly lent Becca. They're all Somewhere.

'I want those keys found,' I tell Jack and Becca as they lay the table for supper. 'Things don't just disappear.'

'They do,' says Jack. 'Remember Wally Walrus?'

'Yeah,' says Becca with some relish. 'Remember him?'

Wally Walrus was a large soft toy bought after a visit to an aquarium. Wally belonged to Jack, who liked to put the dorsal fin in his mouth and suck it hard while shoving one of Wally's whiskers up his nose. He got such pleasure from this activity that his eyes would close and he would go into a kind of trance. If Wally Walrus was unavailable, there were tantrums and tears. Wally Walrus was invaluable, adored, irreplaceable. And then, one queasy, fateful day, Wally disappeared.

We searched everywhere. Under beds, down the backs of radiators (even though Wally Walrus was frankly too portly to squash himself into such a place). We even looked in the loft just in case, I don't know, Wally had magically managed to lift the trap door himself. But the years passed, Jack grew out of putting things up his nose, the walrus was never found. Wally's case was finally closed.

'Wouldn't it be funny if we found him now?' says Ed.

'Yeah,' says Becca. 'Do you think Jack would stick him up his nose?'

Jack ignores this. 'He must be somewhere,' he says wistfully.

Oh no, I think, not Somewhere again. Then again, maybe it's true. Maybe there really is a place lodged – where would it be? – in the tight little space between the fantasy and the reality of our family life. And maybe Wally's there right now, laughing at us all, along with three or four Oyster cards, countless keys, a whole gymful of PE kit and an armful of Jack's watches.*

becca's Clothes

Saturday night and Becca's going to a party. She's been horrible all day – screaming at people, refusing to help with lunch, locking herself in her room and playing the Fratellis so loud the walls shake. Now, as I get ready to go out to dinner, she comes and stands behind me with the face of an angel.

'Mum?'

'Yes.'

'Um . . . I wondered something.'

'What did you wonder?'

'You know your jacket, the light-pink one with the bits of lace on it? The one you got in Barcelona?'

'Yes . . .' I say.

'Yes what?'

---

* But not his latest, I know he would want me to point out. All these weeks on and he still has it.

'Yes I know it.'

Becca works hard to stifle a small breath of impatience. I sharpen my eyeliner pencil.

'Well, I wondered if I could borrow it. I mean, only for tonight.'

As she sees me thinking about this, her eyes widen. 'I'll take such amazing care of it – keep it on a hanger. I'll give it back to you first thing in the morning. It's just that, well, it's so great having a mum who has such cool clothes . . .'

'OK,' I say.

She looks amazed. 'What?'

'I said OK. You can.'

'That's so nice of you, you're so nice,' she says. 'I really, really appreciate it. Hey,' she adds, 'you look really good, by the way. Your make-up, I mean.'

'I haven't done it yet.'

'All the same, it's good.'

I give her the jacket. She carries it away as if it was made of fairy dust. The Fratellis hit the intro again in her room. Not quite as loud as before.

An hour later she appears in the hall, ready for the party. She has on ripped jeans, scuffed biker boots, at least three layers of grubby torn T-shirts, a piece of something that looks like an old curtain slung around her neck, bright-green kohl on her eyes and something sparkly wrapped around the topknot on her head. The poor lacy jacket is almost unrecognisable under a weight of badges, most of which seem to carry the doomed face of Kurt Cobain.

'Don't worry,' she says, as she sees me looking, 'I put them in very carefully. It took me ages. I swear I haven't damaged the fabric.'

It's not that I don't believe her (I don't), it's more that something about her standing there looking like some alien exotic bird sends my heart into a spin.

'Should you have let her do that to your jacket?' asks her father, as we drive to our grown-up, no-badges-required dinner.

'Teenagers have to customise things,' I say, mainly because I don't really know the answer.

The dinner's to celebrate the twentieth wedding anniversary of old friends. They're our age but they married young. They're also much posher than us. The place is heaving with relatives and somehow we end up on a table with the teenage girls – daughters, goddaughters, nieces – most of them Becca's age, all of them gorgeous, dewy-faced, immortal, opinionated and ruthless.

But it takes me a while to work out what's really unnerving about them. 'They look exactly like their mothers,' I whisper to my husband. 'Same blow-dried hair, same pretty earrings, same groomed clothes – look.'

He can't argue. There's not a ripped T-shirt or a Kurt Cobain badge in sight. I sip champagne and listen to the speeches and watch these smiley, shiny girls lick their pudding spoons and suddenly miss my sullen, scruffy, ripped-up daughter. She may kick against everything in sight, but at least she's alive.

When I was fifteen, a vintage clothes shop opened in our town. We used to go and try things on after school – feather boas, fifties cocktail dresses, weird hats, old men's jackets. One Saturday I went and spent £5.50 on an old black crêpe dress. I bought it because when I tried it on I didn't recognise myself. The person who gazed back at me in the mirror was daring and rebellious and ugly in a way I found exciting, even liberating. I had to have it. All the same, my heart banged as I paid for it – I knew there'd be trouble when I got it home.

There was. My mum said I looked dreadful, and insisted I take it back.

'She meant well, but I think she was wrong,' I tell my husband now, as we drink our coffee. 'I mean, I'm sure I did look really awful, but the point is, I should have been allowed to look awful. I was fifteen, for God's sake.'

'Well, what I can't believe is that you did as she told you,' my husband says with all the amazement of someone who has lived with a female teenager for four years.

We get back at 1.30 a.m. The upstairs light is on, a sign that Becca's safely home. There's another sign that she's safely home, too. My jacket, still encrusted with badges, inside out and slightly grubby, one wine stain on the sleeve, flung down on the hall floor.

Eddie's Towel

Though you'd never guess it from the state of his room, head, desk or life, our Eddie likes things to be just so. You could call him a sensory perfectionist or you could call him extremely, almost inconveniently, alert to his nerve endings. Or you could just call him an old lady.

Anyway, he notices things. Tiny things. Put one little, teeny-weeny petit pois under his mattress and I swear he'd feel it. He'd be black and blue in the morning. Or say he was.

'Hey, Mum,' he says, catching me in the kitchen, where I'm stuffing a load of his grubby jeans (checking pockets first for yukky tissues and stray Rizlas and . . .) into the machine with one hand, while carrying the phone around trying to get through to the vet's surgery with the other, 'there's something wrong with this towel.'

I straighten up, phone still at my ear, pour in the liquid soap, shove the dispenser shut. Sigh. Move phone to other ear.

'Mmm? What is it?'

My mind is still on the fact that the dog is booked to have a booster injection but the car is still at the garage having failed its MOT and I'm really praying the vet won't charge us for cancelling at short notice.

Eddie stands there in his boxers and nothing else and wrinkles his nose. 'Well, I dunno, it just won't dry me.'

'What do you mean it won't dry you?'

He makes a feeble rubbing action with the towel on his bare arm. 'It kind of slips off me and the water stays on me.'

'That's because it's a brand-new towel,' I explain. 'It needs a few more washes, then it will get nicely roughed-up. I don't like them when they're new, either.'

And you'd think that would be the end of the story. He's told me the problem, I've given him an explanation. But no, this is Eddie, remember. And our Eddie comes from a rare and delicious world, a world of sensory security, entitlement and privilege, a world where the 'feel' of things really matters. (And before you start, I know I'm responsible. I'm fully aware that somehow we, his achingly careful parents, have created that world for him.)

The noble Eddie looks troubled. 'Well, can you give it some more washes, then?' he says.

'Obviously, when you've used it a few times I'll wash it again,' I say, going off to search for the dog in case I end up having to take him.

The young prince follows me upstairs. 'I mean, can you give it a few washes before I use it?'

I laugh, but it's an uneasy laugh. 'No, Ed, I haven't remotely got the time and the planet can't afford the electricity.'

He stares at me in an injured way. 'But . . . what am I meant to do about drying myself?'

What am I meant to do? It's the undying mantra of Eddie's life.

'Run round the block,' I suggest as I call the dog in from the garden and slip a lead round his neck. He stands for a moment, innocently baffled, trying to work out what I mean.

Some hours later, fully robed at last, if unsatisfactorily dried, he comes downstairs. He looks stricken. 'Mum?'

'Yes?'

'It's just . . . I've got a little thing that hurts on the back of my hand.'

'Show me.'

I peer at the back of his hand. I can't help thinking it's a nice hand. Is it one of nature's sweeter tricks that the flesh of your children somehow remains adorable forever, regardless of how ludicrously unreasonable their personalities turn out?

'I can't see anything,' I say, resisting the impulse to grab and squeeze and kiss the dear hand (however much it hurts – ha!).

Eddie frowns and juts out his lip the way he used to when he was two and liked to spit lumps of Weetabix onto the floor. 'There, look.' He indicates a tiny area of pink. 'It's really sore.'

'It's very small.'

'It really hurts.'

'I think you'll live.'

'I've had it since Friday.' (It's Monday.)

'Seriously, it's nothing. It's a bit of dry skin. It'll go.'

'But can you suggest anything for it?' he persists, this great big man-child who towers five inches above me.

'The only thing I can suggest,' I say, 'is maybe to consider getting some early nights and eating some decent food and not smoking either tobacco or cannabis for a while so your immune system gets a chance to repair itself.'

'For fuck's sake!' Eddie yanks open the fridge door and suddenly looks a whole lot heartier. 'There's no need to be like that.'

'It's a serious answer. You have a little patch of dry skin. It's probably nothing. Or your body may be trying to tell you something.'

Ed thinks about this for a second. 'Hey, do you think it's trying to tell me I'm allergic to the new towels?'

Pasta bake

Five o'clock on a Thursday afternoon. The day is gone; it's dark outside already. It's not normal for me to be lying on the bed at this time of day with my eyes shut, but I am.

I have to go out later to a work thing. I have to be sparkly and look nice. But my eyes hurt, my hair smells of cooking and I feel about eighty-six. And I spent the last hour cooking a nutritious meal for my teenagers, which Becca took and ate in front of the TV, but both boys refused to eat. It was a pasta bake with tuna and tomato.

They said the edges of the pasta were too curly.

'What do you mean "too curly"?' I asked Jack.

'When they twist up like that. They go all dry.' He shuddered.

'It's totally gross, Mum,' Ed (who had picked out all the bits of tuna and left the rest) agreed. 'It's kind of like . . . toenails.'

I leaned against the cooker. Some part of me was starting to hurt but I was too tired to work out which. 'Toenails?'

'You know, old man's toenail clippings – all hard and yellow and thick.'

Jack laughed agreement and, in one evil movement, pushed his plate away.

I stood for a moment, head throbbing. 'OK, you win.'

In a single dramatic gesture I picked up the casserole and tipped it into the sink, where the curly-edged pasta toenails slid obediently down the waste disposal.

The boys stared. That much at least was satisfying.

'I can't believe,' I continued, 'that I have somehow managed to bring up teenagers who still, with everything that's going on in the world, can make a fuss about the texture of the edge of a piece of pasta.'

I pulled off my apron, threw it on the floor.

'Eat what the bloody hell you want,' I said. 'Or don't eat at all.'

They looked at each other.

'No need to swear,' said Jack.

'You think you're so cool, but you know nothing about the world,' I told them as I stomped upstairs. 'Nothing!'

'What's that got to do with the fact that you can't fucking well cook?' Ed managed to shout after me.

And so here I am. Eddie's cat blinks at me from on top of the clean washing. A cat blink is equivalent to a shrug. Although she's not helping – later the top towel will be covered in a mass of tiny grey hairs – she at least understands. Cats never bother doing anything for anyone, and you can see why. Oh well, at least Becca ate it, I tell myself. She's not half as fussy about food as the boys are.

On the radio, people (who probably don't make a fuss about pasta) are talking about blowing each other up. The words slide in and out of my head and then slowly start to make no sense as I drift off—

A scream.

Becca is in the room. I open my eyes, shut them again. Maybe she'll see that I'm sleeping and creep out quietly. Fat chance.

'Mu-um!'

'Oh God, what is it now?' I don't say it very nicely.

'Those fucking boys! They won't let me watch my fucking TV programme. They've chucked me out of the sitting room. They have no right.'

'Becca,' I say quietly, 'I'm trying to rest. But if you want to, go and watch on the little TV in your father's study.'

'Why should I? Why should I be the one to go into that hellhole? I don't see why it should be me. Why can't you get off your butt and do some proper parenting for once?'

OK, I think, stay calm.

'I'm not on my "butt", and by the way I'm not American, either, and I'm actually lying down because I'm not feeling very well.'

Becca throws her head back as if she's about to be executed. 'Why-y is it always me? Why, why, why?'

'Please,' I whisper. 'I'll come down in ten minutes. I just need ten minutes—'

'Ten minutes is no good!' yells my daughter. 'Don't you see? That's you shirking responsibility as usual.'

I sit up, furious and tense. 'No, actually, it's me being ill, OK?'

'You don't look very ill to me.' She snaps the radio off. 'Come now.'

'No,' I say, 'I won't. And put the radio back on, please.'

She does. She puts it back on and swings the volume right up to deafening. Storms out of the room. Then storms back in.

'And by the way,' she says, 'you need to do something about your cooking. I couldn't eat a single mouthful of that pasta. The edges were bone-dry.'

She leaves.

I lie there. I don't cry. Instead, I wait for something to change. A minute later something does. Jack puts his head round the door.

'I do care about the world, Mum,' he says softly. 'I'm making hot dogs for me and Ed and I've cleared up the plates. Do you want a nice cup of tea?'

borrowing Things

My black glossy opaque tights are missing. The expensive ones that make my legs look slinky.

'Have you seen my good black tights?' I asked Becca yesterday, because she has been known to 'borrow' my things.

'What good black tights?'

'You know, the good ones. The expensive ones I have to hand-wash.'

'Why the fuck would I have seen them?' she snapped, nursing a tub of maple pecan ice cream as close to her chest as it would go.

'What're you doing with that ice cream?'

'Waiting for it to get soft. Is that OK or d'you want to have me arrested for that too?'

I didn't remind her that last time I 'lost' an eyeliner pencil it turned up on her floor, cap off, discarded among the dirty clothes and Diet Coke cans. As for my socks and T-shirts, I've given up keeping track of them. There seems to be some (unspoken, unagreed) rule that we share them.

The thing is, I think I'm pretty generous with my stuff. I never mind lending Becca a T-shirt or a jacket or a squirt of this or that lotion. I don't want her sneaking in and helping herself, that's all.

But I know I used to sneak around my own mother's room. As soon as she left the house, I'd go straight up, touching things, trying things on. I remember the chilly fascination of discovering her diaphragm in its scary snap-shut box. The fun of sitting at her dressing table and seeing what I looked like with red lips, dabbing her Diorissimo behind my ears.

Did I feel guilty? Yes, definitely. But it was a thrilling and noble kind of guilt, a guilt where – in my own head at least – I was still the good guy. An agent on a mission to steal the enemy's secrets. Because the enemy was the grown-ups and it was still going to be some time before I got to infiltrate them for real.

Did she know? She must have done. I must have reeked of Dior. But she never once said anything, never once accused me, and I'm mildly impressed by that now.

But then again, I had respect. I would never, not in a

million years, have dreamed of actually taking anything. For instance, I always covered my tracks. I was careful, respectful. I put things back exactly where I found them. If I sat on her bed and flicked through her *Vogues*, I replaced them with the right one on top, at exactly the angle it had been at before – and I straightened the bedcovers afterwards.

Becca doesn't do that. She takes, uses, drops, lies, screams innocence and then somehow manages to accuse *me*. Still, I suppose that also means she doesn't creep around, covering her tracks all the time. Is the way I behaved – so deeply, calculatingly surreptitious – any more or less honest?

'Becs doesn't set out to lie,' her father says. 'She simply can't ever bear to admit that she's wrong. So she gets herself into these messes.'

Messes? I'm confused. 'That's still lying.'

'Not quite. She gets herself to a point where she doesn't want to lose face, don't you see? So by having it out with her, you force her into a corner. Anyway, you're surely not saying Jack and Eddie don't lie to you?'

I think about this. I think of the other morning when I woke Jack up and asked him why he had a curling roach readied on his bedside table.

'It's not a roach, Mum,' he muttered kindly, face still scrunched with sleep. 'It's only a bit of tube ticket that's been rolled up.'

I said nothing. Why? It was early in the morning, I was

tired, I wanted to believe him. Or is it that, unlike Becca, he had the sense not to snap when I accused him?

Now, this morning, I come down to find a fine layer of chocolate powder spilled all over the kitchen floor.

'Who did this?' I ask all three of them as they sit there eating toast. 'It wasn't there when I went to bed last night. Someone must've come down, made hot chocolate, spilled powder and not swept it up.'

They all gaze at me blankly.

'Come on, guys. It has to be one of you.'

More blank stares.

'Which means one of you is lying. Why? Why would you lie to me about this?'

No answer.

'Don't you see?' I hear my voice wobble. 'The mess doesn't matter, but the lie does.'

Of all of them, Becca gives me the dirtiest look. 'Who do you want it to be?'

'What's that supposed to mean?'

Her eyes are cold. 'D'you know that all you do, all day, every day, is accuse us? It can't be good for you. It's eating you up. Seriously, Mum, I mean it – can't you find a new hobby or something?'

I look at her. 'Did you do it, Becca?'

She holds my gaze for a quick moment then goes back to her toast.

After they've gone to school, I go upstairs and sit on her bed. She hates me going in her room, but I decide to do it anyway.

The hot chocolate mug is there by her bed, with its give-away pinkish-brown dregs. And it doesn't take me long, either, to see my tights, balled up on the floor among the fluff and discarded copies of *Metro*.

Eddie's Towel 2

It's 6.30 p.m. I catch Eddie nipping into our bathroom.

'What are you doing?'

'Um, nothing. Getting a towel, actually.' He blinks and holds a crunchy, white, freshly laundered towel to his skinny chest.

'No, Ed, the white ones are ours. You know they are. You have specially bought red ones.'

'But, Mum,' he begins, 'I've no idea where any of mine are and anyway—'

'That doesn't mean you can march in and take ours.'

I take it back. He flinches as if I snatched at his soul. 'My towels don't dry me. They're too new. Little bits of red come off all over my body.'

Oh God, I think, please not this one again.

'Ed, I thought we'd been through this. All they need is to go in the wash a few times. I know for a fact there's a clean, dry one sitting on the landing shelf outside your room right now.'

Eddie's tall, lean body crumples. 'Oh, Mum, for God's sake, please let me borrow it this once. I need to have a shower quickly, I've got to go out to this bonfire thing, I'm on a schedule.'

Eddie's 'schedules' are famous in this house. They tend to involve spaghetti bolognese at 0300, sleeping till 1400, wandering round the house in underpants complaining till 1800, then shower and out again till 0230, just in time to start boiling the water and chopping the onions . . .

I look at him for a moment. 'No,' I say and walk into my bedroom and softly shut the door.

He bangs a half-hearted fist on the door. 'I can't believe you're making all this fuss about one fucking towel,' he says.

'Exactly,' I reply. 'Look at yourself, Ed. It's ludicrous.'

'Fuck off,' he mutters and he opens the door and comes in. I push him out of our room, gently, and lock the door. Slightly shaky, I pick up the newspaper. I hear him slump on the floor outside.

'Have it your way,' he says.

'What do you mean my way?'

'I'm staying right here till you give me a towel.'

I jump to my feet, unlock and pull open the door.

'OK, Eddie,' I say at last, 'I want you to know I'm finding your behaviour threatening. You have a perfectly good clean towel you can use. You're not having one of ours, and if you think that I'm going to give in now, you're wrong. Go away.'

I shut and re-lock the door, and turn on Radio 4. Slowly Eddie beats his fist on the door. I say nothing. I try to listen to *The News Quiz*. But all I hear is Eddie's fist – bang! bang! – as if I'm trapped inside some low-rent horror movie. I feel like crying, and hate myself for feeling it. I can't believe I've brought up a child who'd do this. To me, to anyone. I seriously cannot even begin to picture Adam doing this to his mother.

Twenty minutes later, he's still sitting out there and I'm still sitting on the bed. Complete stand-off. The front door bangs: his father's home. Footsteps on the stairs, rescue. By the time he comes in there are tears on my cheeks. I try to explain, but his father takes one look at Eddie and hands him a towel.

'Take it,' he says. 'You've won. Congratulations. Enjoy the towel. But don't think you're not a complete tosser.'

Eddie walks away, smirking.

'You shouldn't have done that,' I tell my rescuer as I reach for the tissues.

'Given him the towel or called him a tosser?'

'Neither.'

He turns to me and he looks suddenly very tired. 'OK, you tell me how I should have handled it. Because you were clearly doing brilliantly.'

107

When Eddie was two years old and had moved from a cot into a big bed, he wouldn't stay in it. You'd put him to bed all happy, read him a story, give him a kiss and a cuddle, say, 'Night-night.'

'Night-night,' he'd go and you'd creep downstairs, hoping.

But five minutes later, as if all of that had happened to another Eddie, he'd be out of bed and down in the kitchen, sobbing his heart out.

We tried everything. We tried coaxing, we tried stern talking, we tried a star chart. In the end we installed a stairgate so that when he left his bed he couldn't get downstairs. He'd stand and rattle the gate, sobbing furiously, until he fell asleep on the carpet. Then we'd carry him back to bed, where he'd stay till morning. It was a solution of a kind.

After three or six or nine months, or however long it was (when your child is small, a day feels like a year), he finally gave up doing it and we (and he) forgot all about it. But how would I have felt if someone had told me then that, almost sixteen years later, he'd be employing identical tactics and this time I'd be the one in tears?

Omega-3

I've decided Jack must start taking Omega-3 capsules. The papers are full of convincing evidence that it might be good for boys. In spite of its potential attractions, I don't tell him that much of the research was done on young offenders.

'You have to take six every day for twelve weeks,' I say, reading the label. 'Then after that, when your body's built up its supplies, you can go down to two.'

He looks at me in an alarmed way. 'What, for ever?'

'Of course not for ever.'

'How long, then?'

'Look, let's see if it does any good, OK?'

'How will you know? What's it supposed to do?' Becca asks with her mouth full of brioche. 'I mean, will it make him less of a little creep or what?'

I hesitate. It's not exactly any of Becca's business, and I don't want to put Jack off. In fact, I'm rather pleased and amazed that he's not putting up more of a fight. But then again, we did just say he could have a sleepover on Friday night.

'It makes boys healthier and more organised,' I tell her, realising as I say it how it sounds. Straightaway everyone in the room bursts out laughing.

'But I am organised!' Jack protests. 'I haven't lost my watch.'

'Yet,' I say.

'But you've lost three school ties this term,' says his father firmly. 'You leave your PE kit all over the place. And you can't even wake up in the mornings.'

Every school morning at 7.30 when I go and wake Jack,

109

he's lying in his room with the light on and the radio blaring out some vague rap sound – and he's fast asleep. I always have to shout to get him to open his eyes and even then he shuts them as soon as I leave the room and goes straight back to sleep.

'That's just called being a teenager,' says Eddie.

'But he used to be the best at getting up in the morning,' I say, 'and now he's the worst.'

It's true that Jack was always the early riser. He was the toddler who'd wake all bright and alert at six in the morning, sometimes earlier. He'd climb out of his cot and stagger into our bedroom in his terry-towelling sleep-suit, with his thumb in his mouth and trailing a large blanket behind him, and climb into bed with me. There he'd lie, sucking, occasionally twiddling strands of my hair so I'd stay awake with him. I remember the sweet, soaked-nappy smell, the warmth of his hair, the slightly cold patch on his sleep-suit where the nappy had leaked.

I didn't really mind him climbing into bed, but as it got earlier and earlier – 3 a.m. was the record – we decided we had to do something. It was the Bunny Clock that saved our lives.

'Remember the Bunny Clock?' I say. 'Remember when we used to have to trick Jack to stay in bed?'

A strange, almost embarrassed grin spreads over Becca's face. 'When his ears were down, you couldn't get up,' she

110

says slowly, 'but when they were up, you could. Jack used to stand in his cot for ages and ages just waiting for them to pop up.'

'I did not,' says Jack.

'You don't remember the Bunny Clock?'

'I do remember it, but . . .' For a moment we all look at Jack. He frowns at the bottle of Omega-3 capsules. 'One small problem,' he says. 'I can't swallow pills.'

'Oh, for God's sake,' says his father. 'You're almost fifteen years old. Of course you can swallow a pill.'

'He can't,' says Becca, who ever since Jack was small has adored cataloguing what he can and can't do. 'He still has to have Nurofen Meltets, remember?'

'It's like nothing will quite manage to go down my throat,' says Jack in total seriousness.

'The thing is' – Eddie leans back, ready to offer his thought for the day – 'you read some half-cock report in the paper and decide to bung these pills into him. But you've no idea what they contain.'

'That's rich,' says his father, 'given what you're prepared to put into your body.'

'And do you realise the report's been written by some money-grabbing hack who's looking to make piles of money out of selling these pills to stupid, liberal health freaks like you?'

'Because,' his father whips in at lightning speed, 'the

111

tobacco industry doesn't profit in any way whatsoever from getting kids like you to smoke, does it?'

'Hang on,' says Becca, and she narrows her eyes at Jack. 'You did once manage to swallow something.'

'What?' says Jack warily.

'You told me you'd once tried half an E.'

'He what!?' both parents explode simultaneously.

'I didn't swallow it,' says Jack going bright red. 'I tried to take it in a bit of food, but I couldn't so I spat it out.'

I say nothing. I pass him the capsules.

Jack's Late Night

On Friday night – against my better judgement, because his recent behaviour hasn't really earned it – I said Jack could have friends to sleep over. His father told me it was absolutely the wrong decision. I told him I felt Jack really wanted to turn over a new leaf. He laughed.

'But,' I said to Jack, 'you have to promise me – you have to absolutely swear – that you'll go to bed early enough on Saturday to get a good night's sleep and concentrate on getting your homework done on Sunday. And you mustn't pick a fight with us the way you always do when you're overtired.'

He solemnly swore.

'I'm optimistic,' I told his father. 'I think he really did get the point about not starting pointless arguments.'

I've no idea what time he and his friends got to sleep on Friday night. And on Saturday night he messed around with Ed and – he admits now – didn't go to bed till 1 a.m. So now, on Sunday, he's worn out, shadowy-faced and refusing to eat. Because not eating is usually his opening gambit.

'I don't like that type of bread,' he says when I try to offer him a nice sandwich.

'Not eggs. Don't feel like eggs,' when I say why don't I fry him a couple?

'This is ridiculous,' I say, aware all the time of his father's cool eyes on me. 'You normally love fried eggs. OK, boiled, then?'

'The white's all slimy. I can't take slimy when I'm this tired.'

'Exactly,' I say. 'You're exhausted. You did the one thing you promised not to do, didn't you? And now you're absolutely worn out.'

'And you're surprised?' his father says to me.

'You can fucking well stay out of it,' says Jack.

I go right up to Jack and look him in the eye. 'How dare you talk to him like that? Say sorry right now.'

Jack says nothing.

'Do it.'

'Sorry,' he mumbles, 'but you—'

'No buts. Now, let's work out what you might eat so you can go and do your homework.'

'He's almost fifteen,' his father points out, 'not five. He should be mature enough to deal with his moods and make himself eat.'

'Don't talk about me when I'm in the room,' says Jack. 'You're always doing that.'

'There he goes again,' his father jumps in.

'Going where? Where am I going? Tell me!'

'You're picking a fight.'

I'd like to say that actually they both are, but I sense that to withdraw parental solidarity at this crucial point would be a mistake.

'I wish you wouldn't do this to me,' I tell Jack with a sigh.

'Do what? What am I doing?'

'Proving me so wrong. I swore to Dad you'd behave.'

'That's all you care about?' says Jack. 'Being in the right?'

'I'm saying nothing,' his father says.

'But you're not, are you?' I snap at him. 'In fact you keep on saying the most unhelpful things.'

'Well,' he says slowly and reasonably, 'what you mean is they're not the things you want to hear.'

Jack gets up and goes over to the fridge and stares into it. After several minutes he grabs the sandwich I've made for Becca's lunch tomorrow.

'Not that,' I say, because it's the one thing – the only thing – it would inconvenience me to have him eat. Which of course is exactly why he picked it.

'Why not?'

'Because it's for Becca and because you know it is and anyway you don't even like hummus.'

Jack chucks it back in the fridge, glares at his father, and throws himself on a chair.

'Pancakes, then. Will you make pancakes?'

His father looks at me. 'Don't you dare even think about making him pancakes. Not when he's been so rude to you. And me.'

I hesitate. One part of me knows he's right, of course he is. No way in a million years does Jack deserve pancakes now. On the other hand, if he'd only eat a pile of pancakes with a banana, he'd have the energy to do his coursework, which is due in tomorrow. Then I remind myself that he's almost fifteen and likes Bacardi Breezers and spliffs and girls.

'I'm not doing pancakes.'

'Why not?'

'Too much work for me, not nutritious enough, and you weren't very pleasant just now.'

He throws his head back in despair.

'If you want another reason,' I tell him, 'every time I cook you pancakes my hair smells of frying, and I'm sick of it.'

His father laughs and leaves the room.

'Good riddance,' says Jack.

'Don't say that.'

'Oh my God, this day is turning out so shit,' says Jack and

115

something about the way his face crumples reminds me of the promise he made me and how passionately I needed to believe he meant it.

'Yes,' I agree, 'isn't it?'

Becca's Door

Sunday afternoon in early December, three o'clock. The light is dying and so is my energy. The phone rings in the hall. It's not going to be for me, but I answer it anyway.

'Hello?'

All I hear on the other end is a sob.

'Who's that?'

'It's me.'

'Becca? Where are you?'

Another sob. 'Up here, on my mobile,' she whispers. 'Can you come?'

'Come where? Where are you?'

'Where d'you think I am? In my room. I'm trapped.'

'What do you mean "trapped"?'

'I can't get out. I'm trapped. By spit.'

'Spit?'

'Saliva, OK?' A pause. 'They're out there right now,' she says, 'those bastards. They're standing there and' – another sob – 'gobbing on my door.'

'Why?' I ask as calmly as I can.

'*Why??!!*'

'Yes,' I say, trying hard not to laugh. 'Why are they doing that?'

'Because – because – oh God, Mum, I don't know why! Because they hate me? Because they're arrogant shits? Because they like threatening me with . . . Oh, Jesus, I really don't think I can live like this any longer!' Her voice topples over into full-blown crying.

I push Jack's PE kit, Becca's muddy trainers, *Anna Karenina* and two Topshop carrier bags off the only chair in the hall and sit down. The dog is watching me carefully, chin on paws.

'OK, Becca. Now listen. If you guys are having a fight up there, I just think, well, shouldn't you be able to sort it out yourselves? I mean, you're sixteen years old. Are you really saying that you need me to come running up to intervene like I did when you were six?'

The dog blinks approval. Crashing silence from my daughter.

'Well?'

Still silence.

'I mean, I'll come if you want,' I continue, 'but I'm wondering whether it's either necessary or the right thing.'

I hear her take a breath. 'That,' she says slowly, 'is just so totally fucking typical.'

'And what's that supposed to mean?'

'What it's supposed to mean, dear Mother, is that I should have realised how little you care about me and how you're actually probably rather happy to have me held hostage up here by actual saliva from your own darling sons' mouths.'

This time I can't help it, I do laugh.

'Becca, pull yourself together. Of course I don't want you trapped. Look, can't you simply tell them to go away?'

'Oh, that is such an insulting thing to say.'

'I only mean—'

'OK,' she interrupts. 'OK, you asked for it. Listen. You just listen to this.'

I hear nothing. Silence.

'OK,' she says. 'You heard that? So what do you think now about your little darlings?'

'I didn't hear anything,' I tell her.

'I can't believe it! You're actually on their side. She's on their side, oh my God, oh my God . . .' and she hangs up.

I put the phone down, look at the dog. He looks at me.

'What would a good mother do?' I ask him softly. He has no answer.

It's very dark upstairs. Ed and Jack are both sitting on the floor of Ed's room, mouths open, Playstation flickering over their faces.

'Have you been spitting on Becca's door?' I ask them briskly.

'Why would we do that?' asks Ed. Jack blinks at me.

118

I knock on Becca's door.

'Who is it?' she calls tearfully.

'Me. The cavalry. Open up.'

'Have you punished them? I'm not opening this door till you tell me you've punished them.'

'Look, Becs,' I begin, 'they're both denying it. I'm not saying I don't believe you, but—'

'Feel my door,' she interrupts in a low voice.

'What?'

'Feel. Feel how wet it is. Go on, put your hand there, feel it!'

I look at it. It doesn't look at all wet. I run wary finger-tips over it. (Why am I doing this?) It's bone dry.

'So?' comes Becca's voice from inside. 'Do you believe me now?'

'I'm not continuing this conversation unless you open up,' I say firmly.

A scrabbling as the key turns in the lock. My daughter stands there, white-faced, dishevelled, wet-eyed, anorak on.

'Why're you wearing your school coat?' I ask.

'Because . . . because I didn't know how long I was going to be stuck in here, did I?'

'Have you got provisions?'

She glares at me. 'What d'you mean "provisions"?'

'Tins. Stuff to eat over the next few months. Blankets. Water. Kendal mint cake.'

119

Despite everything, she cracks a smile. We look at each other for a long moment.

'Oh, Mum. Those boys,' she whispers.

'I know,' I whisper back. 'I know.'

She lets me escort her downstairs. If this were a movie, there'd be a crowd down there, helicopters, blue lights flashing, a melancholy crane-shot. Instead, the dog has used the diversion to rip open a bag of cat food and is waiting for us with guilty triumph in his eyes.

Eddie's Christmas Spirit

Eddie comes into my study and finds me wrapping presents. His eyes travel swiftly over the mess of tissue paper and ribbons.

'What's all that? Who're they for?'

'Oh, nothing,' I tell him. 'Just some little surprises I'm giving Dad.'

'Giving him when?'

'For Christmas, of course. It's his stocking.'

'He's having a stocking?'

'Don't tell him.'

'He won't appreciate it one bit.'

'What a funny thing to say. How do you know?'

Eddie stands there with his hands in his pockets, and sighs. 'I don't know,' he says gloomily. 'But I do think it's rather sickening, that's all.'

'What do you mean? What's sickening?'

'It's just . . . you spend all this money on him and, well, me and Becca and Jack seem to get nothing these days.'

I put down the Sellotape, laughing. 'I've never heard anything so spoilt and ridiculous in my life. You guys get way too much, actually.'

'Not last year we didn't.'

'You got a table-tennis table!'

'Yeah. Shared.'

I look at my son carefully. There's an uneasy blend of indignation and shame on his face. The shame is a start.

'But you all loved it,' I remind him gently, 'and you got loads of other things, too.'

'Yeah. Great. Some spot cream.'

'You mean some very expensive toner for oily skin. Which you begged for.'

'Yeah, but I didn't want it as my Christmas present, did I?'

I stiffen. 'Actually, if we're talking about Christmas, I was going to have a word with you. Because no way are you going to do what you did last year and not give anyone anything.'

His eyes go wide. 'I gave presents last year!'

'Paid for with my money. I had to give you cash to buy them, remember? Even my own present. Because I thought it was horrible for you to be left out of the giving.'

'Wouldn't have bothered me.'

121

'I know it wouldn't. You'd quite happily have received and not given. That's exactly what I found so disturbing.'

'I had no money.'

'Because you'd spent your allowance on drink and drugs and refused to do anything to earn any.'

'I just didn't see why I should slave away for Dad simply so that I could participate in some cynical consumerist nightmare.'

'And yet you were very happy to participate in the so-called nightmare when you opened your own presents.'

'That's not the same.'

When the kids were still quite little, and when letters to Santa had become no more than unattractive lists of every expensive thing they'd seen advertised on TV, I decided to do something. So every December we'd clear out the toy cupboard and pack any stuff they no longer played with into a nice box for the local children's home. 'Taking toys to the poor children', it was called.

The children's home was very happy to have the toys. But if I'd had some *Little Women*-style vision of the four of us arriving with our baskets on our arms, it didn't quite work like that. More often than not, by the time we'd got around to sorting out the stuff and found time to take it, it was late in the day and the children were cranky and tired. Mostly I ended up leaving the car on a yellow line while the three of them fought and moaned inside and I struggled to take the box in all on my own.

But at least we talked about what we were doing and why. And we did it. And I suppose I passionately hoped the experience might catapult the children into understanding that there were people out there who had much, much less than they did.

'Do you remember when we used to give toys to the poor children at Christmas?' I ask them all later.

'What poor children?' yawns Becca. 'When?'

'Oh, you mean like the time I had to give them my Power Ranger transformer?' Jack says. 'I was so upset about that.'

'Oh no,' I say uncertainly, 'I would never have made you give away anything you still played with.'

'Well, you did. When I saw it in the box, I cried and cried.'

Eddie grins. 'Yeah, well, it was one of Mum's little fantasies, you see. The idea that if we gave away all our toys we'd grow up less spoilt.'

'I'll never make my kids do that,' Becca says. 'I think it's really cruel and fucked up.'

'It was never all your toys,' I protest. 'And you guys had so much. You still do. Have you any idea how much money Dad and I spend on you every year?'

Eddie flashes me a look. 'I just personally think, Mum,' he says, 'that you're forgetting about the real spirit of Christmas. It's not supposed to be all about money, you know.'

I shut my eyes, open them again, take a little breath.

Morning After

Eddie, Becca and Jack are laying the table for supper and discussing something in low, urgent voices. I hear the words 'morning' and 'after'.

'What're you guys talking about?' I ask.

Becca looks at Ed. Ed looks at Jack, who's picking away at one of the windows on the *Simpsons* Advent calendar with his thumbnail. Ed snatches it back.

'Pill,' says Becca with a shudder. 'Morning-after pill.'

'Someone Becca knows had to take it,' says Jack a little too quickly, 'and then they threw up all over the house and—'

'Shut up, Jack. Just shut your fucking mouth, OK?'

'Who had to take it?' I say as casually as I can as I start chopping onions for supper.

Becca stops chewing the end of her hair. 'Oh – someone. No one you know.'

'So what happened? Did a condom break, or what?'

I feel Jack's eyes on me.

'Don't think they used one,' says Becca, 'the dumb-clucks.'

'That's so judgemental,' says Ed, who is lying on the rug with the dog to get out of laying the table. 'You don't know why they didn't use one. They might have had a perfectly good reason.'

'Is there such a thing as a perfectly good reason for not using contraception?' I ask him.

He hesitates. 'For instance, they might have been skint.'

'Tough! Don't have sex, then!' cries Becca as she chucks a fork across the table.

'Or not penetrative,' I agree (a small shock-wave as they hear me say that word).

'Becca's only saying that cos she never has,' observes Jack.

'And neither have you,' she snaps back, 'because your penis is the size of a—'

'Enough with the personal stuff!' I say. 'I'm very glad you haven't had sex yet, either of you.'

Now that most of the table is safely done, Ed sits up on the rug.

'But you're all talking as if sex is always planned,' he says. 'Doesn't spontaneity ever come into it?'

'Hold on,' I say. 'You're saying that if you feel like having sex and you have no condoms, or no money either, it's fine to go right ahead as long as you have the urge?'

Ed shrugs. Becca picks up the Advent calendar and inspects the state of the last windows.

'Anyway, Mum,' says Jack, 'why're you saying it's good I've never had sex? Plenty of people my age are doing it, you know. By the way, Becca, the next chocolate in the Advent calendar is mine.'

'It is not!' shouts Becca. 'You opened the day before yesterday.'

'I did not!'

'You did, because you weren't there the day before because you were at Liam's having a sleepover, remember, so we swapped.'

Jack looks confused.

'He thinks he's old enough to have sex, but he can't remember which day he's supposed to open the Advent calendar,' his sister remarks to no one in particular.

'I hope,' I say, turning back to Ed, 'that you'll never ever dream of having sex without contraception. I'm serious, Ed.'

He shrugs. 'What if you don't have money for a condom? Anyway, there's always the morning-after pill – that's what it's for.'

I stare at him. I'm finally shocked.

'That's not what it's for at all. It's far better than a pregnancy, but it's a last resort. When a girl takes that, she's getting a great big dose of hormones. Why do you think Becca's friend was so sick? I'd be really shocked if I thought you were putting any girl through that except in a dire emergency.'

Ed smiles. 'Easy for you to go quoting all the stuff you've read in the papers.'

I pull off my apron, chuck it down, walk over, pull out a chair. 'I've taken it,' I tell them.

Silence. Serious shock-waves now. Jack looks at me. Ed looks away.

'When?' says Becca.

'When I was young. At university.'

Ed rolls his eyes. 'It didn't exist back then.'

'It did, but only a doctor could give it to you,' I tell him. 'I slept with a boy, and the condom split. He said it would be OK, but I was terrified. I didn't sleep all night and as soon as it was light I left his place and waited outside the surgery. They gave it to me. I was very sick. It felt so lonely.'

'Did you sleep with him ever again?' says Jack, cutting straight to the chase.

I try to remember. I do remember. I wish I didn't.

'I did,' I say. 'I was madly in love with him. I was an idiot. Looking back, he didn't treat me very well.'

'Poor Mum,' Becca takes my hand in both of hers and pats it. 'But he must have been well buff, yeah?'

'Not especially,' I tell her. 'He was just a boy. A bit scared, a bit arrogant, a bit chaotic and all over the place.'

'A bit like Eddie,' says Jack.

We all look at Eddie, even the dog. No one says anything.

Eddie's Towel 3

The day after Boxing Day. I have to go and do a brief stint at the office and then come straight back to start cooking as we have people coming to supper. I could really do with some help. Eddie sits in the kitchen, tipping back on his chair as far as it will possibly go.

'Mu-um,' he begins, 'you know my towel?'

127

I look up. He hasn't mentioned The Towel in weeks. I had actually begun to let myself believe we were over The Towel.

'Do you realise I waste about six minutes every morning because it's so pathetic?'

'Really?' I stay breezy, swipe the bowl of cat food from under the dog's nose a split second before he lunges. 'Is there any chance you could peel some potatoes for me, Ed? Either now or at some point later today? I'm trying to get ahead for tonight.'

'Six fucking minutes,' he says, tipping even further back.

'I need the potatoes done, or else you can top and tail some sprouts.'

He freezes, mid-tip. 'Six! Did you hear me, Mother, darling?'

'That's really awful for you.'

His father comes in, picks up the full kitchen bin. 'What's awful for him?'

'That nothing fucking well works around here,' says Eddie, grabbing the table to stop himself falling backwards.

'It would be lovely,' says his father, 'if just very occasionally someone else would think to empty this bin.'

Ed rolls his eyes. I sort cutlery into the drawer.

'I really could do with some help,' I say again.

'But you've no idea what it's like!' he says, once his father is out of earshot.

128

'What what's like?'

'Trying to use a towel which the water just runs off. In a freezing bathroom with no heating.'

'Of course your bathroom's heated!' his father shouts from the hall.

'Not today, it isn't.'

'Then learn to turn up the thermostat.'

We hear a door slam.

Eddie looks at me. 'When I run that towel over my body,' he says, 'I want to weep.'

'Oh, Eddie, listen to yourself. I am so bored of this subject.'

He juts out his bottom lip. 'All very well for you. You don't have a scrotum.'

'What?' I say, laughing.

'My scrotum. The towel kind of slips on it.'

'Anyway,' his father, who missed that last bit and is now back, trying to keep his suit clean while replacing the bin and washing his hands, 'what I'd like to know is who came down in the night, tipped the crumbs from the toaster all over the counter and left the light on?'

'Fucking toaster. That doesn't work, either. It would be good to have either the grill or the toaster working.'

'It needs a new element,' his father says. 'It's low on my list of things to do. My long list. And we know who broke the grill.' He walks out again.

'"Low on my list of things to do",' Eddie imitates as sarcastically as he can.

'Goodness,' I say. 'Can't you be a bit more mature?'

'Can't he be a bit less fucking grumpy?'

'He probably would be if you didn't give him so much to do. Honestly, if the toaster needs to be tipped out, clear up the crumbs. If you come down in the night, turn the light off.'

'You know, Mum,' Eddie says, doing the light, reasonable voice that is always so seductive to teachers, friends, parents of friends, 'let's forget who broke the grill, OK? The point is, any normal family would have got it mended by now.'

I don't know what to say to this. Some days I feel like it's all I do – organise and pay for things to be repaired. Some days it feels as if his father and I are disappearing under a heap of broken things.

His father strides back into the room carrying a washing basket just as Eddie is moving – very slowly – over to the sink to peel the potatoes.

'Well done. Well done for throwing wet clothes all over the utility room.' He turns to me. 'He only yanked his own boxer shorts out of the machine and left everyone else's clothes scattered across the floor. Nice work, son.'

'Oh, Ed,' I say, genuinely disappointed. He doesn't wait. He seizes his opportunity, chucks the peeler down in the sink.

'What's the point of trying to help if I always get blamed for everything?' he says, and his face looks genuinely injured.

Ten minutes later, I'm upstairs getting changed. Suddenly Eddie is in the room.

'Sorry,' he says as I jump.

He glances at my bra, then quickly glances away. 'Sorry, Mum. I just wondered . . . if there'd be any chance of a bit of money?'

'What for? Where are you going?'

'We're meeting up in Camden. Me and Adam and some of the others. And I've been trying really hard to smoke less. But you see if they all decide to go off for coffee and I don't have any money to join them, then—'

'You're forced to stand on a street corner and shoot up?'

Eddie grins. The thing about Eddie is you can always make him smile.

I sigh, pull on a T-shirt.

'Look, Ed, my darling, it goes like this. I want to give you coffee money, I really do. There's nothing in the world I'd like to do more. But one, you refuse ever to earn any money, ever. And two, how can I hand you money when you trashed the kitchen last night and probably will again because you're too immature to take any responsibility around this house?'

Ed looks at his feet. 'OK,' he says.

'OK?'

'Well, I see your point. It's fair.'

'You have a lovely quality,' I tell him. 'Do you know what it is?'

He looks surprised. Shakes his head.

'You're rude and you're lazy and I sometimes find you unbelievably selfish, and I do so wish you'd shut up about the towel, but . . . you light up a room. You always did. There's something so . . . lovely and lovable about you. But oh, Ed, you've got to stop leaving chaos and destruction in your path, OK? Do you see that? I'm only telling you because it would be such an easy thing to change. A small thing which would make all the difference in the world. I'm being honest with you now, darling, do you believe me?'

He sighs and stuffs his hands into his pockets. His jeans are ripped and halfway down his bum, his sneakers have holes in them. He looks like he used to look when he loved Thomas the Tank Engine and wore worn-out stripy dungarees bought second-hand at the shop down the road. He looks like a six-foot-tall three-year-old. I love him so much.

'What?' he says.

'Nothing. But have a good day, OK?' I say.

'Yeah. You too.'

As he goes, I want more than anything to call him back and give him his coffee money. But I don't. I keep my mouth shut.

Jack's Nails

Becca's drinking apple juice straight from the carton. There is a sparkle coming off her I've never seen before. Last night she went to a party and today every bit of her looks different.

'Can you put it in a glass, darling, please?' I ask.

She smiles and grabs a glass and pours it in. 'Sorry,' she says, and her eyes are warm and sweet. I glance at her father to see if he's noticed. He smiles. We both smile. We don't say anything.

'Anyway, Mum,' says Jack, 'you know how you promised me twenty quid if I grew all my nails?'

'You didn't!' His father rounds on me instantly. 'I hope she didn't,' he says to Jack.

'She did, so you stay out of it.'

'Don't you even dream of speaking to Dad like that!' I look up and almost risk burning the porridge.

Jack looks grumpy. 'Well, he shouldn't wade in when he hasn't a clue what he's talking about.'

'I'm not going to begin to discuss this till you apologise to him.'

'Sorry,' growls Jack.

'It's OK,' says his father. 'I'll stay out of it from now on.'

'I never promised you twenty,' I say carefully, 'and I didn't say cash. I think I said I'd get you a small present if you could show me ten nice long fingernails.'

'And you had to cut them twice, remember?'

'You're right,' I sigh. 'I'm sorry. I meant to get you something. I've been so busy.'

'Get him a pool table,' says Becca in a voice that sounds half serious. 'A full-sized one like in a pub. Cos that's what he wants.'

'Shut up,' says Jack quickly. 'Cash is fine.'

'I'm not giving you cash. That's not what I said.'

He looks sulky. 'There's no present I want right now, but I always need cash.'

That is horribly true. It's not Jack's fault that his birthday comes at a bad time of year – a couple of weeks before Christmas – but it was pretty depressing this year to discover that all he wanted to be given for either occasion was money. And not even money for buying CDs or clothes or saving for one amazing, spectacular thing. He just wanted 'money for going out'.

'Hold on a moment,' says the Father Who Was Going to Keep Out of It. 'How are the nails now?'

'They're OK,' says Jack quickly.

'Show me.'

'No way.'

His father looks at me. 'I think that speaks for itself.'

'They're OK,' mutters Jack.

'Then get him a mini-pool table,' says Becca brightly. 'You know, a toy one.'

'Show me,' I say to Jack.

He holds out eight of the dirtiest, inkiest fingers I've ever seen. He keeps the thumbs hidden.

'Thumbs?'

They're not so good.

'OK, four are slightly bitten, six are good. Six out of ten's not bad, though.'

'And you're going to reward six out of ten with a cash prize?' his father says.

'I wish you'd managed to keep them unbitten,' I sigh to Jack. 'They were so great a few weeks ago.'

'But I had no incentive! You didn't reward me. If you'd handed over some cash right then, I'd have kept them long.'

'I'll give you something,' I say, 'because that's only fair. I need to think about what, that's all.'

'Fair?' his father exclaims. 'He has bitten nails! You're going to reward him for biting them?'

'They weren't bitten before. It's my fault they got bitten because I was too busy then to get the present.'

His father laughs loudly.

'Not everything's your fault, Mum,' says Becca in such a soft and unusually kind voice that I glance over at her in surprise.

'It's not fucking fair!' says Jack. 'Either you reward me like you said or not at all. In which case hurry up and decide because I'm meeting Liam and Jon in a minute.'

'Oh no you're not. You're grounded, remember?' says his father rather too happily.

Jack looks at him. 'Since when?'

'Since last week. Since I found Rizlas in your blazer. All weekend.'

'I am not!'

As Jack bangs both fists on the table, Eddie comes in. 'What's going on here?'

'They're going to buy him a pool table,' says Becca sweetly.

'Seriously?'

'No,' she says, and twists her hair onto her head, looks in the mirror, pouts, lets it go.

Jack looks at his father. 'Please not today. It doesn't suit me.'

'And since when was a punishment meant to be convenient for the offender?'

'I do think,' says Eddie, grabbing the carton of apple juice and tipping the rest of it into his mouth, 'that you guys get it a bit wrong with punishments. I mean, if you could just be civilised and consult us about them.'

Now even I start to laugh.

'Like, before you grounded him,' says Becca, 'you might have let him check his diary at least.'

'Or,' says Ed, completely missing her sarcasm, 'instead of grounding and all those meaningless little sadistic tricks, how about some system of fining us? And in the end you use the fund to buy us something nice?'

'Like a pool table!' says Becca.

'So if I'm getting this right,' says his father, 'your approach to punishment is this: the more badly behaved you are, the more you get what you really want anyway.'

'We could encourage the whole country to do it,' adds Becca. 'Want a new hospital in your neighbourhood? Go out and park on a yellow line every day. Double yellow line if you want it more quickly.'

Jack looks at her. And we all watch as he tries to decide whether it's worth his while to laugh.

The Sparrow

Tuesday, 6 p.m. I've brought my mum to hospital for a scan and I should be back by now but it's taken longer than expected. So I call home.

The house phone rings and rings. I try Ed's mobile. Off. I try Becca's. It rings and rings. I try Jack's. Off. I try the house one again. It keeps on ringing, drowned, I imagine, by yet another repeat of *South Park* or *The Simpsons* at full volume. In the end I give up, ring off, wait, try again. And then:

'Eh, man!' says Jack.

'Hi, darling. You OK?'

'Eh.'

'Why on earth does no one ever answer this phone?'

'Eh.'

'Look, everything's taking longer than I thought here. Is Daddy back yet?'

'Nah.'

'Have you eaten anything?'

'A piece of bread. I think.'

'That's not enough.'

'Some butter on it.'

'Look, Jack, can you ask Ed to cook something now, some pasta or something? Because I'm not sure there will be any proper supper.'

'Ed's not here.'

'Where is he?'

'Dunno.'

'Then tell Becca—'

'I'm not tellin' that girl anything.'

I take a breath. 'Jack, you've got to be helpful. I'm looking after Granny and it's stressful. You haven't even asked how she is.'

'She OK?'

'She's all right, but we've been waiting ages. All I'm asking is that you eat something proper, then do your homework. You won't concentrate if you haven't eaten.'

A pause.

'Can I make a cake?'

'No, no, no! I don't want baking.'

'Why not?'

'Jack! I can't talk long. I want you to eat something decent. I'm going to call you in ten minutes to see if Ed's back and to check you've eaten, OK?'

Silence. Huge sigh.

'Bye, darling.'

'Bye.'

'Bye.'

Twenty minutes go by. Mum and I are still waiting. An episode of (no escape) *The Simpsons* is playing on the TV in the waiting area. My phone vibrates. I dive into the corridor to take it.

'Are you all OK? Is Ed back yet?'

'Mum,' says Jack, 'it's just that something has happened—'

'Oh my God! What?'

'I opened the front door a minute ago and there on the step was the dearest little bird you've ever seen, all brown and a bit speckly with kind of strange, like, markings on the top of his head. And he was just sitting there and—'

'Jack. Stop. Answer me for a second: is Ed back?'

'Yeah, but—'

'And have you eaten anything?'

'Listen! This bird he just stood there all trembling and trembling and so I picked him up and—'

'It's in the house?'

'We-ell, look, what we were thinking is, Becca hasn't really got a pet at the moment and well he seems so tame and—'

'No.'

'What?'

'You can't keep him.'

'Oh, Mum, please! He's so completely tame and we've never had a bird of our own before—'

I sit down on a plastic chair in the corridor. I shut my eyes, open them again. Every last bone of me feels tired, every part of me wiped out. A very old lady is wheeled past on a trolley. Her eyes are shut, her skin white as paper.

'Jack, I have to go back to Granny. Put the bird back in the garden and tell Ed to cook. I'll call you when we're on our way back home.'

'Oh, by the way,' says Jack, 'Ed was attacked.'

'What?'

'Yeah, on the way home he was mugged by this bunch of rudes and—'

'Wait – you're saying he was really attacked? Is he OK? Can I talk to him?'

'It's nothing to worry about, but he was hassled cos they wanted to take his phone and—'

'Can you put him on the phone right now, please?'

Ed comes on. 'Has he told you about the bird?'

'Eddie, what happened? Are you OK?'

'It was nothing, a bit of hassle that's all. I could make a cage for the bird out of—'

'Did they take anything. Were you hurt? Did you call the police?'

Ed doesn't sound as if he's listening. The phone goes muffled.

'Hold on, Mum . . . Oh, shit . . . Something's just happened. I'll have to call you back.' He rings off.

I march back into the waiting room, check our place in the queue, come out again, redial. Line busy. I wait. Try again. Eventually I get Becca.

'What now?'

'Becca, what's going on? You've got to tell me – I need to know that everything's OK.'

'Wait.'

Silence. Then Becca comes back on the line. 'It's, well . . . the cat just got the bird. It's . . . yeah, it's in her mouth now and Ed is trying to shoo it out of the cat-flap and its wings are flapping and – oh dirty! – there's blood all over its beak and—'

Ed snatches back the phone. 'Mum? Relax. The bird's dead. The cat's locked out. I'm cooking some pasta, OK?'

KFC

It's a bleak and cold night, a school night. For supper we had fresh tuna with rice and peas. Stewed apple with cinnamon for pudding. Eddie ate most of the tuna and left the rest. Jack left the tuna and ate only the white rice grains, picking them out from among the peas. Becca ate everything after smothering it all in tartare sauce. No one wanted pudding.

Now it's eleven o'clock and Jack's light should be out. Instead, he appears in the sitting-room doorway in hoodie and hat. 'Hey, I'm popping out for a minute. Won't be long, yeah?'

'What!'

'No, you're not,' says his father.

'You're supposed to be ready for bed,' I tell him.

He gazes at us blankly. The shadows under his eyes are deep and scary. 'I'm hungry, man. I gotta get something to eat.'

'Then you should have eaten your supper, man,' his father replies.

'There's plenty of food in the fridge,' I say. 'Or cereal. Have some cereal.'

'There's nothing,' Jack says, 'There's no cereal I like. And anyway I want KFC.'

His father and I look at each other. 'No way,' says his father. 'Forget it.'

'It will take me two minutes. I'll be so quick. You can time me.'

'It's not remotely safe for you to go all the way to the High Road at this time of night,' I tell him.

Jack rolls his eyes. 'KFC's the safest place in the world, man. Everybody's there at this time.'

'How do you know?' his father says. 'When have you been there at eleven at night?'

'Stop treating me like a baby, man.'

I stand up and start turning off lights. 'The answer's no. You're not going out. You were offered a perfectly good supper and you left it. If you're hungry, there's cereal. Now go and get ready for bed.'

Jack stands still. Very still.

'Go on.'

'Make me,' he says, and his eyes are dark with fatigue.

Luckily I don't have to decide what to do next because just then the big shape of Eddie bursts in, pushing past Jack, who simply ricochets against the wall. Suddenly the room feels full of men.

'I need the cleaner's number right now,' says Ed, running his hands through his hair.

'You what?' says his father.

'I need to ask her about something, yeah?'

'About what?'

'Some money of mine's gone missing and I need to know where she's put it, don't I?'

'I'm going,' says Jack and he turns round.

'Don't you dare,' says his father.

'There's no way Carmen would touch any money she found in this house,' I tell Eddie, 'and it would be deeply embarrassing for us to let you phone her.'

Eddie makes an impatient noise. 'It has to be her. I had ten quid – this guy who owed me finally paid me back. And it's not where I left it last night and she was here this morning and—'

'Where did you leave it?'

'On the kitchen floor,' he says, as if it's obvious.

Now things are getting interesting, Jack allows himself to slump onto the sofa.

'Hold on,' says their father. 'Let me get this straight. You left ten pounds on the kitchen floor and you're surprised it's not there any more?'

Eddie flings his arms out. 'For Christ's sake! I dropped it there last night and went to bed. I knew exactly where it was. And when I came to get it this morning, it was no longer there – get it, duh-brain?'

Jack starts laughing. Then he yawns. Then he remembers why he's here. 'OK, I'm starving. I'm off,' he says.

'No!' shouts his father.

'I'm going.'

'You walk out of this house now and there will be ... consequences,' I say, but my voice is shaky and he knows it. He blinks at me and walks out of the room.

My heart starts banging and at this moment Becca comes in. At least she's pyjamaed and ready for bed. At least she ate her supper. I smell freshly washed hair. Incense. Vanilla and pineapples. Becca has recently started washing because she has a 'person', the one she met at this party, who rings her up all the time. As far as I can tell, they don't see much of each other, this 'person' and Becca. But her phone rings constantly and she won't answer it if we're in the room. And she has a bath every night. And she smells nice. And sometimes she even is nice.

'Hey,' she says, 'what's going on?'

'Have you seen the money I left on the kitchen floor?' Ed demands.

Becca puts her head on one side. 'Hmm, now let me see. Would that be cash or cheque?'

'Fuck off,' says Ed. 'The tenner Joe paid me back. It was my entire going-out fund for tomorrow night! My entire social life was based on it. So just tell me, dear Mum and Dad, what exactly am I meant to do?'

His father and I look at each other for a long time. We can think of so many answers. Where do we start?

At that moment Jack reappears. He's taken off his hat and he's carrying a bowl of Weetabix, drowned in milk, and his face is soft again. My heart turns over with relief.

Smoking Draw

What do you do if your eighteen-year-old baby gets a monthly allowance that's supposed to include enough for clothes, but chooses instead to spend it all on 'going out', and walks around in rags?

And I do mean rags. Eddie stands in front of me in a pair of jeans so full of holes they make me feel shivery and sad. I've worn cheap clothes in my time – as a student I was dressed exclusively by Oxfam – but never clothes like these. I've never had to wear two pairs of trousers simply in order to stop the wind whistling past my knees. I've never worn a jumper at least two sizes too small. Or a cotton jacket in February. Or trainers which flap open at the toe and let in the freezing winter rain.

I want to take my boy shopping. I want to dress him like I used to be able to when he was seven or eleven or even fourteen. I want his clothes to fit and be warm and comfortable and appropriate for the time of year. I want him to have two pairs of things. Scarves and gloves. Enough boxer shorts not to have to dry them on the radiator every other evening. I want it to be like the old days, when the lady with pursed lips in Peter Jones's shoe department used to watch him walk up and down the beige carpet for ages before she could be sure the width fitting was exactly right.

'If you take him out and buy him shoes or clothes,' his father says, 'all you're doing is increasing his budget for drugs and alcohol. Simple as that. Think about it. Is that really what you want to do?'

He sounds harsh when he says this, but there's grief in his eyes.

'I can't bear seeing him in those jeans,' I whisper.

'It's his choice. If you care about that boy, you'll help him face the consequences of his actions.'

'Which are?'

'Being bloody cold. Shivering at the bus stop.'

Listen to us. Go back seventeen years and I remember anxious conversations about cot bumpers, bonnets, blankets and (were we for real?) scratch mits. Was our boy too hot or too cold? Should he sleep on his back or his side? Were sheepskin fleeces really a hygienic option? And now here we both are consigning to him to the bleak, midwintry streets of London without a proper coat, just to make him see what happens if you blow your allowance on vodka and E.

'Where does all your money go?' I ask Eddie. 'Can't you at least buy yourself some cheap jeans in the sales?'

As usual, he tips back in his chair. 'I'm really poor. How the hell am I meant to buy jeans?'

'Your allowance was worked out so you could afford some clothes. You get more than Becca and Jack. I don't see how—'

He yawns. 'I have debts.'

'But what sort of debts?'

'I always seem to owe people, that's all. And the people who owe me never pay up.'

'I hope you pay up.'

His eyes widen: 'Why the fuck d'you think I'm so poor?'

Later on, when Jack is standing by the (recently mended) toaster cramming bagels into his mouth and I've put Eddie's last few remaining threads of clothing into the washing machine, I fling a couple of tiny plastic bags onto the kitchen table.

'OK, how much cannabis are you guys buying?'

Jack reddens. Eddie doesn't.

'Where'd you get that?'

'Your pocket. If you can still call it a pocket. It's really no more than a flap of fabric hanging off another flap.'

'I don't want you going through my pockets.'

'Then empty them before you put them in the wash.'

'You know we smoke draw,' Ed says.

'But hardly any,' says Jack quickly. 'I swear. We don't smoke on weekdays. If you don't believe us, test our urine.'

'You're not testing mine,' says Ed in a voice so languid it hurts my heart.

I ignore him and turn to Jack. 'You're fifteen,' I say. 'Have you any idea what you're doing to your brain?'

Jack sighs. 'Mum, you think you know all about drugs because you once tried a tiny bit at university—'

'Jack,' says Eddie, 'look, shut up, OK?'

'Just about everyone we know smokes some draw at weekends,' says my youngest, who only really finally put his Lego away for good a year ago.

I said we used to worry about cot bumpers, but actually it was more than that. It was life and death. Especially death. I'd often get up in the night and tiptoe across the landing just to look at my babies in their beds. They slept so soundly that it sometimes took a while to be sure they really were still breathing. I'd have to stand there and wait for a sigh, a snort, any little noise or movement. And, exactly like now, my own heart would stop while I waited.

Revision

Eddie's revising for mocks. We know this because he walks around the house very, very slowly, carrying an armful of books and saying things like 'By the way, I'm going to be working for the next two hours, so please don't anyone disturb me' or 'How the hell can I wait an hour for supper when I need some protein inside me for all this fucking revision I have to do?'

He sighs a lot. He scratches his head. He undoes his belt and does it up again. He frowns at his reflection in the mirror and checks the side of his nose for spots. What he doesn't do is a) go upstairs to his desk, b) sit down with his books, or c) actually do any work.

He does, however, take breaks. Discovered sprawled on the sofa halfway through an episode of *Malcolm in the Middle*, he observes, 'The good thing about this programme is it's really, really therapeutic. It kind of clears my head when I'm having to take in so much information, you know?'

He also stands staring into the fridge as if it might offer him all the answers. Then he closes it. Then he opens it again and takes out a yoghurt. Becca's yoghurt.

'That's Becca's,' I tell him. 'The last vanilla one's hers.'

'Why?'

'Because I bought three and you and Jack have each had one and she hasn't.'

He slams the door so the milk bottles clink. 'Great. So what am I meant to eat when I'm revising, then?'

'Any of the other yoghurts. Apricot, strawberry, mango.'

'Mango. I hate mango. Whoever invented that flavour needs therapy.'

'It's not an invention, it's a fruit,' I remark as he scowls at me.

When he's not looking in the fridge, Eddie boils the kettle a lot.

'Hey, that kettle's way too full,' I tell him as he splatters it up to max. 'Think of the planet, Ed!'

'I can't think of anything right now except revision,' he says with the sobriety of an elder statesman contemplating a land invasion with heavy casualties.

Meanwhile, Jack is quietly getting on with some maths at the kitchen table. Quietly, because he's turned over a new leaf recently, which means he gets on with homework without

150

being reminded. I cannot tell you how much easier this has made life for his father. So much less shouting, so much less stress. The other day he even admitted that he's enjoying schoolwork a bit more.

'That's so great,' I said as steadily as I could, afraid that if I betrayed my unmitigated, undying relief, the illusion might just go pop.

'It's like I suddenly have a reason to work,' he said, 'a purpose. As if I can suddenly see the point of it all.'

Unfortunately, the sight of someone else genuinely working proves irresistible to our Ed. He plonks himself down on the chair next to Jack and sighs loudly. He says he needs to start revising so could Jack please try and be very, very quiet?

Jack looks at him. 'I wasn't sayin' nuttin', man.'

'I mean it,' Eddie growls. 'Shut up.'

'Shut up yourself, man.'

'Ed,' I say, 'this is ridiculous. If you need peace, why pick the one room in the house where there are other people? Go to your own room, for goodness sake.'

'I can't,' says Ed quickly. 'My room stinks.'

'What do you mean it stinks?'

'Becca left some Weetabix in there and it's going green.'

Jack looks at me, waiting to see what I'll say about this.

'Becca doesn't eat Weetabix,' I tell Ed. Jack goes back to his work. It's the right answer.

'I don't know what she fucking does or doesn't do, but can you please shut up so I can work!'

'He's distracting me,' says my youngest child. 'Do something, Mum.'

'The little squirt just wants to make a fight,' says Eddie. 'If you can't see through him, you're very blind indeed.'

'I was here first,' says Jack, who has put his pen down and is scraping his chair back. My heart sinks as I watch all the good intentions and concentration drain from his face.

'He's right, Ed,' I say. 'He was here first. And you have a perfectly decent room to go to.'

'So does he.'

'That's not the point.'

'Really, dear Mother? So what exactly is the point?'

Ed looks at me and there's real triumph in his eyes. He's wrong. He's mean. And he's trying to undermine everything I'm doing with Jack. If all this is so obvious to me, then why do I feel so panicky?

At that moment Becca walks in. She goes to the fridge, takes out her vanilla yoghurt, picks up a spoon. Silence. Everyone watching.

'What?' she says after a moment. 'What?'

Then, catching the tension and Ed's smirk and the look of desperation and exhaustion on my face, 'I'm not on your side, you know,' she informs me quickly.

Cheese

I'm home early from a meeting, not feeling well. As I put my key in the door I find it's still double-locked. No one back from school yet. Empty house. Bliss.

I turn up the heating, turn on lights, swallow two ibuprofen and breathe in the silence. But after less than two seconds, the front door shudders shut. The Richter scale tells me it's Becca. The thud of her rucksack hitting the hall floor. A sob of impatience as she kicks off her shoes. But even though my peace is evaporating, I've never not felt a mad surge of happiness when my kids come home.

She comes through, cheeks rosy with cold, gum in mouth, white iPod earphones in ears. An instant scowl: 'What are you doing here?'

'No need to look so disappointed.'

'I just wasn't expecting you to be here, that's all.'

'Well I wasn't going to be here, but I felt bad so I came home. Hope I'm not getting flu. Good day?'

'No.'

'Oh dear, why not?'

'Nothing you can help me with.'

'Try me.'

'I don't feel like talking, OK?'

OK. I don't say any more. I head upstairs.

When I was sixteen and my mum was under the weather,

153

I'd offer to make her tea, fetch her aspirin. My mum was a strong character, generous and loving and relentlessly charismatic. Some days I wanted her approval so much I was ready to burst. Sometimes in struggling to please her, I almost forgot there was a person called Me. Not a problem my Becca has. Will her daughter bring her tea when she's ill?

As I slide into bed I hear the front door slam hard. Jack. Good. I close my eyes and maybe I sleep for a bit because the first clue I have that Eddie's also home is when he flings open the bedroom door and turns on the light. 'OK, the sliced cheese in the fridge, is it for packed lunches or not?'

'The what?' I blink. 'Ed, please, I'm trying to rest.'

'Sorry, but I've absolutely got to get this straight. Becca says it's for packed lunch but there's two packs there and I urgently need some to make cheese on toast.'

'Eddie, turn off the light, please.'

'Not until I get an answer,' he says, but then, possibly realising how close to a Gestapo agent he sounds, he turns it off anyway.

I put on the bedside one and take a small breath. My head still hurts.

'It's for lunches. Now please go away and let me rest.'

'Fine. If you're going to be like that, I'm taking some anyway.' He starts to walk away.

I sit up. 'It's not to be used now,' I call after him. 'There's some unsliced cheese, I know there is. I bought the sliced specially for packed lunch. Eddie!'

His head reappears round the door. 'OK, fucking hell, Mum, no need to get in such a state. Listen to your-self, you're so uptight. No wonder you have to lie down all the time. Why can't you just leave me alone and learn to chill?'

I stare at him. Me? Leave him alone?

'I'm not well enough for this conversation,' I mutter, as his footsteps recede.

Darkness. Peace. But a minute later the light goes on again and there's Becca.

'Right. Listen to this. Ed has taken three slices of cheese. He has removed them from the packet in the fridge and is stuffing them into his big fat mouth as I speak.'

'Oh dear. Has he?'

She takes a breath. 'That's all you can say? Oh-dear-has-he?'

'Look, darling, please, I don't feel good. Can it wait?'

'Do you think it can wait?'

'Yes, I do. I actually think it can.'

'Your son is viciously plundering cheese from the fridge and you think it can wait?'

'Becs, come on, he's only doing this to get attention. I'll talk to him later, but right now—'

I break off because Becca is looking at me with such extreme coldness.

'Mum, you know what? It's not about Eddie. Forget Eddie. This isn't about him. It's all about you.'

'Me?'

'Yes! You're impossible to talk to about anything because you don't care about anyone except yourself.'

'Oh, Becs—'

'And you know what? If I had a real problem right now, you're the very last person I'd turn to.'

She leaves the room and slams the door. Then reopens it. 'I mean even if the world was fucking obliterated and the last person left was you, I would not confide in you.'

'That's tough,' I admit. 'But, Becs?'

'What?'

'Do you have a problem?'

She looks away for a quick second. I pat the bed. 'Tell me about it.'

She says nothing. She sits down. She still can't look at me, but all the anger leaves her face.

'Oh, sweetheart. Try to tell me.'

I hold her little hand for a moment. It feels cool and dry. I know if I looked at it I'd see ink smudges. She doesn't tell me anything, but we sit there for a few moments without talking and eventually she knocks a tear away with her hand and tries to smile.

'I'm sorry about the cheese,' she says.

Swearing

'What's this about you owing three homeworks?' I ask Jack as I read a stern note from his German teacher. My younger son, standing by the fridge as usual, looks at me for a quick second and licks chocolate milk from his lips.

'Oh, well, no,' he says carefully. 'It doesn't quite mean that.'

'What does it mean, then?'

He takes a breath. 'Well, you see, the first one, she thought I hadn't given it in, but it turned out it was just quite near the bottom of the pile, so she hadn't had a chance to look at it, and then the second, well, because it was the day of the snow, remember, and I missed the beginning of the class so I wasn't there when it was set, so that wasn't my fault, and then the third one, well, I know about that and I'm doing it tonight, but, you know, anyway, you should ignore anything that woman says because she's a cunt.'

I sit for a moment and take this in.

'Jack,' I say, 'never, ever say that word about anyone, please.'

He wipes his mouth with the back of his hand and gazes at me with the wide-apart angel eyes that remind me of the time when he still sucked his thumb day and night.

'But she *is* a cunt.'

'Oh, for fuck's sake, it's only a word, Mum,' pipes up our

Eddie, fearless campaigner against family injustices every-where.

'I have nothing against the word itself,' I tell him calmly, 'though some people have and you ought to be aware of that. It's an old word, and I don't especially mind it being used to describe a woman's vagina under the right circumstances. But I will not listen to any of you use it as a derogatory way of referring to someone. I won't hear it used as a curse.'

'Why not?' asks Jack, who quickly poured more chocolate milk when I said the word 'vagina' so he didn't have to look at me.

'Because it's lazy and very, very offensive. I hope you're going to drink that, Jack.'

He gulps it down.

Eddie grins at me. You can tell he's loving this. He blinks. 'The thing is, Mum, can you please chill. It's a word, right?'

'You already said that.'

'Yeah, well, all I mean is, what's so scary? You've no idea how middle-aged and uptight you sound.'

'I am middle-aged, but I'm not scared and I'm not uptight. I've never been uptight.'

When the kids were younger and had just discovered the zingy deliciousness of swearing – when Eddie was busily introducing the younger two to 'bugger' and 'bloody' and 'fuck'

– we decided the only way was to fight fire with fire. So we'd be driving along and one or other of them would start swearing and, rather than ban it, I'd yawn and say, 'OK, take two minutes and say all the words you need to say and then, when you've got that out of your system, we'll talk about something more interesting.'

And at first, of course, they thought this was thrilling and funny. Giggling, they'd lob endless 'fucks' and 'shits' across the car. But after a few minutes of such permitted (and therefore strangely futile) cursing, the power of the words would eerily diminish. And, almost without realising it, they'd move on to something else. Exactly as we'd hoped and planned.

'You know, Mum,' a nine-year-old Eddie (an Eddie I can now barely believe ever existed) once observed, 'it's not that swearing's so amazing, is it? It's more that humans always long to do the one thing they're not allowed to do.'

Great, I thought, it's worked. And I felt so happy, such a good mum. I was smug. But I was also wrong. Well, it didn't work, did it? Somewhere, somehow (how, exactly? I wish I knew), boundaries were overstepped, standards dropped, relaxed. Somehow, against my wishes, I ended up living a life surrounded by 'fucks' and 'cunts'.

Actually, not 'cunt'. That one is still rarely used in our house. But for how long?

'Anyway, Mum' – Jack is delving around in the bottom of

159

his rucksack and once again not looking at me – 'what are the right circumstances?'

'Right circumstances for what?'

'For using it to describe a woman's . . . you-know.'

'Vagina?'

'Mmm.' He blushes. Eddie – who would himself have to blush if his brother wasn't kindly doing it for him – turns to watch us both, an expression of relaxed enjoyment on his face.

'Well, it's a tricky one,' I begin. 'It's really about context, isn't it? But, Jack, darling, you know what?'

'What?'

'I find it quite funny, and maybe a bit sad, that you're quite happy to describe someone as a "cunt" but you can't quite bring yourself to say "vagina" without going red.'

He carries on blushing. My baby. And for once I don't particularly feel like helping him out.

Not Recognising Jack

Jack comes home on Saturday afternoon, having been at Luke's house since the day before.

There's mud on his trainers and he has a look on his face I don't like – as if his brain's been sucked out of his skull, whacked hard and put back in the wrong way up.

I ask him if he's put his school uniform in the wash yet.

He sucks his teeth. 'I'll do it, OK?'

I say I really need to have it now as I don't want to have to do washing on Sunday.

'I said I'd do it, didn't I?'

'I want to put it on before lunch.'

'You haven't had lunch yet?'

'Dad's doing some in a minute,' I say. 'Are you hungry? Did you have breakfast?'

He looks at me and for a second his face goes blurry, as if he's about to burst into tears.

'Hey, sweetheart.' I go over to him. 'Hey, darling, what is it?'

He gives me a look as if I kicked him.

'What on earth's the matter?' I'm seriously concerned now.

'Please leave me alone. I mean it. I'll get the fucking uniform in a minute, OK?'

He sinks into a kitchen chair. 'Get off me,' he growls, although I haven't touched him.

Two days ago, I was walking back from the High Road at about five, pavements crowded and cold, and there was this tall, thin man walking in front of me and something about the shape of him was familiar. Was it his walk? His clothes? I couldn't decide.

Then I saw that the crotch of his trousers came right down below his anorak – just like Jack's. The guy was all in black, hooded, rucksacked – could be school uniform, but . . . and he was huge, at least six foot.

In the end I decided to overtake him.

'Yo, Mum.' He grabbed my shopping bags, happy to see me.

I was happy to see him, too, but couldn't believe that this tall, black-clad man was my child. That, on a crowded street at dusk, my child could be a stranger to me.

'For God's sake,' says his father now, 'leave the boy alone. Even if something is wrong, why should he always have to give you a full written report?'

Jack shoots him a look – half grateful and half wary.

'D'you want some pasta?' his father says. 'I'm making it for Becca and me. Speak now if you want some.'

'Yup,' says Jack, and he goes to wash his hands.

'His face,' I whisper as soon as he's gone.

'What about it?'

'Didn't you notice? He looks weird.'

'He looks normal to me. Tired, probably. Stop crowding him. Seriously. Don't you see what you're doing?'

'But he was on the verge of tears a moment ago.'

'So?' His father puts spaghetti into boiling water. 'Sometimes people want to cry but they stop themselves. He's fifteen. Stop acting as if he's eight.'

It's true, I think. The size and shape of Jack when he was eight or nine years old – small and bendy enough for me to grab him and kiss the top of his head, smell the biscuity smell of his hair – that's what I'm still looking out for when I'm on the street. That's why I don't recognise him when he's walking right in front of me.

The new six-foot Jack comes back in and eats lunch. All seems fine. We chat. Afterwards he goes up and gets his uniform.

As I stuff it in the machine, he comes close. 'Mum? Can I tell you something?'

I wait.

'Last night when we were out, we were attacked.'

'Who?' I find I am surprisingly calm and still.

'Me and Luke. And Jon and Solly. We were in the park, it wasn't even dark and these rudes came over and asked us to empty our pockets so we did and, well, they took everything we had and then they told me to put my hands on the ground and they stamped on my fingers with their boots and then they pushed me down in the dirt and that's why' – he opens the carrier bag he's holding behind his back – 'that's why these jeans are so filthy. I'm sorry, OK?'

I stare at him. 'Did you tell the police?'

He blinks. 'Come on, Mum, what can they do? It's not the first time I've been attacked.'

We stand looking at each other.

'Are you all right?' I say.

He shrugs. 'Don't overreact, OK? I can't tell you these things if you overreact.'

He goes, and I hear the TV being turned on in the sitting

room, the clatter of plates going in the dishwasher. I put the soap in and I press the button and I stay calm and still. I do everything I can not to overreact.

Father and Daughter

Becca and her father are very similar and very close. Both clever, volatile, emotionally distant at times. They share a bitter sense of humour, a love of pickled vegetables and an ability to outwit me in any argument, any conversation.

'You don't get it, do you?' Becca will say when I've asked her for the eighteenth time to please disentangle her knickers from her jeans before she puts them in the wash.

'Don't get what?'

'Oh' – she tosses her hair and looks out of the window – 'it doesn't matter. Never mind.'

'Please tell me what you mean.'

She sucks her teeth. 'It's not worth it. I know what you'll say.'

'What will I say?' I ask with a vague panic that already I'm losing the thread.

She smiles. 'Well . . . you're so predictable, that's all.'

'Stop distracting me from the fact that I'm asking you to do something!'

She smiles again. 'There you go.'

'There I go what?'

'Don't worry,' she sighs. 'I swear to Holy God on High that I'll disentangle in future, OK?'

'Thank you,' I say and she goes and I am left with the feeling that I've both got what I wanted yet also somehow lost.

If I go into a room and Becca and her father are watching TV, they raise their heads to look at me with a mixture of affection, bafflement and amusement. Like a pair of leopards at a waterhole, sizing me up, finger ready on the PAUSE button so they don't miss a frame.

'Yes? What do you want?' Becca asks.

'I came to offer you some food,' I say.

'We're fine,' says her father.

'Yeah, we're fine.'

'Thanks,' I add rather pointedly.

Now they both turn to gaze at me in wonder. 'We said thanks!'

'You actually didn't. Not that actual word.'

And they both sigh and look back at the paused picture on the screen. Beige men conversing in a beige corridor in Boston. The kind of TV I can never get into. I go and leave them in peace.

But when Becca and her dad fall out . . .

I find her now on the landing, pale and furious. 'What is it, Becs?'

'It's *him*.'

'Eddie?'

'No, not Eddie. *Him*. That stupid man you're married to.'

'What's Dad done now?'

'Only refused to let me have the one piece of software I need to complete my fucking homework, that's all. So petty! So babyish! I can't believe it. He needs his head sorting out.'

I think about this. 'Were you rude to him?'

She throws her head back in disbelief. 'Why the fuck do you always have to side with him? He's so fucking unreasonable. I really don't know how you can fucking well live with him.'

Downstairs I find her father at the kitchen table with his head in his hands.

'Do you know what she did?' he says. 'I asked her to empty the dishwasher and she refused. And when I said I was sick of her laziness, she threw the white jug across the room.'

I take a breath. 'Did it smash?'

'What do you think? How can she be so destructive?'

I go to the bottom of the stairs and call up. 'Rebecca! Come down here right now!'

Rather surprisingly, she trails downstairs, morose and shadowy-eyed in jeans and slippers. 'What?'

'You smashed a jug.'

'So?'

'We don't throw objects in this house.'

She raises an eyebrow.

'Now, empty the dishwasher, please. You're the only member of this family who's done nothing to help so far today.'

She folds her arms. 'I'm not doing it till he says sorry to me.' She eyes her father and he looks up wearily.

'Sorry for what?'

'For speaking to me like that.'

'Like what?'

'Like . . . like I never do anything around the house.'

We can't help it. We both laugh.

'But you don't,' we say.

She stifles a small scream. 'There you go! There you both go! Oh, forget it. I don't need the disc. What does it matter? I'll just go and fail all my fucking GCSEs and you can both enjoy seeing my whole life in ruins!'

She marches back upstairs and we wait for the customary double-door slam, and sure enough it comes, followed by a third for good measure.

I empty the dishwasher.

Two hours later, I find the two of them in the sitting room, socked feet up on the sofa, shoulders touching, thick as thieves, drinking Coke together in front of one of their beige urban programmes.

This time I don't offer food. I don't offer anything. Instead, I think how much I would have given to have such a relationship with my own father. I never argued with him – I

167

never dared. I feared him. And maybe if I'd been allowed to smash a few jugs, or even just watch some crap TV with him, I might have felt more when I held his hand as he lay dying.

Portobello Road

A bright spring Saturday: Becca and I are driving to Portobello Road. Becca is keen. She actually got out of bed 'early' (11.30 a.m.) to come.

She wants to get a tight black dress, some red stripy tights, maybe some vintage cowboy boots and some incense sticks. ('You can't burn them in your room,' I remind her, even though I know it's a lost cause. 'Yeah, yeah, I know.') I want olives, flowers, herbs.

'I really cannot imagine,' says Becca, frowning and putting her feet up on the dashboard, 'ever in my life getting to the stage when I'm more excited about herbs than clothes.'

'Feet off the dashboard,' I tell her. 'And I do like clothes.'

'Why?'

'Why what?'

'Why can't I have my feet on the dashboard?'

'Because if we had an accident you'd break your back.'

'Oh, right, and like, we're definitely going to crash, driving through Camden, yeah?'

'You can crash anywhere. You can die anywhere. Worse,

do you really want to be in a wheelchair for the rest of your life?'

She tuts and rolls her eyes but puts her feet down.

'Something really awful happened to someone at school.'

'Mmm?'

'Someone in year ten. They went on holiday and they went walking on some cliffs and their mum fell off and was killed.'

'That's terrible,' I say. 'Who? When did it happen?'

'A few weeks ago. I mean at half-term. Everyone was really upset. We had an assembly about it.' She goes silent for a minute. 'You know the covered market under the bridge?'

'You mean at Portobello?' I say, taking a moment for my mind to switch.

'Right. Can we go there first? Because last time I was there they had some quite good stuff.'

But we end up parking nearer to the other end and walking back. She leads and I follow, once or twice almost losing her in the crowd. Finally, she grabs the cuff of my jacket and pulls me along as if I'm her child.

'Oh, wow, oh my God, awesome!' She's stopped and is staring up at an old black tailcoat. 'That is just so . . . Oh, I've been looking for one of those for ages,' she sighs.

'Ask how much.'

She shakes her head. 'It'll be too much.'

I ask the man. Seventy pounds. Becca is horrified. She bites her lip.

'It looks a bit tatty, actually,' she says. 'It would probably suit Eddie. He'd probably think seventy was reasonable. But he never has any money, anyway.'

She laughs and the thought of Eddie not being able to afford it seems to cheer her.

I think how Becca has always had this sensible, frugal streak, an ability to resist, to square it with herself when she can't have something. Even as a toddler, she was the only one of our kids whose Christmas list didn't read like a Toys R Us catalogue. Her requirements were quaint and homely: 'A Nice Pencil. Some Brown Hairy String. A Tin To Put My Special Buttons In.'

Becca looks at me. 'Mum? I feel a bit funny.'

'In what way funny?'

'I don't know. A bit . . . like my legs are all wavy.'

'Hey,' I remember, 'you haven't had any breakfast.'

We go to a Spanish café. I have coffee, Becca has a Coke and some octopus salad.

'Octopus for breakfast?'

She grins. 'It's nearly lunch.'

'The thing is,' she says, as she skewers the white rubbery rings onto her fork, 'that mum who was killed. It was the first time, you know, that someone I knew died. Well, I didn't exactly know her, but you know?'

I nod.

'The only thing that has ever died in our lives was Jackson.'

Jackson was an old dog which her father and I had before she was born. Jackson just keeled over one day when the children were little. They were unmoved.

'Even though I didn't know her – that mum I mean – I keep remembering her at a parents' evening with Anna. The one before half-term. And, well, she was in the queue for Mr Rigby and she had long curly hair and she looked . . . nice. And, well, she had no time at all left to live.'

Becca sighs a long sigh and puts down her octopus-laden fork. 'I don't know what I'd do if something happened to you,' she says.

I touch her hand, her warm, grubby teenage hand. Life is fragile, I want to tell her, life is precarious and short. Relish the moment. Don't waste any time on anger.

'I love you,' I say.

She looks at me thoughtfully, takes a swig of her Coke.

'That jacket,' she says at last. 'I was thinking, it would really suit you. Why don't you try it on? And if you like it, you can buy it and then, when you've had enough of it, you can give it to me, yeah?'

Springtime

Becca has a late start for school today and last night she gave me strict instructions not to wake her up, so I didn't. Now, at ten past ten, while I'm hanging on the phone trying to get through to Parcelforce, she appears in the doorway, panda-eyed and flustered.

'Why the fuck didn't you wake me?'

'Morning, darling.'

'Well, why didn't you?'

'Because you told me not to.'

She blinks at me. I give up on Parcelforce and hang up.

'Muuuuum! I mean, have you seen what time it is?'

'Becca,' I say, as calmly as I can, 'you expressly told me not to wake you. You said you wanted to sleep in a little longer, remember?'

'Yes! A little longer! Not a whole lot longer! If it got this late, I obviously wanted to be woken, didn't I? For fuck's sake, Mum, can't you try and use what little brain you have?'

I take a deep breath. I look out of the window at the daffodils, the big tree bathed in morning sunshine. Spring is going on out there. Plants and animals waking up. All by themselves, with no one else to blame.

But teenagers don't have seasons. They don't clock that moist smell in the air, that sudden, swervy-wobbly quality to the light. Becca's world is a relentlessly indoor one – artificially lit, with a perpetual backing track by the Killers.

'How could I possibly know what you considered to be too late?' I ask her. 'I thought you'd set an alarm. What time do you have to be in, anyway?'

She gives me an impatient look. 'I haven't got time to talk,' she says and slump-stomps downstairs. I hit redial and I'm back to Parcelforce.

But half a minute later, she's back, flushed and panting. 'Have you seen my tie?'

'What?' I'm trying to listen to a mechanical voice which is calmly laying out my options. 'Shh, just a minute.'

'My tie. My tie! Quick! T-i-e. That black and yellow stripy thing that goes round my fucking neck, remember?'

'No,' I say quickly, 'I haven't seen it.'

She bangs her fists against the wall and then lays her cheek against it, eyes shut in gothic dismay. 'I don't believe you.'

'What reason would I have to lie about your tie? And why would I have seen it, anyway?'

'Because it's not where I fucking well left it on Friday, that's why!'

I sigh and put down the phone again. I was so close.

'OK. Where did you leave it?'

'I don't know.'

'Then how do you know it isn't where you left it?'

She gives me a filthy look. 'I haven't got time for your mind games.'

This time I start to laugh.

'It's not funny,' she tells me, scowling.

'All right,' I tell her, 'there's a secret spare one in the cupboard above the cooker, behind the rice. But it's the only spare. It's Jack's spare one, too. It means you absolutely have to find the other one and put the spare one back.'

But she doesn't answer. She's gone.

A minute goes by. I hover over the phone, wondering whether I dare re-enter the world of the Parcelforce automata.

I was right to wait: she's back, hair pinned on top of her head, fingers fumbling with the tie round her neck.

'Hello again,' I say brightly.

'How cold is it out there?'

Again I glance out of the window. The sky is soaring and blue.

'Quick! Tell me! I need to know.'

'It's spring,' I tell her.

'Yeah, I know that. How cold is it?'

'Well, let me see . . . I haven't been out yet, but I would guess there's a slight chill to the air at this exact moment, but that it will slowly get warmer as the day goes on. No rain is forecast. Have you seen those daffodils?'

She looks at me as if I'm on day release. 'I hate this weather.'

'Do you really? Why?'

'It's so fucking bright. It hurts my eyes. You stand at the bus stop and you can't even see the number on the bus, it's so dazzling.'

I think about this. A teenager's take on sunshine. Suddenly Kafka seems an incurable optimist.

'But doesn't it cheer you up?' I suggest.

'What?' she snaps. 'What about it would cheer me up?'

'Well, you know, everything getting warmer. Things growing.'

'I hate warm and I don't care what grows.'

'But . . . summer coming and all that?'

'I hate summer.'

'Do you?'

'Yeah. Everyone looks so horrible with their clothes off. I hate it. Speaking of clothes, I was going to say, I could really do with some new jeans, you know.'

'Don't you have to go?' I say. 'I thought you were in a hurry?'

She glances at her watch. 'For fuck's sake, Mum, are you trying to get rid of me or something?'

Eddie's Lies

Eddie went away for the weekend to stay with a friend at university. He said he'd be back Sunday afternoon in time to finish an essay. But when we went to bed he still wasn't back and at about 3 a.m. I heard the front door shudder shut.

Now, on Monday morning, I find his rucksack dumped in the hall with our nice cocktail shaker sticking out of it. Becca comes down to find me holding it.

'I said you'd go mad if he took it,' she says with a sideways glance bordering on pleasure, 'but he took it anyway.'

I try to unscrew the shaker but it's stuck. It's really sticky. Becca opens the bread bin and peers in.

'You mean you saw him take it?' I say, rinsing my fingers under the tap.

She shrugs, puts a slice of bread in the toaster, reaches for the Marmite. 'What was I meant to do? Oh, and he filled it up with vodka by the way.'

'Our vodka?'

'Whose do you think? He topped up the bottle with water so you wouldn't know.'

'He topped it up?'

'Mum? Are you just going to stand there repeating everything I say or what?'

I try to think. 'Becca,' I say, 'you did actually see him do this?'

She sighs. 'Of course I saw him. Why would I bother to lie about it? Have you seen my PE shirt anywhere, by the way?'

I tell her I haven't. She lets out a quick yowl of fury and stomps back upstairs.

Jack comes down, carrying a football, an art folder, two pairs of trainers and a wet towel. His trousers are riding so low on his thighs that, minus the usual hand to hold them up, he has to keep his legs wide open to prevent them from falling right down.

'This morning,' I tell him, 'when I let the dog out, I found two cigarette butts on the lawn.'

'It was Ed,' he says straightaway.

'They were right under your window.'

Calmly, he puts down his stuff and pours Weetos into a bowl. 'I told you, it was Ed. He does it on purpose.'

'Does what on purpose?'

'Goes and smokes in my room so you'll think it's me.'

'But . . .' I hesitate, confused. 'He goes in your room?'

'If you don't believe me,' Jack says, 'go and look in his room right now. On the chair by his bed you'll see every-thing – baccy, Rizlas, lighter.'

'But,' I say, not getting it, 'I mean . . . when did he smoke in your room?'

'Last night. I don't know when. Late. He's evil. He woke me up, man.'

I run up to Ed's room. He's asleep in T-shirt and boxers. Light snoring. An odour of bad milk, sweat and incense. I pull up the blind. On the chair by his bed, just as Jack said, is the full smoking tackle.

He groans as daylight hits his face. 'Get up,' I say.

'Free period,' he lies.

'Don't lie.'

I sit down, not caring that I'm squashing his legs. 'And

why did you take our cocktail shaker? And our vodka? Why did you wake Jack in the middle of the night to smoke in his room?'

He opens his eyes. 'How d'you know?'

'I found stubs under his window this morning.'

'No, about the vodka?'

'Never mind.'

'That bitch—'

'Don't use that word, Ed. I mean it.'

He's silent a moment. 'Don't be fooled by anything that little squirt Jack says, by the way. They're his stubs, I can promise you that.'

I look at my elder son. He has the nicest eyes of anyone I know: frank, intelligent, open, kind.

'I swear to you,' he whispers, as if he's seen a chink.

I close my eyes. 'I'm sorry,' I say. 'I don't believe you.'

He leans up on one elbow. 'Mum, think about it. What evidence do you have? Why's he any more likely to be telling the truth than me?'

I look at this boy–man's face, and a long-ago random memory floats into my head. I see a nine-month-old Jack strapped safely into his Mamas and Papas pushchair, a four-year-old Eddie and a two-year-old Becca holding onto each side as I push.

'I don't know,' I say as, in my head, the mum and the three kids start to cross a busy road. They're being so careful. The mum is checking all the time that they're holding on. She looks left and right.

'But you believe him and not me?' says Ed.

I nod and a tear slips down my cheek.

'What the fuck's up now?' he says. 'What the fuck're you crying about?'

'I don't know,' I say, as the long-ago mum and kids safely reach the other side; and the tear reaches my mouth and I taste the welcome hotness of salt.

TV Supper

Becca, Jack and I are having our supper on the sofa in front of *ER*. Or trying to. Jack's in a bad mood because he thought it was just going to be us two.

'I don't want that cow joining us,' he says when he hears Becca's home.

'Don't be so horrible,' I say. 'Of course she can watch it with us if she wants.'

'But why?'

I yawn. 'Because she's a part of this family.'

'She doesn't act like one.'

'What's that supposed to mean? Don't be so silly.'

I put some cauliflower cheese on his plate. A glass of wine would be nice, I think. But then again, I promised myself I wouldn't drink tonight.

'Cauliflower,' sighs Jack. 'The one vegetable I don't eat.'

'You hardly eat any vegetables.'

'Well, I never eat cauliflower.'

'Well, tough, because that's what we're having.'

'Can't I just have the sauce?'

'No, you can't,' I say, wondering if there's any Sauvignon in the fridge.

'Why?'

'Because it would be impossible to separate the cauliflower and the sauce, that's why. And because you're fifteen not five and— Oh, for goodness sake, Jack!'

Suddenly exhausted, I bang the saucepan down harder than I meant to. One glass might be counted as medicinal.

'No need to be like that,' he says.

'I'm just so bloody tired, that's all.'

'You shouldn't have bothered cooking cauliflower cheese, then,' says Jack. 'I'd have been happy with pasta.'

And now here we all are on the sofa: Becca joylessly separating each cauliflower floret before licking off the sauce; Jack, who's settled for a piece of bread and butter, ketchup and a pea-sized blob of cauliflower cheese; me with no glass of wine. And someone at County General lying on a gurney and vomiting blood.

'Move your leg,' Jack suddenly snaps at Becca. She keeps her eyes on the screen.

'I said move it!'

'Oh, Jack, really,' I say. 'Leave her alone.'

Jack puts his plate on the floor and picks up his glass of squash – that awful pink stuff that smells of air freshener. I always swear I won't buy it for them and then I always do.

'This is a three-seater sofa,' says Jack. 'There're three of us. That lump over there is taking up way more than one seat.'

Wearily I glance over at the lump, who is actually rather elegant and birdlike and seems to be sitting in a perfectly reasonable, normal and confined way.

'She's fine,' I say.

'I'm fine,' growls Becca.

'Oh God,' says Jack, 'I don't believe you can't see it. Are you blind, man? Look at her leg. Look at how it's spilling over into my space.'

I look at the leg in question. A part of it could be said to be drifting about 3cm from the top left corner of the sofa cushion that Jack is sitting on.

'Becca,' I say, 'move your leg a bit, can you? I'm sorry. Jack's being incredibly immature. But I just want to watch *ER*.'

Becca scowls and moves her leg. Then straightaway lets it flop back over into Jack's space. I try not to see. I close my eyes and try not to think of Sauvignon.

'For Christ's sake!' Jack bangs his fork down on his plate. 'What?'

'Her leg! Her fucking leg! It's back!'

'Becca?'

'Now what?'

'Please – I beg you – don't wind him up.'

Becca puts her plate down and glares at me. 'How can you say I'm winding him up when it's so fucking clear that he hates me and doesn't want me here?'

She lets out a forlorn little sob.

A gunman has somehow got into the ER and is letting rip. I wish I was there. It seems almost peaceful – a nice safe place where things are settled with gunfire or hypodermics.

'Too right I don't,' mutters Jack. 'Fat cow.'

'Did you hear that?' Becca shouts. 'Did you hear what he called me? Or are you deaf to your little golden boy?'

I get up and pause the tape. 'OK, I give up. It's like trying to watch TV with a couple of two-year-olds.'

Jack lowers his eyes, but Becca is on fire. 'Both of us? You're saying that both of us are doing this?'

I try to remember exactly what I said. 'Jack started it,' I say, 'but you haven't exactly been very mature, either.'

Big tears are rolling down my daughter's cheeks.

'I'm so tired,' I tell her truthfully. 'I really haven't got the energy for this.'

'You should have thought about that before you started it.'

I'm speechless. 'Started what?'

'This . . . fight. You think it's Jack I have a problem with,

182

but it's not, it's you, Mum. You're the only problem in this house!' And she storms downstairs.

Jack and I continue with *ER*. But not before I've fetched myself a large glass of wine.

Stealing

Two pound coins have gone missing from the pot of parking-meter money in our bedroom. It's not the first time this has happened. A couple of weeks ago, a five-pound note disappeared from my handbag. At least, I was pretty sure it did. But what if I was wrong? What if I'd spent it and forgotten? This time, though, there's no such doubt.

'I wasn't exactly setting a trap for them,' their father tells me in a voice that is sad, baffled and weary all at the same time, 'just that I did make a mental note of exactly how much was there.'

'It's not so unusual for teenagers to nick money from their parents,' I say, but even as the words come out I wonder if I'm making it up to comfort us.

Either way, he's not buying it.

'Did you steal from yours?' he says.

I hesitate. 'I do remember being about nine and taking coppers that my father emptied out of his pockets at night. But I felt so guilty that I stopped.'

This is the truth. I remember it so well: the slow and

horrible realisation that neither possessing nor spending those coppers gave me any pleasure at all.

'But you were nine,' he says with a huge sigh. 'There's a big difference. And it made you feel bad. The trouble with our kids is they have no sense of guilt. No moral centre.'

I say nothing.

'Well?' he says. 'Don't you feel that?'

'I don't know,' I say, and I look at him and try to work out why the terrible weight of disappointment on his face makes me feel that I'm the one who's let him down.

But we agree the situation can't continue. So next day we announce that no pocket money will be paid to any of them until the culprit confesses.

'Not to any of us?' gasps Eddie.

'Not until someone confesses, no.'

'But that's so fucking unfair on us innocent ones!' Becca immediately shouts.

'Well, tough,' I say. This is the new me: gritty, determined, unswayable and a little bit scary.

Eddie looks appalled. 'A measly couple of quid goes missing and suddenly all pocket money's on hold?' he says. 'Seriously, how the hell can you justify that?'

The new Nazi me shrugs quite convincingly. 'Tell me why we have to.'

He stares at me. Becca sucks her teeth and looks out of the window.

'It's not the money,' says their father. 'It's the principle. If one of you is stealing from us, we need to know who.'

'Why?'

'So we can talk about it. Help whoever it is.'

'Oh.' Becca rolls her eyes. 'You mean therapy.'

'We mean,' says her father, 'a basic sense of right and wrong.'

'I don't see why we should all suffer when it's pretty fucking obvious it's Jack,' she says, banging the parmesan grater down hard enough on the table to make cheese spray out everywhere.

Jack is the only one so far remaining silent and placid. He licks his finger and starts picking up bits of cheese.

'Anyway, you guys are so tight,' Eddie says. 'You give us so little allowance that you shouldn't be surprised if we steal from you.'

'Is that a confession?' his father asks him sharply.

'Of course not,' he says, flushing. 'We all know it's Jack.'

'What makes you think it's him?'

Certainly, of the three of them Jack looks the least guilty. He slices up a pear and when, as he starts to eat it, the juice dribbles down his chin, he trots off to get a piece of kitchen towel.

Becca watches him as if he's Beelzebub. 'I'm not saying anything,' she says, 'but if the little fucker doesn't confess . . .'

'What?' says Jack calmly. 'What will you do?'

'Just fucking tell them,' she hisses.

'Maybe you should fucking tell them,' Jack replies.

Becca pulls her hair over her face. 'I would. I fucking would. If I had anything to confess to.'

A week goes by. A week during which Becca moans that there's no point looking forward to the weekend because she can't go to Camden and get the bright-yellow nail polish she's seen. A week during which Eddie says his life might as well be over if he can't go to a club on Saturday night with his friends. A week during which Jack carries on pretty much as normal.

Then, late one night as we're going to bed, he asks to have a word with us. He sits on the clothes-strewn chair in our room and carefully strokes the nap of his jeans.

'I stole the money,' he says after a second or two.

Silence. His eyes barely flicker. There's a deadness there that frightens me.

'So can I have my pocket money now?' he says.

To be continued . . .

Stealing 2

Previously on *Living with Teenagers*:

Two pound coins have gone missing from the pot of parking-meter money in our bedroom . . . No one will 'fess up to the heist . . . And it's not the first time money has taken a walk . . . After an announcement that no one gets pocket money until the culprit spills the beans, Jack has finally come to our room and sung like a canary.

It's late at night. We're not that surprised it's turned out to be him. But I'm shocked by his face: tired, defiant, dead.

'So can I have my pocket money now?' he says.

His father takes a breath. 'Look, boy, well done for owning up, but this is very, very serious.'

'Why?'

There's something slightly menacing about the loose-shouldered way he says it, as if now that he's confessed to one crime he can simply relax into further yobbishness.

'What?' says his father, confused.

'I don't see why it has to be serious.'

'Jack,' I say slowly, 'you don't think it's wrong to steal?'

He thinks about this for a second. 'Well . . . it depends, doesn't it?'

'Sorry? What exactly does it depend on?'

'On who I steal from, right?'

We stare at him. 'Have you stolen from us before?' his father asks in a rougher voice.

Jack is furiously ironing a crease in his jeans with his finger and thumb. The crease is getting sharper and sharper.

'Once or twice,' he says, still in that deadpan tone. 'I'm not going to lie, am I?' He flushes when we both say nothing.

187

'Fivers have gone missing from my purse,' I say quietly.

He looks genuinely appalled. 'Never a fiver!' he says. 'And never from your purse.'

'How do we know whether to believe you?' his father sighs.

'You'll just have to, won't you?' he frowns.

Something occurs to me: 'Have you ever stolen from anyone else?' Suddenly I really need to know.

And our youngest boy, the baby I gave birth to so easily one lunchtime, the toddler who was so straight and guile-less, the boy who sent a full month's pocket money to help the poor children when he saw a documentary about starving babies on TV, says, 'Well, if, like, a guy in a shop is fuckin' rude to me, I might take something, yeah.'

Our mouths drop open. We can't help it.

'What might you take?' I whisper.

He shrugs. 'I dunno. Just something small, like. A choco-late bar or whatever.'

'Because you want the chocolate bar,' his father says, 'or because you want to get back at him?'

Jack thinks about it. 'Both, I guess.'

We're not so much shocked (though we are, we are) as trying to pick our careful way through a deep, dark, tangled forest. A place we've never been in before.

Suddenly Jack looks impatient. 'I don't know why you have to make such a big thing of it.' Then, when we still don't answer, 'You said we could have pocket money once someone had confessed. Well, I've confessed, so stick to your side of the bargain, man.'

The door is yanked open and Becca's there, wet-haired, in T-shirt, shorts and slippers.

'We're in the middle of a serious private talk with Jack,' her father says. 'So unless it's really urgent . . .'

Becca's eyes flick around the room. 'So he's confessed?'

'None of your fucking business,' Jack growls.

'Only I need to know,' she says, 'because it kind of affects my plans for the weekend – how much money I'm gonna have and so on, yeah?'

'Please, Becs,' I tell her. 'It's late. We can't do this now.'

'OK.' She looks once happily round the room, clocking each of our faces and, satisfied, she goes.

'Anyway, she's not so blameless,' Jack mutters as her feet scutter down the stairs.

'What's that mean?'

'All those mini-pot mousses that went missing from the fridge? It was her. Look in her room if you don't believe me. She flings the empty pots down behind the shelves.'

'But, Jack,' I say, 'that's bloody annoying and typical of Becca's rampant selfishness, but it's a whole different thing from stealing from a shop. Do you really not see that?'

Jack's face is dark and tight.

His father's head is in his hands. And when he looks up

at his son, there is so much pain and bafflement in his eyes. How did we come to this?

'Jack, darling, darling,' he says, 'stealing from a shop . . . it's immoral. I mean, there are no shades of grey. You know that.'

And I don't know what it is – maybe the unexpected gentleness of that word 'darling'? – but suddenly Jack deflates, as if someone has punched all the air out of him.

We wait. I hear him swallow. None of us says anything. I wonder for a second if he's going to cry. If he does, I think, at least I'll be able to hug him. But instead he just sits there and so do we, waiting for something to change.

Eddie's Girl

Sunday morning, and there's a girl in Eddie's room.

Jack saw her first. 'I went in there to get the PSP and I just saw this long, blonde hair all over the floor,' he says in the awed voice he usually reserves for reporting football scores. 'I don't know who she is, but she's well buff.'

'She's not in his bed?' checks his father. I can see him trying to decide what to feel. Eddie's had people in his bed before – not girlfriends, exactly, just people, male and female, who drift back from parties in the small hours and doss down like so many sardines.

We don't like it very much. It's not so much that we're

worried about the possibility of sex – though our children, of course, love to tell us that we are. It's more the disorganised casualness that depresses us, the fact that they never get up, and when they do they wander round the house half dressed and unable to utter an enunciated word. In fact, in some ways, it's the very sexlessness of these sleepovers that seems so odd. Does none of them want the fun and emotional satisfaction that one-on-one brings?

But this is different. This morning I noticed that a bottom sheet, duvet cover and pillowcase had disappeared from the shelf on the landing. Ground-breaking. I have never, ever known Eddie make up a bed for someone in his life. Not even for himself.

'And a towel!' exclaims Becca. 'There's a towel in the bathroom and some contact-lens stuff. She must have washed her face.'

This really is rare. None of Eddie's friends washes.

'She really is quite buff,' says Jack again. 'It's weird. I mean, I can't believe she'd go out with Eddie.'

'She probably isn't,' Becca decides. 'I mean, not "out".'

'Hey,' I say, 'hold on a moment, guys, that's not quite fair. Eddie's very good-looking and he's lovely when he wants to be.'

'Are you his mum by any chance?' says their father.

Eddie's never really had a girlfriend. He knows plenty of girls, has girls as friends. And I think he's had sex. In fact,

I'm sure he has. We've found condoms in his pocket and just been glad he's using something.

But he's never brought a girl home or, to my knowledge, met up with a girl, one particular girl, for a date or anything. I'm never sure whether this should bother me. At his age, I was still nowhere near having sex, but I was high on the romance, the uncertainty, the sheer poetry of knowing boys. Sometimes I worry that Eddie will never have this.

'He's not a girl,' his father points out when I sporadically express this worry. 'Don't expect him to be like you were in 1978.'

At about 11.30, the girl comes downstairs, closely followed by Eddie. We all try not to stare. Eddie is never up before lunchtime on Sundays.

'Hi,' smiles the girl.

'This is Sarah,' says Eddie gruffly.

'Hi, Sarah,' we all say, trying not to speak in unison.

Sarah is nicely dressed in skinny jeans and a white broderie-anglaise smock thing. Cowboy boots. A pretty smile. Dimples. I see Becca quickly clocking the details.

Eddie is also fully dressed. Unheard of for 11.30 on a Sunday morning. He flips on the kettle.

'There's some real coffee on the stove, if you want it,' I say, trying not to sound too eager, or too much like I want to invite Sarah to move in and have my grandchildren.

'Sit down.' Their father hastily shuffles chairs to make a space for Sarah. You can see Jack wishing he wasn't wearing a dressing gown over his T-shirt and tracksuit bottoms.

'Hope you don't mind that I stayed over,' Sarah says, 'but the last bus had already gone.'

'Of course we don't mind,' I tell her warmly. 'We wouldn't want you going home on a night bus.'

'What time did you come in?' their father asks.

Ed grunts a monosyllable and Sarah laughs as if she already knows what he's like.

Now I'm with Becca. She probably isn't his girlfriend. Yet. I mustn't rush things. I mustn't like her too much.

We ask her if she goes to Ed's school. She does. Year below him. What AS Levels is she doing? English, French, Drama and History. She wants to do History of Art, maybe Edinburgh.

'Ed isn't going to university,' Becca announces and Ed shoots her a quick look.

'I haven't decided,' he mutters. 'I'm still thinking. I may apply this month, actually.'

His father and I try not to exchange too excited a glance.

Eddie pours out coffee for Sarah and – another first – offers us some. Then he looks at his watch. 'We need to get on,' he tells Sarah, 'if we're going to Tate Modern.'

I make sure not to look at Becca's face.

Good Parenting

Last Saturday at lunch Jack called his father 'a cunt'. When challenged, he said, 'Well, he is, isn't he?' He also called me a 'pathetic little piece of shit'. He then knocked over a glass of squash on the table, refused to clear it up, and left the room.

We called him back and told him that the night's planned sleepover was cancelled.

His eyes stayed level: 'Then I'll have one next weekend.'

'You're not having one next weekend,' I replied, 'or the weekend after that, or—'

'Careful,' warned his father, who says that one of my big parenting faults is that I'm always threatening mega-punishments which my kids know full well I will never carry out.

'—or any night after that until you apologise for what you just said,' I added, heart sinking as I felt myself wading in deeper.

'Great,' said Becca, helping herself to all the olives off the top of the feta and stuffing them in her mouth before anyone could stop her. 'All he has to do is apologise and you give in.'

'You stay the fuck out of this,' growled Jack.

'Don't speak to your sister like that,' I said. 'Stay out of it, Becca.'

'But she's right, anyway,' said Jack. 'You know she is. You won't keep it up. You never do. Tonight you might, but I bet you anything I'll have friends to stay next weekend.' And he smiled at me joyously.

'You won't,' I said feeling more and more out of my depth.

Jack looked me over kindly. 'You'll give in,' he said. 'You always do.'

Fast-forward a week. It's Saturday lunchtime again. Jack has laid the table without a murmur and done over an hour's homework and now he's asking if he can possibly have three friends to stay the night?

'I don't see why not,' I say happily as, at his own request, I ladle more of my healthy, home-made, fresh tomato sauce onto his pasta.

His father is staring at me, deliberately allowing his jaw to fall open.

'What?' I say.

'Have you any idea what you're doing?'

'Doing?' I look at the spoon, the sauce, the pan.

'Did you hear what you just said?'

'What did I just say?'

'You really do have the memory of a mongoose,' remarks Becca and even Eddie shakes his head.

And then it starts to come back: last weekend, the cunt episode, the threats . . . And yes, I'd totally forgotten, because today is another day, a bright and sunny day, and Jack has been so helpful and sweet. That other Jack – the Jack of a week ago – has long since faded.

Their father is still gazing at me. 'You're amazing, you know. The way you completely blot things out.'

I rub my eyes. 'A lot has happened since last Saturday,' I say truthfully. 'I can't spend my life hanging on to the bad things.'

'OK,' says their father. 'But last Saturday Jack threw down a gauntlet. He challenged us.'

'Come on, Dad,' says Jack, who does in fact share my tendency to move on. 'OK, look, I'm sorry I called you a cunt.'

'It wasn't your behaviour,' says his father, 'though that was bad enough. But you challenged us. You told us we wouldn't punish you. You said your mother would forget. And you used that certainty to excuse yourself from showing any remorse whatsoever at the time.'

Jack bangs his fork down in his bowl – a tactical mistake on his part because a small sliver of the fury I felt last weekend returns.

'He's right,' I say. 'It's you, Jack. You've made it impossible for us not to go through with this.'

He makes another noise of incredulous frustration and pushes back his chair. Then his face softens.

'I'm sorry,' he says. 'I'm really, really sorry. I know how I behaved last weekend was out of order. I knew I was being shit. I was only . . . It was out of order, OK?'

I say nothing.

'Please, please forgive me,' he says. 'It was wrong.'

His voice is real this time. He means it. I find myself looking at his father.

'Is there any other kind of punishment we could give him? Like cleaning or gardening or a pocket-money fine or something?'

'For God's sake!' Eddie and Becca both explode in unison.

Their father looks at me. 'You think this is good parenting?'

And I think about it and I don't know what to say because . . . what exactly is good parenting? Do we really feel we've pinned it down? And will a middle-aged Jack look back and think how lucky he was to have parents who were rigid and consistent? Or will he, when struggling with his own difficult kids, remember those moments when his parents – just like so much else in life – showed themselves to be wobbly and uncertain and capable of the occasional loving compromise?

Jack's Illness

Jack has been off school since Thursday with a nasty sort of virus which involves a temperature, a dry, hacking cough and a constant need for jam sandwiches. It may be a slightly Munchauseny thing to admit, but a part of me quite likes it when my kids are ill. It's the only time when they go back to being what they once were – nice, passive little people who let me take control and who look at me with soft, loving eyes when I tuck them in and bring them hot-water bottles.

Now, though, it's Saturday lunchtime and the patient is saying he feels a whole lot better.

'Hmm,' says his father, 'and it's the weekend. Interesting.'

'Why d'you always wanna stop me having any kind of life?' Jack wails when I suggest that if he's determined to go out and see his friends, he should at least be home by ten.

'You've been seriously unwell. You've had two days off school. You've been let off all homework and table-clearing duties. I'm not saying you can't go out. I'm just saying be back in time to get a good night's sleep, that's all.'

Jack tips his whole body back in his chair and rolls his (glassy, red) eyes.

'That's fucking unfair, man.'

'What is it you're so desperate to do?' his father asks. 'What do you want to do that can't be done before ten?'

Jack gives him a quick, vicious look. 'You wouldn't understand,' he says.

'Try me.'

'Just fucking see people,' Jack says. 'You wouldn't understand because you've never had a fucking social life.' He tears a piece of bread off the loaf and stuffs it in his mouth.

'Oh, God.' Becca's whole being shudders into action. 'Did you just see that? Anyone?'

'What?' I say.

198

'He just used his fingers on the bread. You don't know where those fingers have been.'

At this moment Eddie walks in, wearing just a grubby T-shirt and boxer shorts.

'Out,' says his father immediately. 'Go and get dressed.'

'After lunch,' Ed growls.

'No, now. I'm not having you at this table in your under-wear.'

'Go on,' I tell him. 'Everyone else is dressed.'

Ed stands for a second and scratches himself. 'What's so wrong with underwear, Father dear? Does it offend your eyes?'

'Since you're asking, yes, it does.'

Eddie yawns, leans forward and tears a chunk of bread off the other end of the loaf. On cue, Becca yowls.

'You're letting him do that? When he's just been touching himself?'

'I have not been touching myself,' sighs Eddie.

'By the way, I need some more school shirts,' says Jack.

'I don't want him using mine,' Becca snaps. 'He makes them smell and he turns the collars green.'

'Why would I want to fucking well use yours?' says Jack, picking all the cherry tomatoes out of his salad and lining them up on the edge of his plate. 'Yours are girl shirts and they smell of . . . blood.'

'That's an unnecessary thing to say,' I tell him, 'and please eat those tomatoes. Eddie please go and get some clothes on.'

'I don't see why my body is so offensive to everyone,' says Ed with a genuine frown.

'I am eating them,' says Jack. 'I'm just eating them last.'

'Vitamin C,' says his father.

'Like that's going to encourage him to eat them,' laughs Eddie.

'Your body is offensive because you don't wash,' says Becca.

'OK,' says Jack with a sigh, 'I'll be back by ten.' He puts a tomato in his mouth and chews it quickly, then swallows it down with water as if it's a pill.

'I do wash,' says Ed. 'Every morning I take a fucking shower.'

I look at Jack who is shivering. 'You're not well, are you?'

'I'm fine. I'm just a bit cold. I'll wrap up really warm.'

'Jack, it's twenty degrees outside. It's weirdly hot for the time of year. And humid. If you feel cold then you probably have a temperature.'

'I don't think he should go out at all,' says his father.

Jack gives me a baffled look. 'I said I'd be back by ten,' he says. 'Is he deaf or what?'

He leaves at two. At five he calls us from the tube station to say he feels really bad and could we please come and collect him. His father picks up the car keys, whistling in an I-told-you-so way.

Jack looks grey and shivery. I give him Nurofen and make him a jam sandwich.

'Make sure you use the raspberry jam,' he mutters weakly as he heads upstairs. 'Not the one in the fridge, the seedless one.' He eats the sandwich and sleeps for a couple of hours, and at nine comes down and says he feels completely better and can he go out now if he promises to be back by eleven?

His father and I just look at each other.

'What?' says Jack.

Ketchup

Supper was going to be salmon, new potatoes and broccoli, but the salmon is a day past its sell-by date. It smells fine, but we don't dare serve it. Becca is going through a phase of sniffing everything you put in front of her at the moment. So we find some burgers in the freezer and grill them instead.

We could call the kids to come and lay the table, but frankly the cost (loss of peace and upbeat mood ten whole minutes earlier than necessary) is just too great. And yes, it does occur to us that this fact is woeful.

So here he is boiling and chopping and grilling, and here am I laying the table. Some days we feel like one of those Edwardian 'downstairs' couples, cleaning, cooking and chauffeuring for the three teenaged lords who live 'upstairs'.

'The really awful thing,' their father says as he turns the burgers and I sift through the cutlery drawer, 'is that they've won. They've bullied us into doing all the work.'

'Not bullied us exactly.'

'With their consistent bad temper, yes, they have.'

'They did all help yesterday,' I point out, wondering why on earth I'm sticking up for them.

'Yes, but only when you lost it with them. Until you shouted, they'd done the barest minimum. And they never actually come and offer any help, do they?'

Now I hear the thump, thump of Jack's hefty trainers on the stairs. He's grown so tall recently that he looks strangely windblown, like a young tree that needs staking.

'What is it?' he asks gloomily, hands in pockets.

'What's what?'

'That.' Eyes on hob.

'It's supper,' I say brightly.

'Yeah, but what?' He continues to eye the cooker as though it were an unexploded bomb.

'Burgers,' says his father, 'and potatoes and broccoli.'

Jack falls backwards into a chair as if his feet have been kicked from underneath him.

'Oh no! But we don't eat broccoli.'

'Hey, don't panic,' I say. 'No one's going to force anything green down your throat.'

He sticks his lip out like a toddler.

'Well you should remember that no one here fucking well eats broccoli.'

Their father has his back to us, but I see him take a deep

breath and stand motionless for a moment, oven glove in hand.

'Where are you going?' he snaps at Becca, who has drifted in and is heading straight for the bread bin. She flinches dramatically, as if he's just hit her, and widens her eyes.

'Just getting some bread.'

'What for?'

'To have with the burgers.'

'No!' her father shouts, a little too loudly.

'For Christ's sake,' says Eddie from under the towel with which he's come in drying his hair. 'Why all the shouting?'

'I tried to get some bread,' whispers Becca in a victimy voice.

'No one needs bread,' says her father.

'Why not?'

'It's not that sort of a meal.'

Jack stares at him and so does Becca.

'But it's burgers.'

'Yes, but not that sort of burgers.'

Eddie laughs.

'What sort of burgers is it then, Father dear?'

'It's burgers served with vegetables.'

The kids all look at each other.

'What's so strange about putting a burger between two slices of bread, Dad?' says Becca carefully, in the kind of voice you'd use to address a certified lunatic.

'Yeah,' says Jack more nastily, 'don't be so fucking uptight.' And he grabs the ketchup from the shelf.

'Not ketchup,' says their father with a little wail. 'Oh please, not ketchup.'

'Does ketchup really matter?' I ask, having kept out of the bread débâcle. 'I mean, it's quite good for you.'

'Lycopene,' agrees Ed, and his father shoots me a look which means he'd now quite like my head on a stake at Traitor's Gate.

Silence. Everyone stares longingly at the bread bin.

'After supper I'm watching the match,' announces Jack.

'Not until you've done an hour of homework, you're not,' I tell him.

'I'm not doing an hour. I can't be arsed,' and he shoots a look at his father, who immediately takes the bait.

'I hate that expression,' he says.

'Well, tough,' says Jack, 'because I'm using it.'

'Well, I'm asking you not to.'

'Well, fuck off then.'

Silence.

'Right,' I stand up, 'that's it. Go to your room, Jack.'

'Don't threaten something if you're not prepared to carry it out,' warns his father.

'I am prepared to carry it out. He's not telling us to fuck off. Please go,' I tell Jack.

And I hold my breath as – luckily for me because I hadn't

got a plan B – he leaves the table and goes upstairs. And in the few seconds that it took for us to watch him go, Eddie has managed to squirt ketchup onto his plate and Becca's.

Squash

Eddie and Becca sit down to supper. Eddie has just got himself a drink and – rather amazingly – some for his brother and sister too. Three pink glasses of Summer Fruit squash sit on the table. Eddie glugs his straight down in one go and turns to Becca.

'Can I have a bit of your drink?'

Immediately she clamps her arms around it and juts out her bottom lip. 'No. Why?'

'Because I got it for you.'

'Just because you got it, doesn't mean you can have it.'

Eddie frowns. 'For fuck's sake, Becs, you're not even drinking it.'

'I'm about to.'

'You haven't even touched it.'

'I'm about to take a sip.'

'Go on then.' He waits. She pulls the glass a little closer.

'For goodness sake, you two,' I say.

'I'm waiting,' says Eddie.

'I'll do it when I'm ready, thanks,' says Becca.

'Do it now or I'm taking it.'

'Dad!' Becca looks straight past me and yells to her father, who's trying to fix the broken waste disposal – broken ever since Jack dropped a spoon down it. 'Eddie says I've got to drink my drink straightaway or he's gonna take it.'

'Just spit in it,' mutters her father from under the sink.

'Do something!' shouts Becca. I look at her crumpled-up face. It looks exactly as it used to do when she was two and someone tried to work a beloved piece of Duplo out from between her sticky, furious fingers so they could wipe them with a flannel.

Their father comes out from under the sink and straightens up very slowly.

'Why does he want your drink?' He looks slightly mystified, as if for a few golden seconds he's forgotten what manner of offspring he has spawned.

'Because I was the one who got it for her,' says Ed simply.

'It's not fair!' shouts Becca, doing the two-year-old face again.

'Not fair!' mimics Ed. Becca swipes at him, misses and knocks a fork to the floor.

'Drop dead,' says Becca.

It's just as bad as the train, I think. At half-term they embarrassed me so much by fighting in First Class (they begged for a Saturday upgrade and I relented). First Jack shoved Becca's elbow off the arm-rest, then Becca shoved back, then finally they started pummelling each other. I thought about moving away and pretending they weren't with me, but then I realised that I actually had a responsibility to the other (full-fare-paying) passengers.

Now Becca picks up the fork and threatens Ed with it. 'Fuck off,' she says.

At this moment, enter Jack. As usual, Jack is planning his social life. If Jack put the same amount of effort and flair into his school work that he throws into his partying, he'd definitely be on track for 12 A-stars. Now he frowns as if solving an especially fiendish Sudoku.

'If I work really extra, super hard all tomorrow and get my homework done, all of it I mean, by Thursday night, yeah? Well, is there a tiny, tiny chance I could have a sleep-over on Friday and stay out late Saturday night as well possibly?'

I look at him. 'Very unlikely,' I say.

'Jack,' says Eddie politely, 'while you're up, do you think you could possibly get me a drink?'

Jack regards his brother coolly. 'No,' he says.

'Please,' says Ed.

'Give me one reason why I should.'

'Because I got you one?'

'You didn't get me one.'

'I did.' Eddie looks at Jack's drink and suddenly a light bulb comes on in his head. He picks it up and gulps it down.

'Hey!' Jack darts over. 'You said that one was mine.'

Eddie eyes him steadily. 'Well, it was, but why should I get a drink for someone who won't get me one?'

Now even Jack looks confused.

If these kids were five or six, or even eight or nine, none of the above would be very extraordinary. But my children are fifteen, sixteen and almost nineteen. When I had toddlers and tried to imagine them as teenagers, I envisaged tall, strong, interesting people, helping me with shopping, talking about art and politics, offering perhaps to cook the evening meal.

'Listen to you all,' their father tells them. 'Don't you realise how old you are? People of your age have actually fought wars, and here you all are squabbling over a glass of pink water.'

Jack eyes him thoughtfully. 'I wouldn't mind fighting in a war,' he says, 'as long as I could still see my friends.'

'There are no sleepovers in a war zone, you moron,' Becca points out.

Meanwhile, Eddie has been grating some parmesan cheese.

'Give me some of that,' says Jack, holding out his plate.

'No,' says Ed.

'Come on,' says Jack reasonably.

'No,' says the almost nineteen-year-old who could have been in the trenches, in the Falklands, in Basra. 'Why should I share my cheese with someone who won't even get me a drink?'

Exams

Becca slept badly last night. Now she comes back from her History GCSE frazzled and tired. I give her head an affectionate stroke and ask how it went.

'OK.'

'Just OK or really OK?'

She fills a glass up with ice and pours in pink squash. 'Well, all the questions I'd been expecting came up and I don't know quite how I've done but I think I probably did about as well as I could have.'

I tell her that's brilliant. How can anyone do more than that?

'Yeah, well, I'm so shattered though,' she says. Worried she may be heading for her bed, I warn her not to lie down.

'If you sleep now, you won't sleep tonight,' I tell her, 'and then you'll be exhausted for French tomorrow.'

She says she's just going to 'shut her eyes' for half an hour, but I must please wake her if she falls asleep. I go up the High Road to get dishwasher tablets and return to an ominously silent house.

'Becs, honey,' I put my head round her door, 'you need to wake up now. That's forty-five minutes.'

She opens her eyes and regards me as if I'm covered in slime. 'What is it? Get out! Get away from me.'

'You said you didn't want to sleep.'

She growls and turns to the wall.

'Darling—'

'Just get the fuck away. Seriously! I'm so fucking sick of your interfering.'

I hover a moment, unsure what best to do.

'There's a chocolate muffin downstairs if you want it,' I tell her, adding in a slightly tougher voice, 'and I strongly advise you not to go back to sleep.'

Actually, Becca has always been cool about exams. She's always worked hard and, though the state of her desk might make you think otherwise, she's pretty organised about revising. Her exam timetable – carefully marked up in different coloured felt-tips – is pinned up on her wall next to her Bob Marley calendar, and she actually follows it.

'Thank God we have one child who knows how to work,' her father had sighed to me the day before.

I knew what he was thinking. He was thinking that both Eddie's and Jack's approach to exams are slightly different. Eddie doesn't work, but at least gives the impression that he knows what he's doing. As for Jack, not only does he not have a timetable on his wall, not only does he not know when his exams are, but he assures us that neither do the teachers.

'We've got some kind of early GCSE exam tomorrow, by the way,' he told me on Tuesday, just as we were leaving to go out to his father's office summer drinks party and he was busy kicking a tennis ball against the hall skirting board.

'A what?!' I stood in the hall, trying to get my earring through the hole in my ear.

'Don't worry. They're not really expecting us to know much. Even the teacher didn't know we were having it till yesterday. It's a new thing, doing part of it this early.'

'But . . .' I glanced at my watch, wondering for a few wild seconds whether I should actually skip the drinks (please God) and stay home to supervise revision. 'You can at least revise tonight, can't you?'

He moved the ball backwards and forwards under his foot. 'Revising has never ever made my marks go up.'

'What, so you're the only child ever in the history of education who needn't prepare for exams?'

'It won't make any difference.'

'Of course it will. Even if it makes the smallest difference, it's worth it.'

He didn't look at me. 'I'll try, OK?'

'Like hell he will,' said his father as we drove to the do. 'My God, does he actually think he stands a chance of getting to a good university with this attitude?'

'University isn't everything,' I muttered.

Jack sat his exam the next day. When he got home – shirt dirty and flapping from playing football after school – I asked how it had gone.

He hesitated for a quick moment, as if he were trying to remember what I was talking about. Then: 'Oh. Fine.'

'You could do it?'

He shrugged. 'I could do some parts of it. The parts I couldn't do, I just left them.'

That was yesterday. Now Becca comes harrumphing downstairs, face still pink with sleep.

'I know you have exams,' I tell her, 'and I'm doing everything I can to make your life smooth at the moment, but I won't be spoken to the way you spoke to me upstairs.'

She says nothing.

'Do you still want me to test you on your French?' I ask her.

She does what she always does at such moments – grips her stomach and winces as though she has an inoperable pain. She gives me an injured look, then helps herself to a chocolate muffin and disappears into the sitting room, from where, three seconds later, *The Simpsons* theme tune starts up.

Jack and the £5 bonus

About three months ago, we devised a brand-new scheme to encourage Jack to work. The idea was that as long as he spent a whole hour on his homework every night – regardless of how little he might have been set – he'd be paid an extra five pounds a week.

Jack seemed to think it was a pretty good deal, and so did we. If he had plenty of homework, as he mostly does, then it meant there was nothing to be gained from rushing it. If he hadn't been set an hour's worth, then he had to stay at his desk but could do something else constructive, such as read a book.

'You know, I really like this new system,' he told me after about a month. 'I seem to work harder when there's no choice. And it's kind of relaxing to have all this time to read.'

'I really think it's working,' I rushed to tell his father. 'It's just so amazing to see him willing to sit at his desk and concentrate.'

His father agreed it was good that it was working.

'I wouldn't get too excited though,' he said. 'It's only been a month.'

'What do you mean "it's only been a month"?'

'I just mean . . . you know Jack.'

'What do you mean "you know Jack"?' I asked him. 'Surely you're glad he's co-operating with this?'

His father shrugged. 'He wants the fiver.'

'OK, but even so—'

'I'm not saying anything. I just don't want you disappointed, that's all.'

I thought about this. 'I don't see why you have to be so down on everything,' I told him. 'We devised a scheme. He's showing willing. What more do you want?'

His father said nothing.

Now it's half past six and Jack should have been home by quarter past five.

'Where is he?' demands his father as soon as he gets home, his tone somehow implying that I'm complicit in this. When the front door finally slams at twenty to seven, I ask Jack where he's been.

He tuts with impatience as he chucks his rucksack on the floor. 'I got caught up, didn't I?'

'What do you mean "caught up"?'

He gives me a thuggish look. 'Just, you know, caught up.'

'Come on, boy,' his father says. 'You know we need more explanation than that.' Jack glances at me.

'Well, you see, I didn't have my watch on and I didn't know how much time was passing and—'

'You haven't lost your watch?!' I almost shriek, because Jack has managed to keep his current one now for a record number of months.

'No, I think it's by my bed. Anyway, then we were all about to go home and these rudes come along—'

'Came along,' corrects his father.

Jack scowls at him. 'Came along. And they didn't exactly attack us but, well, we had to hang around a little bit longer just to be sure and—'

'All right, it doesn't matter,' I say, because Jack's excuses can sometimes go on forever. 'You're home now. Do you want to do your hour straightaway or after supper?'

Another impatient noise. 'I don't need to do an hour,' he says.

'Of course you do,' I say, my heart plummeting.

'Mum, I literally haven't got any fucking homework.'

'Then lucky you,' his father says. 'You get to read a book for an hour.'

Jack flashes him a sweaty look. 'I'm not doing it. You can't make me.'

'I don't get it,' I sigh. 'Why are you suddenly being like this? What about the scheme?'

'I'm sick of the stupid scheme,' he mutters. 'It's not working.'

'But . . .' I struggle, intensely conscious of his father's eyes on me, 'you said you loved it, you said it was working.'

'I never said "loved". I said it was OK. Anyway, I was just saying that to keep you happy.'

'Fine,' I say, anger mounting as my optimism slips away. 'If you don't want the fiver, then that's that, there's nothing we can do.'

'For fuck's sake! None of my friends have to do this!' Jack explodes. 'They all get extra money all the time, whatever homework they do or don't do. No one makes them sit in a room and read a stupid book like they're still in Year 7.'

'Look, Jack,' his father says carefully, 'if you're suddenly feeling differently about the scheme, then maybe that's something the three of us need to discuss, but there's no way we can go on paying you the fiver unless you do the hour.'

Jack looks at him coldly. 'Why not?'

His father tries to smile. 'Give me one reason why we should.'

'To prove you're not the most fucking stingy parents in the whole fucking world perhaps?' And with a small sob of frustration, he grabs his rucksack and goes upstairs. Three seconds later, his door slams.

His father looks at me.

'What?' I say.

'I didn't say anything.'

Eddie and becca

Ten o'clock on Tuesday night and I find Becca sitting halfway up the stairs, wrapped in a big bath towel and weeping silently into her phone.

'It's nothing,' she gulps, when I put my arm around her and ask what the matter is. 'It's just – it's me. I feel so very stupid.'

It's rare for our Becca to call herself stupid. This and something about the resigned, almost womanly way she says it makes my heart go out to her. 'Why, darling? What did you do?'

She looks at me for a second, hair all twisted up on her head, face flushed from the steam, eyes rimmed with teary kohl. She lets out a big sigh and another tear rolls down.

'I trusted Eddie, that's all I did.'

She bites her lip and looks down at her nails, which still reveal her age – scruffy boy's nails. Becca has grown recently – lengthened and filled out in all sorts of places – but her hands are still the babyish, Play-Doh-kneading hands she had when she was small.

I take both of them in mine. 'OK. You'd better tell me. What did you trust him with?'

She shakes her head miserably. 'You'll think I was stupid. You'll think it serves me right.'

'I'm ready.'

She sighs again, but she lets me keep on holding her hands. 'You know my canvas shoulder bag? The one I got at Portobello with the picture of Kurt Cobain on? The one I looked all over for and couldn't find anywhere and then I finally found one on a stall for three pounds and I couldn't believe it?'

I struggle to remember which bag this is, but I nod anyway.

'I didn't want to lend it to him. I really so didn't. But he needed something to put his stuff in when he went to Andy's thing last week and he was literally begging me and so . . . He swore to me he'd take such great care of it because I'd told him it was totally irreplaceable and—'

'What's he done to it?'

Becca pulls her hands out of mine and puts her head on her knees. Big, heavy, heartbroken sobs. 'He's . . . it's gone. I phoned him just now at Sarah's. I thought it must be in

217

his room, but he just said he hadn't seen it and shouted at me to leave him alone and then he practically hung up on me.'

'Oh, Becs.'

'The thing that really hurt was that he practically denied ever having borrowed it!'

'Sounds like Eddie.'

'I don't know how he can do this to me!'

I pull her to me, kiss her sweaty forehead. 'I feel so fucking depressed,' she says softly. 'I don't know what's the matter with me, I really don't.'

'Nothing's the matter with you,' I tell her. 'You're just very overtired after a week of exams and your brother has let you down in a big way. Again. So here's what you're going to do. You're going to go and dry yourself and put your pyjamas on, and then you can come and get into bed with me until Daddy gets back and we'll watch a bit of TV and have some hot chocolate until you're feeling better enough to go and sleep, OK?'

Becca gazes at me with big eyes. 'OK,' she says.

'It's not so much the bag itself I care about,' she tells me ten minutes later as she sips her hot chocolate, 'it's more that I really can't forgive myself for being so stupid as to trust him. I should have known, shouldn't I?'

I think about this. 'You weren't stupid,' I tell her. 'You did the right thing, the good-person thing. We all have to give the people we love second chances, even if they let us down again and again.'

'Why do we?'

'Because it's the only happy way to live, that's why.'

Becca sighs, puts down her mug and spreads her fingers out on the duvet. 'Do you think I've got babyish hands? Do you think my nails are shit?'

I lie: 'You've got lovely hands.'

'But look at my nails. They're all flaky.'

'Do you want me to paint them for you?'

Becca wants dark purple, but I don't have that so we settle on a brightish red. She snuggles up close to me and I file and paint her small, square boy's nails.

And it takes a long time and we don't really talk. Instead I take in the warm, dark smell of her scalp and listen to the slow in-and-out of her breath. And I think how Eddie's got this little person here at home, this embryo-woman who adores him, who'll forgive him just about anything, who'll even lend him her most precious possession. Yet he's too stupid to see it, he doesn't know how lucky he is, and he tramples on her heart without a second thought.

Becca's New Phase

Just recently – it's hard to pinpoint exactly when it started – I've found myself actually enjoying being with Becca. When she's with her brothers, she can still be her old, angry-sulky, impossibly rude and argumentative self. But when she and I are alone together, there's a new softness to her – a tentative, almost vulnerable quality that just wasn't there before. I find myself startled by this. It's something I never considered before – the possibility that the plump, frowny, hiccupy baby I gave birth to sixteen years ago could one day turn out to be such lovely company.

The other day, for instance, I was sorting out some old clothes to give to charity and I suddenly thought that I ought to offer them to Becca first. It was a long shot – she's certainly never deigned to accept any cast-offs of mine before – but I put them on the bed anyway and called her in.

The old Becca would have stood there, twiddling her hair and surveying the clothes as if they had some peculiar, off-putting smell. 'I'll be all right, thanks,' she'd have said, half annoyed, half amused, before flouncing quickly out.

The new Becca doesn't do this. The new Becca gives the bed of clothes her full, solemn attention. This Becca tenderly examines a sparkly cardigan from Whistles that I've begun to feel a bit too old for. 'Hey, I've been wanting something like this for ages,' she says.

'It's got a little hole in the sleeve.'

'That's cool. I actually prefer things a little bit worn.'

'Well,' I say, trying to hide my flush of pleasure, 'it's yours if you want it.'

She tries it on. 'What do you think? It might be really good with my black jeans.'

The old Becca would never in a million years have sought my opinion on how she looked.

'It looks lovely on you,' I tell her. 'Far better than on me.'

She beams. 'It's just my style,' she says, and then she picks up a stripy T-shirt. 'And this is good too. Yes, please, I'll have this.' Then she sees my old denim jacket and grabs it. 'You're saying you seriously don't want this any more?'

I shrug and again try not to look too pleased. 'I like it, but I never ever wear it.'

She pulls it on. 'Wow. Exactly the right size.'

'I wasn't sure you'd want that,' I tell her, 'but your style's changed a bit recently, hasn't it?'

She looks at herself in the mirror with critical but excited eyes. 'Yeah, my style's definitely changing.'

My darling, I want to say, it's not your style that's changing, it's you. Look at you, you're opening up – to people, ideas, clothes, everything.

'You look completely gorgeous,' I tell her.

She sighs. 'I don't know why, but there are just so many clothes I want in the shops at the moment. I mean, there never used to be anything. If I went looking for a T-shirt or whatever, I could never find even one I liked. But just now it's like every single thing I try on seems to suit me. And I want it.'

221

'It's called being sixteen and suddenly feeling attractive,' I say.

Later, when I tell her father about the clothes episode, we both agree that Becca's in a really nice phase at the moment.

'Or maybe it's not just a phase,' he suggests. 'Maybe this is actually the real Becca and this is who she's going to be. Have you thought of that?'

I hadn't. Is it really possible that, as so many parents of twenty-somethings breezily insist, teenagers do eventually turn into human beings? Suddenly a whole new sunny horizon opens up before me. I see the five of us gathered at the kitchen table – everybody, even Jack, smiling.

'Well, let's not get too excited,' I tell him.

Meanwhile, though, Becca and I seem to go from strength to strength. It's as if she actually likes me.

'You're such good company these days,' I tell her when she agrees – with hardly any persuading – to come and help me shop for food. 'I mean, we've been spending quite a bit of time together recently, haven't we?'

She eyes me cautiously. 'Er, Mum, hello. I've been living with you for the last sixteen years.'

I laugh and hand her a bag to carry. 'Well, I feel somehow like I'm getting to know you better, that's all.'

'Yeah,' she says, 'isn't it funny? Sometimes it feels like I've known you all my life.'

'Now you're sending me up.'

She smiles, and her face is different, both familiar and strange at the same time. 'It's OK, Mum,' she says, and she won't let herself look at me. 'I know what you're trying to say. It's OK, it's cool.'

'I love you.'

'Yeah. You and me together, we're awesome.'

Theatre

It's 6.10 p.m. I put my head around the sitting-room door. Jack is lying on the sofa staring dully at the TV. In his lap, a plate of bagels spread with Nutella. Each half bagel has been carefully ripped open, had about three bites taken out from near the centre, and then been discarded.

'Hey,' I say (wondering why a child who always leaves crusts has a preference for bread that has a hole in the middle), 'remember we need to leave by half past.'

'Leave? Why?'

'The theatre, remember?'

He frowns and I tense. Jack agreeing to come to the theatre ('only if it's a school night. I'm not giving up my weekend') is a recent thing. He said yes when he was in a good mood. There's always the danger he'll change his mind.

'What time does it start?'

'Half past seven.'

223

'And we're leaving a whole hour in advance?' He looks horrified.

'We need to pick up the tickets and the bus is unpredictable.'

'Why bus? What's wrong with the car?'

I stay calm. 'I don't want to drive to the West End.'

'Why not?'

'Because it's hard to park and the traffic is even more unpredictable and . . . Oh God, Jack, I just don't want to, OK?'

He sighs.

'What's the matter?'

'I just don't want to be hanging around, that's all.'

'Who says you're going to be hanging around?'

'We'll be so fucking early.'

'So what? We'll get a drink. It'll be fun. Just you and me.'

An hour and a quarter later (we made it with just eight minutes to spare), we're in our seats waiting for curtain up and he's busy telling me about the wonderful parents of some friends of his ('I'm not telling you who they are, because I know what you and Dad are like') who are incredibly laid-back and put up with all sorts of 'appalling' (his word) behaviour from their son and his friends.

'Such as?' I watch as the theatre slowly fills up.

'Oh, well, you know, one time they came home to find us

all smoking draw and they were just so completely relaxed about it.'

I say nothing. I've run out of words for these mythical parents who are apparently content for their offspring to consume all manner of illegal substances in front of them.

'And then another time we were all taking it in turns to lean out of the window, yeah, and spit on this car—'

I yawn and think about this.

'Hold on. What do you mean spit? How come a car was so close to the window?'

Jack gives me a triumphant look.

'It wasn't,' he says. 'It was well far away, across the street.' He pauses for effect. 'I can spit that far.'

'You can?' I'm genuinely surprised.

He glances across the rows of seats. 'You see the bit of space over there, the bit where you can walk between the seats?'

'The aisle?'

'Yeah.'

I nod. It must be thirty feet away.

'Well, if I wanted to I could make my gob land over there right now. If I wanted to, I could.'

'Wow.' I'm actually impressed. Jack sees this and laughs.

'You want me to show you?'

'Absolutely not. But that's an awfully long way to be able to spit.'

'Thanks.'

'It's a pleasure.'

We talk about the play we're about to see. I chose it because it's had good reviews and sounded energetic and a bit anarchic. Jack says he doesn't mind the theatre, 'But there's never a bit when I'm not completely bored.'

I agree with him that theatre takes a different energy than watching a film. 'That's because you give something to it, which means when it's good it can be amazing.'

'But when it's boring,' says Jack loudly, 'you just want to fucking kill yourself.' The lady in front of us looks round.

The play begins well. Some swearing, lots of action, plenty of laughs. The audience seem very up for it and Jack glances around with interest. I try not to watch his face too hard as the story unfolds, but I can feel him next to me and I've never known him sit so still. When, after quite a long first half, the interval comes, he makes a sound of loud annoyance.

'Why do they have to stop now? What's going on? Can't they just keep going?'

'Don't you want to stretch your legs? Do you want a drink?'

He glances impatiently at the stage.

'Not really. I think I'll just sit here, thanks.'

In the end he agrees to a chocolate ice cream which he demolishes with one eye on the stage. 'You're quite enjoying it then?' I dare to ask him, as people come back to their seats.

He gives me a long look. 'It's the best fucking thing I've ever seen,' he says, and the lady in front looks round at us again.

Eddie's Girl 2

Eddie's met a new girl. 'The thing is, Mum,' he tells me, screwing up his eyes as he licks a Rizla, 'I've only known her six days and already it's like . . . wow.'

We're in the garden courtyard of a café on the High Road – Ed's bonus for helping me with the shopping. Not that he really demanded a reward, but I've always loved sitting in cafés with my kids.

'And what I feel about her right now,' my eldest continues as he fumbles in his jacket for a lighter, 'well, what's amazing is I felt it after just two days.'

I skim the froth off my cappuccino. 'What's her name?'

'Aliza. It's – I don't know – Scottish or Portuguese or something. She's the cousin of . . . do you remember the guy who was drumming in the band that Adam was once nearly the singer in?'

I must look blank because he goes on: 'Well, her and me, it's almost spooky. It's like, seriously, Mum, we can even have the exact same thought at the same moment sometimes.'

I smile at my boy. 'But,' I say, knowing it's the wrong question, 'what about Sarah?'

I'm never very sure whether Sarah is or isn't Eddie's girl-friend, but she's been a big part of his life for several months and he likes her. Or maybe what I mean is, I like her. She's frank and intelligent, and when she smiles, there's something real going on in her eyes.

Ed gives me an unbothered look. 'Oh, Sarah's great and a very nice person and all that, but—'

'But?'

He's holding a roll-up and he still hasn't found his lighter. 'I just don't know if Sarah likes me that much, to be honest.' He stands up. 'Look, can you just hold on a sec, Mum?'

And I watch as my eighteen-year-old son, his jeans so ragged they barely cling to his legs, walks purposefully towards a young, bob-haired woman of about twenty-five. He bends towards her and says something and she pulls a lighter out of her bag and hands it to him. He cups his hand over the flame and as he hands it back, she returns both his eye contact and his smile.

Mission complete, he plops back into the chair in front of me and turns back into Eddie. Eddie who loves his cat. Eddie who picks the mushrooms out of mushroom lasagne. Eddie who doesn't like the feel of a normal towel on his skin.

He sighs and takes a drag of his cigarette. I feel the sun hot on my head.

'Anyway,' he goes on, 'she's got to go up to Manchester,

to see some aunt or something. So I thought I might pop up there too, you know? Spend a bit of time chilling.'

I put my cup down and sit up. 'Ed, can you really afford to go anywhere right now?'

He rolls his eyes. 'I knew you'd do this.'

'I'm not "doing" anything, but you promised you'd start looking for a summer job. You owe Dad and me about two hundred quid already, and you certainly can't afford to go buying rail tickets.'

He gives me a fed-up look. 'I really don't see, Mother dear, why you can't let me enjoy myself for a bit. Why does it always have to be all about money? You and Dad, you're obsessed.'

'The reason it's always about money, Edward my dearest, is because you owe it everywhere. And the reason you owe it is you adore spending it. You can't stop yourself. I would say you're the obsessed one. So stop spending it and it won't always be about money. Don't you even owe Sarah some money?'

He gives a wave of impatience. 'She says she doesn't need it back yet.'

'She might need it back a bit sooner once she hears about Alicia.'

'*Aliza.*'

'Whatever.'

Ed juts out his lip and frowns into his coffee. And I

remember a time when I would take all three children shopping for something boring like school shoes, and then we'd go to a toy shop so they could spend their pocket money, and then to a café for drinks and cakes.

I'd spoon all the chocolatey froth off my cappuccino into their three sweet, giggling mouths, and then they'd get their new toys out of the bags, just to look at. And because Ed could never quite afford the latest bit of Lego that he wanted, I'd often 'advance' him a bit of next week's pocket money. So he could buy what he most wanted. So he could have his heart's desire right now this minute, without waiting. And yes, I know what you're thinking, because I'm thinking the same thing too.

Teeth and Rain

Becca has an appointment with the dental hygienist. She normally goes to the dentist on her own, but since I'm working from home today, I say I'll drive her. 'You could be a bit more grateful,' I tell her when I get no reaction whatsoever to this offer. 'Do you want a lift or not?'

She stares at me. 'I want the lift. But I feel sick, OK?'

'Feeling sick shouldn't stop a person from saying thank you.'

She says, 'I really don't see what I've done wrong.'

We drive to the dentist. On the way Becca is very pale and

silent and doesn't join in when I try to chat to her, so I turn on the radio. It's *Brain of Britain*. 'Hey, can you get that?' I ask her as a particularly impossible question comes up.

She replies, 'I'm not listening to a word they're saying.'

The dental hygienist says hello to Becca. Becca grimaces. I sit in the room with them while Becca's teeth are checked and cleaned. I can't see her face, but I watch as her hands grip the side of the seat and occasionally flutter up towards her face. 'Are you OK?' the hygienist asks Becca. Becca's reply is muffled, but I think I detect the words 'fucking' and 'hell'. When the appointment's over, Becca looks white and shaky.

'Poor thing,' I say. 'Was it really that bad?'

She mutters in her most sarcastic voice, 'It really was that bad.'

'Well, come on then, let's cheer you up. Shall we get a drink across the road?'

'No.'

'Shall we see if the new Mojo's out?'

She says nothing, just bunches up her lips and stares at the ground.

'OK, well, I just want to nip into the garden centre for three seconds, all right?'

Becca shrugs. As we walk towards the car, I say, 'Come on, sweetheart, cheer up. I know it was a bit uncomfortable and you're not feeling too brilliant, but people do have worse things to deal with.'

Suddenly there's fury in her eyes. 'I don't see what the fuck I'm doing wrong!' she yells at me. 'I mean, why're you doing this to me? Seriously, what the fuck more can I do?'

'It's your face,' I go on as we pull up outside the garden centre, 'it's just so . . . angry. Please, darling, all I'm saying is pull yourself together and start being a bit nicer now.'

Becca stays in the car as I walk into the garden centre. I'm barely past the bedding plants when I hear a ghastly horror-movie scream. Then another. And another. I run back to the car. She's banging her head against the windscreen. People are looking. I pull open the door.

'Becca! Stop that immediately! You simply can't behave like that. People can hear you. I mean it, just stop.'

She gives me a dark, metallic look. 'Being heard. That's all you care about, you self-absorbed bitch.'

She gets out of the car, slams the door and starts to walk away. 'I don't even have my bus pass!' she mutters. I hover by the compost, unsure what to do.

'I hope to God you allowed her to go,' her father says when I call him at work an hour later.

'It was just about to pour with rain,' I say. 'She wasn't feeling well.'

'Jesus . . .'

'I gave up on the garden centre and drove off after her.'

'I can't believe it. After all our talk about boundaries and consequences. Ideal chance to let her walk home.'

'It would have taken her more than an hour.'

'And your point is?'

'She would have got soaked.'

'Her choice.'

'I couldn't do it. But I'm afraid it gets worse. I caught up with her on that main road and I begged her to get back in the car. She did, but then when I said I was just going to pop back to the garden centre, she called me a fucking bitch. Again. Then she tried to get out of the car again.'

He sighs. 'And tell me, please God, that this time you let her go?'

I tell him no, I didn't. I tell him I persuaded her back into the car and I drove her home in terrible, fuming silence. And I know, of course I do, that I should have let her walk off – she's sixteen, for goodness sake – but she made me feel so responsible. I don't know who I was trying to protect really – Becca, or the child I used to be, who never felt very safe and was always anxious that somehow, sometime, she would be left somewhere and have to find her own way home.

Free House

Last Saturday we went away for a night and – since Eddie was away with friends – trusted Jack and Becca alone in the house. As it was the first time, we made a rule that they couldn't have any people round. 'You mean absolutely no one at all?' sighed Jack.

'Absolutely no one,' I said. 'Show us you're trustworthy this time and maybe next time we'll be able to relax the rule.'

Keen to get rid of us, they solemnly agreed. It all seemed to go so well. Every time I phoned home, they answered and were polite. They confirmed that they'd eaten supper, locked the back door, turned off the oven. 'This is brilliant,' I told their father. 'Just think, we might even be able to make this a regular thing.'

He smiled and his smile said 'don't speak too soon' and I briefly resented him for it.

Now we've come back to find cigarette butts in the garden, all the chairs rearranged, a wine glass on the step outside.

I take a walk around the house. Upstairs, the bed in the spare room has one of the best sitting-room cushions as a pillow. On the carpet: scrunched-up Kleenex, a pack of Rizlas, a glass with a straw. The window is wide open. I go over to the windowsill. Ash.

I come downstairs, my heart heavy. Jack is unloading the dishwasher – without being asked.

'Did you guys have people round?' I ask him.

'No.' He carries on putting glasses on the shelf.

'Tell me the truth, Jack.'

'I am telling the truth.'

'Jack! Look at me.'

He looks. His eyes are flat and heavy.

'I know you're lying to me and I can't bear it.'

He throws up his hands. 'For fuck's sake! And if we'd had people round, then would that be such a crime?'

'You said you didn't.'

'We didn't. But if we had . . . I mean, you said if it went well this time then we probably could next time. What's the difference between this time and next time?'

Jack's logic can reduce a person to tears.

'Jack. This is this time, not next time. The definition of this time going well was that you'd do exactly what you promised to do, which was not have people round! If you broke your promise and lied to us, then this time did not go well.'

Jack says nothing.

'You broke our trust. Not to mention smoking in the house.'

'That's ridiculous,' says Jack, and he starts chewing a fingernail. 'I tried to make them smoke outside,' he says.

I go up and fling open Becca's door. She's doing something to her feet. 'You could fucking well knock,' she yells at me.

'Did you have people round here this weekend?'

She looks me straight in the eye. 'I – did – not – have – people – round.'

'Did Jack?'

She says nothing.

'Did any people come round here to this house?'

She puts one trainer back on. 'Don't ask me,' she says, 'I didn't see anything.'

'Did you know that people were smoking in this house?'

She shrugs. 'What the fuck business was that of mine?'

'You were responsible for the house.'

'And is anything damaged?' she says. I struggle to think what's damaged, but in my head all I see are chairs rearranged, rules broken.

'Come on,' their father says later, 'in a way she's right – nothing was damaged. Isn't that the point of trusting them here – to see if they can keep themselves and this house safe?'

Later I take Jack to Foot Locker to buy a new hoodie. We stand there among the gargantuan silvery trainers with the music thumping and he tries on a brown, patterned one. I think it's hideous, but you can see from the careful way he looks at himself in the mirror that he doesn't.

'You could never wear that to school,' I tell him, because Jack has a new thing – which Becca tells me is completely against the rules – of wearing a hoodie under his blazer instead of a jumper.

He turns his baby eyes on me. 'But, well you see, you just pull it off as you go in the gates, yeah? And they can't do you for it.'

I look at the label. It's in the sale at least.

'Jack,' I say, 'you must promise me you won't wear this to school.'

He looks at me. 'OK,' he says.

'Breaking the school rules is like lying to me, and if you lie to me then everything – our relationship, all our good talks – it feels so hollow and pointless. Do you see that?'

'I'm really sorry, Mum,' he says. 'I swear I won't do it again.'

We take the hoodie to the till and I'm certain of two things: that he will wear it to school and that he'll lie to me again.

Jack and the night bus

Jack wants to spend his entire holidays 'out'. His father and I have said that's OK, but we need to agree some basic ground rules. Such as how often he can have sleepovers, when we expect him to be home to eat 'a nutritious meal', how much extra allowance he can have for fast food and so on. We haven't told him what the ground rules are yet, mainly because we haven't agreed on them ourselves.

'OK,' I tell his father on Sunday morning as we drink our coffee in the garden, 'it seems to me it goes like this. He wants to see his friends all the time, which is fair enough. So as far as I'm concerned, he can do that as long as he comes home to eat the odd good meal and he's in a good mood and not too tired and helps around the house a reasonable amount.'

'Far too vague,' says his father. 'He'll never manage it.'

'What then?'

'We need to set it out properly. Like: every fourth night he's allowed to have friends to sleep over here, but he's not allowed to have a sleepover anywhere more than two consecutive nights in a row, so he can only go to someone else's house if it's been at least two nights since he had someone here.'

'But that's exactly where we always go wrong!' I laugh. 'You do these complicated mathematical equations of when he can and can't sleep over and I just get so confused, I can't enforce them.'

His father sighs. 'You said rules, but your idea is just to keep it vague and have a row every single time. Would it kill you to learn to enforce things?'

'Yes, when I need a bloody calculator to work out what he's allowed to do.'

Later, Jack – who has been out at Luke's all night – comes to me with a fed-up face and says, 'Have you and Dad decided yet? About the rules?'

'Not quite,' I tell him.

'Because I wondered, if I ate a nutritious meal now and unpacked the dishwasher, can I go to a gathering tonight and stay out?'

'A gathering where?'

'It's a girl's house. You don't know her.'

'But where in London?'

'Um, near Edgware.'

'Edgware's miles away!'

'Not that far. But I need to leave in half an hour.'

Since he's asked me nicely, I throw together a quick salad for him. 'Not tuna,' he begins, 'you know I don't eat tinned tuna.' But then he hears himself and sits and swallows most of it down. Then, having had me check which buses go to Edgware, he leaves.

'At least we can get an early night,' says his father, who thinks I did absolutely the wrong thing in letting him go.

At eleven, we've just put our light out when my mobile rings. 'Mum?'

'What is it, darling? Are you OK?'

'Yeah, but . . . well, it turns out there's too many of us to stay over and, well, I wondered, could you possibly come and pick me up? Or else can you give me permission to come home on a bus?'

I look at his father, who is mouthing, 'No, no, no.'

I sit up in bed. 'Look, are you actually being told you can't stay over?'

'Not exactly. It's just, there's nine people and there isn't a bed and I'll have to sleep on the floor.'

'You cannot drive to Edgware,' his father hisses. 'I'm not having you do that.'

'Look, darling, sorry, it's too late. You're going to have to stay. You'll be a bit uncomfortable, but at least you're safe.'

'Please can I at least go and see if there's a night bus home? Please?'

Against everyone's better judgement, I arrange that Jack will go out and check and call me in five minutes. He does. 'I'm on the bus. It's only going to take about an hour.'

I look at the clock: 11.20. 'An hour?'

'You don't have to wait up.'

'I can't sleep till you're home safely.'

'I'm really sorry. I'll make it up to you and Dad. I'll do housework and everything.'

I make some camomile tea and go downstairs to watch TV. At 12.40, his key in the door. He comes in and flumps onto the sofa next to me.

'I'm really sorry, Mum.'

'Was the bus all right?'

He smiles. 'It was funny. I bumped into Jason – do you remember, from my old school?'

Jason and Jack were friends at primary school. I remember walking Jason back home after swimming one day, his small, hot hand in mine.

'Well, it's pretty sad. His life's already fucked.'

'What do you mean?'

'He's been expelled from three schools already for dealing drugs.'

'That's awful.'

'And you know what? He was really friendly, but when I

240

first saw him – he's so huge now – I was actually scared. Put it this way, if he hadn't known me, I reckon he'd've definitely robbed me.'

Cotching

When the kids were little, I really looked forward to school holidays. I'd take time off work and we'd do things. Museums, cinema, cricket, picnics in the park. Some days, though, we just sat around and did nothing – whole mornings spent in bed together, eating toast, watching TV, doing jigsaws, just luxuriating in each other's company. 'Slob mornings' Eddie christened them and, looking back, they were some of the best times. These days, the tradition continues without me – and we're not talking mornings, but whole days.

It's 2 p.m., gloriously hot. Eddie is sitting on the lawn in his boxers, smoking a roll-up and drinking coffee, the grounds of which he has managed to scatter all over the kitchen floor. Becca, still in pyjamas, is sitting cross-legged and cross-faced, watching a loud sitcom on TV. Jack's still in bed.

I run upstairs and tell him to get up right-now-this-minute. 'No,' he says, snatching the duvet back, so his surprisingly large man-feet stick out the other end. 'Go away.'

Incense ash is scattered all over the books on his desk, but I detect another smell. 'Have you been smoking in here?' I ask him.

'Go away!' I hesitate for a moment, then run back downstairs and demand that Becca turns the TV down.

'Why?'

'Because I can't concentrate.'

'But you're off work.'

'I'm working from home. And please, for goodness sake get dressed.'

'Why?'

'Because . . . because it's very depressing for me to have to see you in your pyjamas at two o'clock.'

She hurls her face into the sofa. 'Sorry if I depress you,' she yelps, 'but it's the way I am. I just can't help it. You should have thought twice before giving birth to me if you didn't want to be depressed.'

A picture pops into my head. Me sweating and panting as I crouched on that summer morning sixteen years ago to let my plump, dark Becca out. 'Sorry! On second thoughts, can we stop? I just have a feeling this one might turn out a bit depressing.'

On the kitchen table are some brochures I left out last night. I'm about to chuck them in the recycling, when I change my mind. I make some tea, feel faintly optimistic.

'How about this?' I say to Jack when he finally stumbles downstairs. 'How would you like to go on a surfing hol—'

'No,' he says.

'You haven't even heard what I'm offering. You could go

windsurfing in Devon for a week. Just think, no parents, lots of girls and big dangerous waves. Just have a look at the pictures at least.'

Jack's eyes are dull. 'I'm not going on any nerdy holiday unless it's with at least two of my friends,' he says flatly.

'Have you any idea how spoilt you sound?'

He shrugs. Becca tramps in, still in pyjamas. 'Why does it always have to be adventure this, adventure that? Why can't we just stay in our rooms like normal people?'

'I just thought you might like to—'

'Anyway those holiday camp thingies, they're full of geeks.'

'You've no idea who goes on them,' I say quickly.

'We do,' Jack rushes to agree. 'They're for the types who get up early and do everything their parents say and have no friends.'

'Yeah,' says Becca, 'and the only way they can make friends is by doing *activities*.'

'Well, that's how a lot of people make friends,' I say.

'Well, not us,' says Jack. 'We like to do other things.'

'Like what exactly?'

Jack looks defensive. His eyes slide over to Becca. 'We like to cotch, yeah?'

'Cotch?'

'He means hang out,' says Becca, who has been translating for him ever since he was in a highchair and saying 'poo' for spoon.

'So you mean stand in a park somewhere and smoke?'

Jack glances at Becca again. 'And other things,' he says.

'What other things?'

'Don't feel you have to tell her, either of you,' says Ed, who, scenting an inquisition, has drifted in to spill more coffee. 'You have every right to remain silent if you want.'

I look at my eldest, ladling out his unhelpful wisdom, and I sigh. 'Look, guys, the only reason I dared – sorry – to suggest a holiday is, well, you all look so bored.'

'I'm not bored,' says Jack quickly.

'Then why can't you get up a little earlier? Why can't you keep the kitchen tidy now you're all off school?'

'What the hell's tidying the kitchen got to do with it?' says Becca. 'That's what this is really about isn't it? Making us into your slaves!'

'If you really want a break from us,' says Ed, still seductively reasonable, 'you go away. We'd consider a week in this house without you to be a real holiday.'

Shit Parents

When I was expecting my babies, I did not drink alcohol, eat runny cheese or (biggest sacrifice) tint my hair. Once they were born, I tried hard to find a balance between taking their health ludicrously seriously (what mother doesn't?) and coming to terms with the fact that you can't protect your babies from absolutely everything.

So, while they were all breastfed for months, I tried not to worry when they crawled around with the dog on the floor. As they got older, we saw no point in banning chocolate or the occasional Fanta, but generally we made sure our babies led a wholesome, wholefood, Start-rite kind of life.

Now my son Jack – fifteen years old and ashen-faced – stands in front of me, demanding to know why I won't buy him a cigarette lighter. 'You fucking well promised! You said you'd give me twenty quid if I stopped biting my nails.'

'I never said cash. I said I'd buy you a game for your computer, something like that. I never said anything about a lighter.'

Jack tuts. 'But you know I use lighters. It's not like I'm pretending I don't. All I want is one of those smart Zippo-type ones. What's wrong with that?'

I take a breath. 'What's wrong with that is that I will not under any circumstances buy you a single thing that enables you to smoke.'

He stares at me. 'Why not?'

'Because I cannot bear that you smoke.'

He still stares. 'You really think that's enabling me? Buying me a lighter?'

'Yup. I really do.'

He gives a yowl of dismay, then hurls himself back into the ever more circular argument. 'But you know I smoke. I just don't see what difference it makes if I spend the money on a lighter.'

I shut my eyes. Yes, I know my baby smokes. I've smelled his clothes, his breath, I've seen it in his eyes, picked up the stubs flung out on the lawn. He has never denied it.

'I know and I can't stop you. But I can't bear it. Don't you see that? I find that knowledge so painful. The idea that any of my kids are prepared to damage themselves in this stupid, mindless way.'

'But you drink.'

'It's not the same.'

'Why not?'

'I'm old. I didn't start drinking till I was about thirty-five. Meanwhile,' I add, in case he's forgotten, 'you need to know that any smoking apparatus your father or I find in this house will be put straight in the dustbin.'

Sensing defeat, Jack tries another tack. 'But just look at my nails.' He thrusts them in my face.

A mistake. The first thing I notice is that, as well as the usual grime, they're encrusted with greenish-silver paint.

'I hope to God you haven't been doing graffiti again.'

Now he gives up. He sinks to the floor and rests his blond head in his arms. The head of an angel. 'You're a cunt,' he whispers.

'What did you say?'

'Never mind. It's just . . .' he raises his eyes and for once they are scarily calm, 'you're such shit parents, you and Dad. You really don't have a clue how to parent us, do you? I mean it, Mum. For a start, you're so immature.'

'Me? Why?'

'The way you burst into tears every five seconds, like a little five-year-old.'

I think about this. It is true that recently there've been a few family spats where I've felt – what? – a lurching despair? Confusion? Simple grief?

'All my friends' parents,' Jack continues, 'they don't erupt all the time the way you and Dad do. They somehow manage to be their kids' friends and their kids respect them. They're far more likely to do as they're told because basically they respect where their parents are coming from.'

I feel tears coming. Five-year-old's tears. I swallow them down.

'I don't want to be your friend,' I tell him quietly, 'I want to be your mother.'

'Well,' he says, 'you're a shit mother.'

There was a long-ago night, when Jack was maybe two years old, when he suddenly seemed to have trouble breathing. His father was working abroad, I was alone with the kids. I was scared. I rushed him to A&E, where he was checked for signs of asthma. The tests were inconclusive, but after some time on a nebuliser he seemed to recover and we were sent home. I took him into my bed, where he fell easily asleep.

247

But I didn't. I lay and watched his impossibly small chest going up and down, up and down. I listened to his breaths, stroked his cheek, his hair, watched his trembling eyelids. It seemed a small price to pay – one sleepless night, in return for the pleasure of watching my baby breathe.

Exam Results

Eddie used to be the brightest boy in the class – so perfectly, shiningly bright that we even worried for him. He scored top in everything, effortlessly and happily, but sometimes he seemed a little too close to his teachers and not quite close enough to his peers. But then again, Eddie was a one-off and everybody loved him, and, anyway, how could you worry about a child who was so attractively open and articulate and passionate? In the end, all you really want for your children is opportunity – and it was clear that Eddie would be able to leave school and burst into the universe and do anything he wanted.

Eddie has just scored mediocre A Level results. No one – least of all himself – is very surprised about this. For the last two (or maybe more) years, he's done no work at all, concentrating instead on Going Out. In fact you could say – given how little time he's spent at his desk, a desk thick with dust, whiskers of tobacco, stray cigarette filters and sticky CD cases – it's impressive that he has any A levels at all. But then life is full of surprises and Near-adult Eddie owes little to Child Eddie.

Eighteen-year-old Eddie is adored by his peers and has countless friends of all ages and both sexes. His teachers have meanwhile found him 'a challenge', mainly because his erstwhile happy respect for authority has mysteriously imploded. Child Eddie did largely as he was told, whereas Near-adult Eddie does exactly as he likes – whether it's writing poetry, smoking draw or cruising the house in his underpants at 3 p.m.

On the day he gets his envelope, our boy seems chipper, but his shrugs don't fool his father or me. I give him a big hug, which he only slightly resists, and then we all take our places in the sitting room. Ed slumps on the sofa and picks at the holes in his jeans and tells us he doesn't want to go to university – in fact, he doesn't want any of the things he imagines we've always wanted for him. 'I know that you and Dad have this image of me as a pin-striped accountant with a swimming pool in Surrey,' he says, 'but I want a creative life. I don't want to be pinned down by anything.'

His father – who has always zealously promoted a creative and unconventional life for our children – laughs despairingly. 'Where on earth did you get that idea?'

Ed frowns and juts out his lower lip. 'Just you and your bourgeois standards, that's all.'

I look at them, father and son. Both are wearing creased

T-shirts, jeans and bare feet. His father hasn't shaved in days. I wonder what a guy has to do these days not to appear bourgeois.

A week later. On the day that GCSE results come out, Becca and I sit in a café near the school. Her hot chocolate is untouched, a skin forming on the top, her eyes closed.

'You don't want a croissant?' I ask her again.

'Shh, just shut up, OK?'

'You're all right, honey, just try to relax.'

She opens her dark-brown eyes. 'Not all right. Very sick.'

'You want to go to the loo?'

She shakes her head, takes a few big breaths, then gets up. Her face is white and solemn. 'I'd better go, Mum,' she says.

I fish in my bag for something. Her eyes widen. 'Your star necklace?' She's wanted it for ages.

'It's yours now. A present. Your good-luck necklace.'

She sighs and fingers the little silver star. 'I won't have done very well, you know. I don't know what you're expecting, but I'm not like Eddie.'

'Eddie hasn't done all that well,' I say, with a slightly uneasy sense that I'm betraying one child for another.

'But all those A-stars he got at GCSE.'

'It doesn't matter how you've done,' I tell her for the millionth time. 'You worked so hard and that's what counts. Whatever your potential is, you're fulfilling it. That's all any parent ever wants for their child.'

She looks doubtful. Turns the necklace over and over in her small hands.

'Aren't you going to put it on?' I say.

'I'm going to hold it.'

She goes. I wait. I order another espresso, but can't drink it. I turn the pages of a newspaper. I carry on waiting.

It's almost twenty minutes before I see her on the other side of the road. Her cheeks are pink and her eyes are bright and that's all I need to know. Ten years of spellings and times tables and capital cities, of sewing name-tapes, packing lunches – it's all worth it for the look on my daughter's face as she comes bouncing back across that grey London road to me.

Pushover

'By the way, Mum,' says Becca, as I give her a lift to Notting Hill so we can sell an old leather jacket of hers at the Clothing Exchange, 'be careful when you do this that you don't seem like, you know, someone who could be taken for a ride.'

'That's rich,' I say. As well as being the much-begged-for chauffeur, I'm a crucial part of this trip because Becca's too young to sell stuff on her own. She needs me because I have a driving licence, I have ID.

'Yeah, well,' she replies.

'Do I really seem like that?' I ask her after a moment or two, not sure whether to be concerned or amused. She glances

251

down at her chipped, navy-blue fingernails, spread out on her ripped-black-denim thighs.

'Not so much that, perhaps. But it's, like, obvious just from the way you talk that you're a real pushover.'

I laugh. Becca doesn't. She picks at her nails.

'Even the expression on your face, actually. The whole way you dress, your smile, your earrings, everything.'

'I didn't realise I was such a liability,' I say, still laughing. Becca gives me a look.

'It's OK. I don't really mind it, not usually. It's just that this is a serious thing we have to do here. I really, really want some money for that jacket, OK?'

'OK.' A moment's silence, then, 'Is Dad the same?' I ask her.

'The same what?'

'A pushover?'

Becca looks shocked, then she laughs. 'Of course he fucking well isn't. Dad's – well, Dad's the complete total opposite of a pushover.'

'Meaning?'

Becca thinks about it. 'You can't trick him, for a start. He can see through things.'

'And you can trick me?'

Becca rolls her eyes. 'Two things, Mum. One, you believe anything anyone says. Two, every single thing you think shows on your face.'

'Not really?'

'Your fairly beautiful but useless face.'

'Thanks.'

'C'mon admit it, you're a terrible liar.'

I do have to admit that.

'Actually,' Becca continues, 'it's quite funny. Eddie takes after you in that way. It's not so much that he's a pushover, but just like you his mouth goes all funny if he tells a lie.'

'That's true,' I agree. Eddie is guileless, transparent. He has a face he pulls when he's not being honest. He can't get away with anything.

'But,' says Becca, who's well into her stride now, 'Ed has a whole other way of being dishonest. It's like he'll never admit to things. I mean he can actually convince himself that a thing hasn't happened. He's been doing it all his life, you know.'

'Such as?'

'Like when we were younger. If we were all fighting and it got a bit rough and he accidentally, say, pushed Jack or me against a piece of furniture and we hit our heads, he'd try to deny it.'

'That's terrible.'

'Yeah, I mean if I hurt one of the boys, I'd go, "Oh God, are you OK? Please don't tell Mum." But not Ed. He'd just grab you by the shoulders and stare into your eyes and go, "Nothing happened just then, do you hear me? Nothing. You're fine. Pull yourself together, you're OK."'

I glance at Becca. 'And what then? What would you two do?'

Becca frowns. 'It wasn't so much that we wanted to protect him. It was more, you know, we almost believed him. That nothing had happened, I mean.' She pauses. 'It can send you a bit mad after a while, though.'

We park and go into the shop. Down in a basement that smells of ironing and is full of rails of sparkly fifties evening dresses, a girl with black punk hair and a ring through her nose examines the jacket carefully. Becca gazes at her with open admiration.

'Sorry,' she says, looking up at last, 'there's a stud missing here, look.'

'Oh,' whispers Becca.

'Oh dear,' I say.

Becca shoots me a look.

'Sorry, but we can't take it,' says the girl, handing it back.

'You mean not even for any money?' gasps Becca.

'We have loads of these and we can't sell anything in this condition.'

We fold the jacket back into its carrier bag.

Upstairs, Becca gives a long sigh. 'I didn't expect much, but I thought at least I'd get something.'

'I'm sorry,' I tell her. 'I thought you would too.'

She squeezes my arm. 'It wasn't your fault, Mum. You were very good in there.'

'Was I?' I say, remembering the 'oh dear' that slipped out by mistake.

'You were cool,' says Becca, adding, 'By the way, did you notice the girl looking at your shoes.'

'Seriously?'

'Yeah. I thought they were a bit chav when you bought them, but they're actually just about OK. Will you tell me when you're sick of them?'

Jack's T-shirt

Tuesday, seven in the morning. Walking up our street, I think I hear screaming. Female, distressed. I can't tell where it's coming from and am just wondering whether I should try to find out (I'm late already and need to change and go straight out again) when I reach our front door and—

I rush inside, dropping my bags. Becca is spreadeagled on the kitchen floor. Jack is standing on her hair and threatening to spit on her.

'Stop this right now, both of you!' I shout. 'Do you realise you can be heard right up the street? I came round the corner and thought someone was being murdered.'

'I *am* being murdered,' sobs Becca. 'Your son – he wants to hurt me.'

I look at Jack. 'Get your feet off her hair right now.'

His face is hard. 'Not until she gives me back my T-shirt.'

'What T-shirt?'

'The one she's wearing. It's mine.'

I look at Becca. She has on a faded old black T-shirt that could be either Jack's or Eddie's.

'You two are screaming this loudly about a T-shirt? Do you realise how embarrassing that is?'

'Oh, what a fucking surprise,' Becca manages to hurl from her pinned position. 'As usual, all you care about is social embarrassment.'

I ignore this. 'Let her up, Jack.'

'No.'

'Do it.'

'Why would I when she has my fucking T-shirt?'

'Just do it, Jack,' I say, as he makes as if to spit on Becca and she screams again, 'or there will be – consequences.'

Jack laughs. Becca screams as he squats down and tries to tear the T-shirt off her chest. More screaming, a scuffling struggle as she springs back up off the floor and throws both arms out as if to hit him, but misses. He socks her back and doesn't miss. She bursts into loud tears. 'Did you see that?' she screams at me.

'See what?' I take a step back.

'What he just did to me, you stupid fucking moron! The violence he just fucking well committed.'

'You tried to hit him first,' I point out, wondering why I'm so set on playing with fire.

'Aaargh!' Becca throws her head back – I don't point out that there's a bit of tinfoil and some dog fluff in her hair – while Jack comes towards her and does a pretend headbutt. I realise I actually don't know what to do. I know what their father would say. Walk away. Leave them to it. Let them kill each other. Let them learn about the consequences that you, their mother, never seem able to dish out.

I try another tack.

'Look, darling, is this really worth it?' I say. 'Do you need his T-shirt anyway? Just take it off and get this over with.'

'Yeah,' says Jack, 'just fucking do it.'

She turns the full blaze of her fury on me. 'You think he should win now? You think his violence should get a result?'

'You've both behaved ridiculously,' I tell her, looking at my watch. 'I'm supposed to be meeting Dad in less than half an hour.'

'That's right. Put your social life before our safety.'

I sink into a kitchen chair. 'Do you know,' I say softly, 'these two teenage sisters – one of them killed the other one in a fight just like this, just the other day. It was in the papers.'

Neither of them reacts.

'Can you imagine living with that for the rest of your life?'

Finally Becca does something. She pulls off the T-shirt and, poised to chuck it in her brother's face, has a better idea. Rushing through the hall, she flings open the front door and, standing there in jeans and bra, hurls it into the street.

Now I lose it. 'You silly, silly little . . . cow!' I tell her. The word slips out before I can stop it. It comes from somewhere buried deep, somewhere that can't bear the sight of a fellow female behaving like this, but I still feel like some horrible fifth-form bully on the school bus.

My daughter freezes. Her face goes tight with horror. 'A cow?' she whispers. 'You call me a cow and you wonder why your son tries to kill me?'

'I'm sorry,' I say, genuinely ashamed, 'I shouldn't have said that. I really didn't mean it. I'm tired and I—'

But she's hit her stride now. She's on fire. Standing there all pink-faced in her little white bra, she has everything she needs.

'If you want to know why we're all so fucked up,' she says as she stomps up the stairs and pauses on the landing for full effect, 'look at yourself. I honestly think you need some therapy.'

Three seconds later, Jack comes back in from having retrieved his T-shirt and he sees my shoulders shaking and asks me what's so funny. I can't tell him that I'm not laughing but crying.

Getting Mugged

Just recently, every time Jack happens to have some of my money on his person, he gets mugged. On Wednesday, he needed three pounds for something at school, but I only had a ten-pound note. I told him he absolutely had to give me back seven pounds at the end of the day. No problem.

But later he told me that 'On the way home, yeah, I ran into two of my mates who were outside the station, yeah, and two rude boys were kind of mugging them and so I went over to help them and I said to the guys if I gave them three quid would they go away, and they said they would, so I did.'

I considered this. '*Kind of* mugging?'

His eyes widened. 'You don't believe me?'

'I think I do, yes.'

'What then?'

I had no answer to that.

That was four days ago. Today, Saturday, I (yes, stupidly) trusted him with twenty-five pounds to get a new rucksack for school. He set off for Camden with a glint in his eye. 'I want a receipt,' I called after him, 'and the exact change. And if you don't manage to get a rucksack, I want all that money back. Every single penny!'

I'm on the bus when he rings. The reception on his mobile is terrible. 'Hey, Mum!' He sounds almost excited.

'Hi, darling, you OK?'

'Yeah, well, look, I need to tell you about something that just happened, right? The reason I'm ringing you right now, straightaway, is so you'll believe me, yeah?'

I pull my bags across so a woman can sit down. 'Why? What's happened?' I ask quickly.

'It's just, well, I just got robbed of five pounds of that money you gave me.'

'Oh my God!'

'Yeah, but listen, right? What happened was this crew just surrounded us.'

'Are you OK?'

'Yeah, but anyway, these guys, they said what you got? And we said nuttin', but next thing we know they take Chad's mobile phone and they make us empty our pockets and take the fiver from me, but not the twenty, as luckily I had that in my shoe, yeah? Anyway, they say if they ever see us again on that part of the street they want fifty quid off us straight-away or they're going to shoot us.'

'They're what?!' The woman next to me shifts in her seat. I lower my voice. 'I want you home right now. Where are you exactly?'

'I'm at Chad's, but we've got stuff to do. I'll be home later to watch the game, OK?'

'No way. You've just been mugged. This is serious and we need to sort it out.'

'Fuck's sake! What's to sort out?'

'For a start, we need to tell the police.'

Jack gives a big sigh. 'But, Mum, it's all over. You don't need to get involved and, anyway, the police don't give a shit what happens to us.'

'You say someone has talked about shooting someone.

That's very serious. I want you home right now.' I hang up as everyone on the bus stares.

When I get home, I'm relieved to see he's already sitting on the doorstep. White face, dark eyes. I stand for a second and look at him. I'm not sure what I'm thinking. 'Where's your key?'

'Dunno.'

'They didn't take your key?'

'Think I left it at Millie's.'

'Who's Millie?'

He frowns as I fish around in my bag. 'Just a girl, OK? Look, Mum, I don't want to hurt your feelings or anything, yeah? But I just wish you'd mind your own business and stop interfering in my life.'

I try not to smile. Sometimes he is so like Eddie.

'Oh dear,' I say as I try my pockets, 'I think Becca's got my key. Oh well, Dad will be home in a minute. OK, explain how I'm interfering in your life.'

'Calling me up all the time, yeah, when I'm trying to deal with the world in my own way, and trying to protect me from stuff you know nothing about.'

'I think you're forgetting,' I say as I sit down on the doorstep next to him, 'that you called me.'

He frowns. 'Did I?'

'You did.'

'Oh.'

261

A moment's silence. 'Jack, if I ask you a question, will you try to answer honestly?'

Elbows on knees, he gazes at the ground.

'Were you really mugged? Or did you just spend the money?'

Silence. We both watch as a small brown bird pecks at a half-open bin bag.

'Does it make such a difference which it was?' he says.

I take a breath. 'I would say it does, yes.'

So there we both sit, mother and son, on the doorstep of our home. I wait for an answer. It takes a very long time to come.

Parmesan

I was going to do a proper family supper – shepherd's pie, carrots, green vegetables. But then I remembered, first that Jack would want to watch the match on TV, second that Becca's been picky recently about eating meat, and though I absolutely don't intend to give in to that, maybe tonight – when, third, I am suffering from incredibly bad period pains – isn't the night to push it.

So I chop some tomatoes instead and make a fresh sauce for spaghetti. Ever since they were toddlers, it's been the lazy-happy option, the one thing they'll always eat.

I'm chopping fresh basil when Becca comes in. 'What's that?'

'Supper.'

'But what?'

'It's spaghetti. Spaghetti with a nice fresh tomato sauce. It'll be about twenty minutes, so could you possibly lay the table?'

She frowns. 'Not tomato sauce again.'

'I haven't done it in a while and the other day you admitted that your main vitamin C intake – since you don't like fruit – is my tomato sauce.'

She's silent a moment, sucking the ends of her hair.

'Anyway, I was going to do shepherd's pie,' I can't resist saying.

'Pies! You always do pies!'

'But I'm not. I'm doing pasta instead.'

'Pie or pasta, what's the difference? Whatever you cook, you somehow manage to fuck it up.'

Deep breath. 'Could you possibly lay the table?'

She's already halfway up the stairs. 'Homework to do.'

Peace in the kitchen. The dog sniffs the bit of onion I've dropped and, realising it's not tasty, throws himself down on the floor with a sigh. Seems like I disappoint everyone these days.

Jack slopes in. 'What's for supper?'

'Spaghetti. I thought we'd eat early so you could watch the match.'

Silence. He goes to the fridge and gets out the parmesan

and starts to grate it. This isn't quite as helpful as it sounds. Jack loves parmesan so much he can't bear to have anyone else near it.

'You OK?' He says nothing. 'I thought you'd be really pleased to have an early spaghetti supper.'

'Don't feel like talking, OK?'

I shout up the stairs that supper's almost ready. Becca stomps into the room and stops dead.

'Oh my God.'

'What?'

'What is it, Becs?' her father says, pushing the dog out of the way so he can sit down.

Becca is staring at Jack. 'I just can't believe it. Yet again you're letting him grate parmesan without washing his hands?'

'He did wash his hands,' I say quickly, because although I'm not at all sure he did, I cannot, simply cannot, get involved in one of Becca's hygiene riffs right now.

She glares at me. 'You complete fucking liar.'

'Don't speak to your mother like that,' says her father.

'Please either sit down or help,' I beg, leaning against the counter because my stomach is really hurting now.

Jack, still grating, looks up. 'What's the matter with you?' he asks coldly.

'I have very bad period pains,' I tell him, wondering why he can't be nicer when I just stuck up – no, lied – for him about the hand-washing. 'I feel like my insides are falling out.'

'Too much information,' says their father gently.

'Typical,' says Becca. 'I'm saying something serious, so she has to get the attention back on herself.'

'Just sit down,' says her father.

She doesn't move. 'That's right. Ignore Becca. Nothing Becca has to say is of any importance. Why? Because she's a girl.'

Her father snorts with laughter. It's the wrong response.

'Becca, could you bring the pan of sauce over please?' I ask her, as I bring the spaghetti to the table.

She pretends not to hear me.

'Do as your mother says,' her father says.

'Not until you admit that your son is grating that parmesan with dirty hands,' she says.

'Enough now,' her father comes in more sternly now. 'Time to leave it, Becs. Grow up, for goodness sake.'

I fetch the pan myself and serve four portions with her standing there. 'Sit and eat or go,' I tell her. 'I don't mind which.'

Delighted, she turns and leaves the room. Silence.

'Very nice sauce, darling,' their father says. Jack looks at him, then at me, then picks up his dish.

'I'm going to have mine in front of the TV,' he says.

'No you're not.'

'Why not, if Becca's been allowed to go?'

'Becca behaved very badly and I cooked this supper specially early so you could watch your match,' I say. I realise I have absolutely no appetite and put my fork down.

'So what? I never asked you to, did I?' My youngest son regards me with eyes that are scary. 'You always like to boast about all these apparently lovely things you do for people, but no one fucking well asked you, did they? Maybe it's time you thought about that.'

Saturday Night

Saturday, 11.02 p.m. Becca's in bed, Eddie's out, their father's away for the night and Jack is due back at any minute.

Well, two minutes ago. He absolutely swore he'd be home by eleven at the latest because he was out even later last night and because I'm shattered and need an early night. Half an hour ago, as I was getting ready for bed, I texted him to check he was on his way. 'On bus,' he replied, '20 mins, OK?'

Good old Jack, I thought. At least he occasionally does what he says he'll do. I made a cup of peppermint tea, tidied the kitchen, tried not to watch the clock.

11.14 p.m. It's at least forty-five minutes since we texted. This makes no sense. I try phoning – it rings and rings. Now I'm worried. So I text: 'Where r u?'

No reply. I try phoning again. No answer. A bad picture

flashes into my mind: his blond head in some gutter, blood pouring. Relax, I tell myself, the bus is late, that's all. But then why isn't he answering? The dog, picking up my mood, stares at me and whines softly.

11.25 p.m. I phone again. He picks up. 'Jack!'

'Sorry, Mum, I'm literally two minutes away.'

'But where—'

'I'm coming, OK?'

I open the front door and look down the road. Nothing. A can rolling around in the wind. At last I spot him. Even though it's a chilly, blowy night, he's wearing just a T-shirt and carrying half his clothes. 'This isn't fair,' I tell him as he reaches the house. 'I thought we agreed eleven o'clock. I'm so tired . . .'

'Sorry, Mum,' he says and staggers backwards for a second, then rights himself.

'My God. Are you drunk?'

He stares through me, blinking. 'Sorry, Mum.'

'OK, what have you had?' I follow him through the hall to the sitting room, where he plops down on the sofa. I turn on the light. His face is white streaked with green. Marble effect. He fumbles for the TV zapper.

'Oh, Jack. You're completely plastered.' I gaze at my son. I've never seen him drunk. I don't think he's ever been drunk.

'I just need to sit here and cool down, OK?'

'You must tell me what you've had.'

'Jus' some beer and some wine.'

'That's all? No drugs? You have to say. I won't be cross. I really need to know what I'm dealing with here.'

'No drugs, I promise. Shit—' He stands up, lurches forward, bends over. Liquid – thankfully clear – pours out of his mouth onto the rug.

I haul him into the kitchen, grab a bucket. 'Sorry, Mum,' he leans over and more liquid comes out.

'You didn't eat anything?'

'No.'

'Jack.'

'I'm so very sorry, Mum.'

I go over and rub his back. His skin feels cold. 'It's OK,' I say, glancing at the clock, which says five to midnight. 'It's not the end of the world. Every teenage boy does this – once.'

'I was sick on my clothes.'

'How many times?'

He holds up four fingers.

'OK, we need to get you to bed. Come on.'

We stagger together up the stairs. In the bathroom, he sits on the loo with the door open. I haven't seen him sit on the loo since he was about eight.

He stands up, wobbling. 'Not sure I can clean my teeth.'

'What the fuck's going on?' Becca stands blinking on the landing.

'It's OK. Go back to bed. Jack got drunk, that's all.'

She chuckles and pulls her door shut.

I put him in bed, stroke his head – cold and clammy. I fetch him a drink of water.

'I'm going to go to bed and read for a bit,' I tell him, 'and then I'll come and check you're all right, OK?'

He stares through me again. 'Thank you, Mum.'

I go downstairs. I am about to go to bed when I remember the clothes. I take his hoodie, jeans, shirt and T-shirt and put them in the machine. Then I get into bed and struggle to stay awake through fifteen pages of a novel I'm not really enjoying. When I creep back upstairs, my boy's fast asleep, snoring gently. I pull the cover over his shoulder and go back to bed. I'm so tired I could cry.

I've said it before – so much of dealing with teenagers is exactly like when they were toddlers. The disturbed nights, the endless worry, the washing of vomity clothes, the smoothing of brows. The only difference is that next day, after I've cooked my boy breakfast, hung his clothes on the line and reminded him gently that he needs to get a couple of hours of coursework done for Monday, he calls me a fucking stupid cunt and tells me to stop interfering in his life.

Becca's Thing

Becca's developed a thing about sell-by dates. When I tell her I'm doing stir-fry for supper, she grabs my sleeve. 'You won't

... I mean, you do know that the Thai sauce in the fridge is off, don't you?'

'What Thai sauce?'

'The one on the middle shelf? The one you bought in, like, early September?'

'I didn't know there was an old one in there, but don't worry, I wasn't doing that anyway. I'm doing it with prawns.'

She wrinkles her nose. 'Prawns. You know they can make you really ill?'

'If they're bad, yes, but since when did I ever poison you with a prawn? Or anything else for that matter.'

'OK, but it's Dad really. Do you know that the brown bread he was trying to make Ed eat yesterday was two whole days past its sell-by?'

'Becs, two days is nothing.'

Her eyes widen. 'You'd trust bread that's off?'

'Not stale or mouldy, of course not. But a few days here or there doesn't matter. Anyway, it isn't "off" as you love to say. It's just past the date the shop thinks it ought to sell it by. What do you think they did in the days before sell-by dates?'

She just shudders.

Later that night, as we all sit and eat the stir-fry (Becca having carefully checked the dates on every single packet I used and picked out each suspect beansprout – 'it looks funny'), her other preoccupation rears its head.

270

'Eddie,' she says, without even looking at him, 'could you please put your other hand on the table?'

'Why?'

'Because I know what you're doing.'

'What's he doing?' asks her father, reaching for more soy sauce.

'Scratching his balls. And it's making me feel quite ill.'

I glance at Ed. His hand seems to be resting innocently enough on his thigh. 'Leave him alone,' I tell her, 'I really don't think he's doing anything.'

Straightaway, Jack sticks his head right under the table. 'Nope. He isn't. His hand's nowhere near his balls, or even his cock actually.'

'Congratulations! You managed to say cock at the table. Again.' says his father.

'Hey, leave my cock out of this,' says Ed, taking up the baton with a grin as he tips the last of the noodles onto his plate.

Becca doesn't smile. 'Well,' she says, as she pushes the food around her plate, turning every bit of vegetable over several times before she eats it, 'Jack would stick up for him, of course.'

'Why would I?'

'Because you're always scratching yours.'

'Yeah, well,' Jack's visibly ecstatic at the turn the conversation has taken. 'I get really itchy bollocks, don't I?'

'That's enough,' I say. 'We're eating supper.'

But Becca's in full swing. 'Seriously, Mum, have you ever tried to watch TV with him? It's disgusting. Unless he's using it to eat, his hand is absolutely always down his pants.'

Eddie laughs loudly. 'You too,' she says. 'In fact, even Dad. All men are the same. They're either using their hands to put food in their mouths, or else they're touching themselves. Simple as that – food or balls!'

Her father smiles. 'What is it with you and men's bodies all of a sudden, sweetheart?'

'It's all your fault actually.'

'Why is it Dad's fault?' I say.

'The way he goes around naked all the time.'

'Dad does not go around naked,' says Ed.

'Yeah,' agrees Jack, 'he doesn't.'

'Thanks, boys,' says their father.

'But that dressing gown of his, it's always about to fall open. I can see his hairy legs and—'

Her father laughs. 'Should I shave my legs?'

'For instance, the other day, right?' she continues. 'You were wiping that dog sick off the hall floor and you had on those low trousers and I could see the curve where your arse started and – oh yuck, I can't even think about it.'

'Well, you didn't have to look,' her father points out.

'I did! I couldn't help it.'

Ed chuckles. 'That's just so fucked.'

'Mum,' says Jack, who has been deep in thought, 'at what age did we stop seeing you naked?'

I hesitate. 'Well, you can see me naked now. You just don't tend to come in when I have my clothes off, that's all.'

'I saw her recently,' confirms Ed. 'If I go in to ask her for money, she always starts taking her clothes off.'

'Works every time,' I agree.

'So if you want to see her fanny,' says Becca, 'just go in there and ask her for a tenner.'

Now everyone laughs – everyone except poor old Jack, who has flushed a deep shade of red. And I'm pleased and slightly surprised to be able to report that I watch his sister clock this, open her mouth to say something, then think better of it.

Becca's Key

Wednesday. I'm really overtired and don't have to work today, so once I've put breakfast on the table for Becca and Jack, I creep back to bed. I feel a bit guilty. So I ask their father – who's leaving the house in about ten minutes – to just pop down and keep an eye on them.

'Aren't they capable of eating their breakfast alone?'

'It's not that. I don't like them leaving the house and going off to school without someone saying goodbye to them. It just seems a bit bleak, that's all.'

He gives a bitter laugh. 'Don't be silly. You're not well and I've still got to shave. Anyway, they don't appreciate it. More to the point, those kids need a bit more bloody bleakness in their lives.'

He leaves. Half an hour later I hear the door slam, which means that one or both of them has left the house. I shut my eyes and try to enjoy the silence, wonder if I can sleep. Suddenly, footsteps pound up the stairs. Becca thrusts her head in the door.

'What is it, sweetie? I thought you'd gone. Are you, OK?'

'Listen, Mum, you've got to wake up, this is urgent. Jack has lost his key and stolen mine, right? So I have to fucking well know right now if you'll be here later.'

I try to make sense of this. 'Later?'

'I'm back at two today, remember? Will you be here? Quick! Just tell me yes or no!'

'Hold on. Jack's what? I mean, how do you know for sure he's taken yours?'

Becca adjusts her voice as if talking to a very truculent and deaf old lady. 'Because it was on the hook by the door, OK? When I came in last night with Ed, that's where I put it, OK? And now the little fucker – by which I mean your precious, darling son – has decided to go off with it, OK? Come on, just tell me if you're here or not, I've got to go!'

'Oh dear,' I try to think fast. 'No, I think I've got an appointment this afternoon.'

Becca frowns. 'An appointment?'

'Yes. Acupuncture. I have to go out at about half past one. But look, have you asked Eddie? I'm pretty sure he'll be here.'

'Ed's asleep. And pretty sure isn't good enough.'

'Oh, darling, look, this is really difficult. I'll speak to Jack later, but right now I need to sleep.'

Becca gives me a look. 'Lucky you. OK, then can you tell Ed he has to guarantee to be here?'

'I'll try.'

'You'll try? Christ, Mum, I'm the victim of a fucking crime and all you'll do is try?!'

'I'll do my best.'

Later, I go downstairs to make a cup of tea and, while the kettle's boiling, have a sudden thought. I go up to my daughter's room and, trying to ignore the magazines strewn all over the floor, the used underwear still tangled in trouser legs, empty crisp packets and drinks cartons that are supposed to be for Jack's packed lunch . . . Ignoring all of this, I stand absolutely still until my eyes fall on Becca's black Levis, worn yesterday and left on the floor exactly where she peeled them off.

Picking my way across the carpet, I lift them up, probe the front right pocket, pull out her key.

I walk back downstairs and place it on the kitchen table, take my tea back to bed.

At supper that night, her father is furious.

'Really, Becca, you had no right to go waking Mum just because you couldn't remember what you'd done with your key. You kids have got to grow up and start taking responsibility for your own possessions.'

'Yeah, but why d'you think I suspected Jack in the first place?' Becca goes. 'Only because the little brute's done it before, that's why!'

'That's not the point. Suspect whoever you like. But you shouldn't have woken Mum. She was exhausted.'

'Oh, well pardon me for thinking she might not want her own child to be left out on the streets after school.'

'Oh, Becs, come on, for goodness sake,' I say, laughing now. 'I have a life too, remember? I'm not going to start cancelling my acupuncture just because you can't be bothered to run upstairs to get your key.'

Jack looks up from his soup. 'Why d'you have acupuncture?'

'To give me energy. To help me feel less stressed when dealing with you three, actually.'

I sigh. Then I see that Becca has that look on her face. The look that means she's spotted her quarry and is preparing to come in for the kill. 'Yeah, and don't you think it's rather ironic that all this acupuncture you're having just seems to prevent you doing stuff for other people?'

Jack's bladder

Jack is in the garden. It's dark and freezing cold outside. I open the door and stick my head out, see his long, tall shape lurking by my lavender beds. 'Jack? What on earth are you doing out there?'

'I'm taking a slash, OK?'

'No, it's not OK.'

No reply.

'Jack?'

'What?'

'I said I don't want you peeing in the garden.'

'Why not?'

'I'd just rather you didn't, that's all.'

He comes back in, zipping up his trousers, tie undone, shirt flapping. 'Too late,' he says, grinning happily. Because anything and everything that involves the discussion of Jack's bodily functions delights him.

'Don't do it again. There are three loos in this house. Please use one of them.'

'But I do it out there all the time.'

'Well, just don't, OK?'

'Come on, Mum, what's wrong with it? I seriously can't see what the hell difference it makes to anyone.'

'Yeah,' says Becca, who is laying the table for supper and would not normally be inclined to defend Jack's urinary habits, 'what difference does it make?'

'It makes a big difference to me. I don't want to smell pee in my flowerbeds for a start. And the neighbours could easily look out and see.'

Becca laughs loudly. This is exactly what she hoped I'd say.

'That's just so fucking suburban,' says Ed. 'First, the thing about it smelling is complete crap. The rain washes it all away. And it's dark out there, so the neighbours would have to switch on the fucking floodlights.'

'Yeah,' says Jack, and you can see he quite likes the idea of a floodlit piss. So does Becca, who giggles. I look at their three faces, all so passionate about their right to urinate in the garden. At their age I was worrying about starving children in Africa.

'Look,' I say, 'can you just accept that I'd rather you didn't? Is that really too much to ask?'

'You're being a bit of a hypocrite,' says Ed, 'given how many times you've peed in public.'

'I have not!'

'Yeah,' says Becca, 'what about that time on the beach in Devon?'

'I was miles from anyone.'

'And on the motorway when we stopped in a lay-by and the wind made it go all over your Birkenstocks.'

I laugh. This one is true. 'That was years ago,' I say, 'and I was bursting.'

'I was bursting just now,' says Jack.

'No, you weren't.'

'Anyway, what about the time you got drunk,' says Jack, 'and peed in the road.'

'I did not!'

'Dad says you did.'

'He's making it up. I never did, OK?'

Becca has just finished laying the table. Now she narrows her eyes at Jack. 'Can I just ask, are you planning to put your hands in the cheese?'

Jack gives her a thuggish look. 'Why?'

'Because if you are, I'm getting a separate piece for myself.'

'Why?'

'Because I don't especially want to eat grated cheese that you've handled, OK?'

Jack turns to me. 'Mum? Did you hear that?'

'Hear what?'

'What she just said to me!'

'I just asked him a simple question,' Becca says.

'Oh, Jack,' I say, 'just answer her, for goodness sake.'

'Did you hear the way she said it?'

'All I said was, are you planning to put your hands—'

'There, Mum! Did you hear that?'

'You two,' I sigh, 'not this silly cheese thing again.'

Their father comes in. 'The cheese thing? I thought I told you, stop bloody well buying them parmesan cheese.'

'It really is quite warped,' says Ed, 'that you get such a kick out of depriving us of things.'

'I actually think it's your sister who's warped,' his father says. 'She's getting way too picky – everything's contaminated, everything's off.'

But Becca – who seems to have forgotten all about the cheese – is sitting at the table striking matches and flicking them out again with a dreamy look on her face.

'Do you remember the time,' she says, 'when we were all quite little and we were on our way back from somewhere, I don't know where, and you forced me to strip and pee in front of the Houses of Parliament?'

Ed laughs loudly. 'Scotland. That was on the way back from Scotland.'

'I did not strip you,' I tell her. 'It was boiling hot and you were all very little and just wearing knickers, and you were really desperate and I pulled in somewhere near Vauxhall and—'

'All the same,' Becca says with a shrug, 'that's what I ended up doing. Peeing naked in front of the whole government. So it just seems a little bit funny that you mind about Jack doing it in our garden, that's all.'

Eddie's Job

Our Eddie has never been very much inclined to earn money. Apart from a brief, honeyed period when he used to babysit for some friends down the road (seven pounds an hour just for watching TV), he's never earned a penny outside this house. Even the babysitting finally petered out because our friends moved and he couldn't be bothered to organise any more for himself.

'Look, it's so easy,' we told him. 'The Taylors will give you a great reference. Just stick some leaflets through people's doors.'

Eddie said he'd think about it, but he never babysat for anyone again. Nor did he take up our elderly neighbour's offer to pay him to mow the lawn. Nor was he interested when I said I'd pay him to hoover the whole house from top to bottom. Or at least, he was slightly interested. 'But it's just not worth my time for only a fiver an hour,' he said coolly. 'I've been slogging away at school all week and I really do value my leisure time.'

His father laughed loudly. 'Really, Ed, you talk as if you're running the World Bank, not fiddling away on that Playstation.'

'Maybe I'd sympathise,' I said, 'if you weren't always going on about being short of cash. It's the same for everyone, Ed: if your outgoings outweigh your income, then it's time to earn some money, simple as that.'

'I really don't see why you can't just raise my allowance,' he said and, looking at his calm, expectant face, I could see he was telling the truth. He really didn't see. How had two hard-working parents managed to produce such a lazy, unambitious child?

'Because it wouldn't be any bloody good for you, that's why,' his father finally snapped. 'Because part of our job as parents is to teach you the value of money.'

But that was then. That was an Eddie in full-time education, an Eddie whose only material desires were gig tickets and bafflingly expensive T-shirts from Urban Outfitters. Now, though, it's crunch time. Eddie has officially decided to defer applying to university till next year – at least. Which means he is now officially doing nothing all day.

Over the summer, we let him chill. He hung out with the guys, played guitar, stayed out late. In September, we told him it was time to look for a job. Either that or let us help him find something abroad.

He crinkled his nose when I mentioned working for a charity overseas, as one of my goddaughters had done. 'I know it sounds a bit worthy,' I told him, 'but she had a really wild time. And just think, at least you'd be able to get away from us.'

'I'm not sure I want to leave London,' he sighed, sounding more and more like an old man afraid of straying too far from his local. 'I mean, you know, all my friends are here.'

'Most of your friends are off to university in October,' we pointed out.

'OK, but my life is here.'

'Your life? What is your life, exactly?' his father asked him. 'It looks to me at the moment as if your life consists of lying in your bed till two and leaving cereal bowls in the sitting room and clothes all over the bathroom floor.'

'I mean my band,' Ed said.

'What band?'

'The one I'm getting together,' he replied.

Now it's late October, and those friends have left town. There's no band and he's still doing nothing. At night in bed, his father and I fret about him. 'Do you think he's depressed?' I say. 'Do you think that now they've all gone, he feels left behind?'

'No,' his father says, 'I think he's just constitutionally lazy.'

We decide we're going to have to give him an ultimatum. Find something to do or – or – or what? We don't get any further, because late one night Eddie comes in and flops on our bed. 'I'm moving out,' he announces, eyes glittering. 'These guys have got a spare room in this place at East Finchley and it's dirt cheap and I can move in in two weeks.'

'What guys?' I say.

'How cheap?' his father says.

'How do you know them?' I say.

'How do you intend to pay for it?' his father says.

'Well, I was hoping you might be able to lend me a deposit, and maybe the first month's rent. But I'll pay you back. You see, one of the guys has a kind of bar, where they do gigs and stuff, and once my band's up and running—'

'What band?' we say in unison.

Eddie just looks at us. 'What the fuck's wrong with you guys? You're so down on me. Don't you want me ever to have any kind of independent life at all?'

Jack's Memories

Jack and I have just been to the dentist. When we walk out into the dark street, he breathes in the air – rush-hour exhaust laced with a million takeaways – and says, 'Ah. Food.'

'You're hungry?'

'I guess I am, yeah.'

'Didn't you eat your lunch today?' (Jack frequently eats his packed lunch on the bus, at break, on the way home – any time, in fact, except lunchtime.)

'Mum. One lunch is never enough.'

I look at my youngest child. He's grown I don't know how many inches this year. Enough inches that he towers over me. Enough that when he went back to school in September, his trousers ended halfway down his calves and I had to do an emergency trip to Brent Cross.

'OK,' I hand him a fiver. 'I need to pop into that shop over there. Go and get yourself something and then wait for me outside.'

He hurtles off down the pavement. 'Jack!' I yell after him. 'Get a receipt and bring me the change.'

He smiles and gives me a thumbs-up.

I buy some chops for supper, some rolls for tomorrow's packed lunches, some orange juice for Becca and – since I sort of forgot to eat today – a sandwich for me. When I come out, Jack is standing cradling a steaming white carton in a white bag.

'You got something?'

'Yeah. Thanks a lot, Mum.'

We go to the car, get in and sit in the semi-dark to eat our food. 'Ooh,' I say, looking into Jack's carton as he takes off the lid, 'you got spring rolls.'

'Mmm. D'you want one?'

I hesitate for a moment. I have a thing about spring rolls. 'It's OK. I don't want to eat your food.'

'Here,' Jack hands me one with fingers that would make Becca keel over in horror, 'have one. I don't need four, after all.'

'Seriously,' I say, 'you're very sweet, but I'm OK. I've got my sandwich.'

Silence as I unwrap it.

'Oh,' Jack sighs, 'this is so nice. Thanks so much, Mum.' When Jack's happy he always says thank you a lot of times.

'It's a pleasure,' I tell him. 'Anyway, I'm really pleased that you didn't have to have any fillings. Well done for looking after your teeth.'

He looks at me. It's at moments like this that I catch myself talking to him as if he's still about seven. And he is kind (or complicit?) enough not to pick me up on it. The guilty secrets of mothers and sons.

'Mum?'

'Ye-es?'

'Do you ever get this thing where you get a sudden flash of something that happened in the past?'

'Mmm, I do. What sort of thing?'

'Well,' Jack licks his fingers, 'I don't know, but it's like at the moment, yeah, my memory for stuff from ages ago is so sharp. Something will just come to me – something that's not connected with what I'm doing or anything. Like, for instance, when I was waiting outside the shop for you just now, I suddenly remembered being in the bath with Becca with that little blue cup thing.'

'The one you used to pour water on each other?' I say through a mouthful of sandwich.

'Yeah, but why did I remember it at that exact moment? Don't you think it's a bit weird?'

'I know what you mean and I don't know why it happens,' I tell him, 'but I get it too. Little moments from my child-hood just come bouncing back to me – just ordinary moments.

286

I don't mean anything especially wonderful or terrible. Just stuff you'd think was pretty unmemorable really.'

'That's it,' Jack nods as he pushes his fork back and forwards among the noodles. 'It wasn't like I so loved having a bath with Becca or anything.'

We both eat. Traffic drones by outside. The sky is purple and black. Far away, a firework sprays over the skyline.

'Where do you think that is?' Jack asks me.

'I don't know. Miles away. Somewhere like Wembley maybe?'

Silence again. 'It's nice,' Jack says. 'Talking to you, I mean.'

'Thanks. It's nice talking to you, too.'

'We are kind of the same in some ways, aren't we?'

'We are,' I say. 'I think you have the kind of memory that I have. You take a lot of notice of things and store it all away. It's a good sort of memory to have. I think it makes you happy.'

'Yeah,' Jack says, finishing his food and folding the carton and putting it back in the bag, 'sometimes it feels like I just have so much stuff crammed in there, like I remember absolutely everything.' He pauses a moment and grins at me. 'Can't remember shit about science though.'

Eddie's Phone battery

Just recently, whenever I'm talking to Ed on his mobile and I start saying things he doesn't want to hear, his battery runs out.

So: 'How're you getting on with looking for a job, darling?'
I'll ask him.

'Look, Mum, I told you. Andy says he knows a guy who
knows this woman who's looking for someone to do bar work.'

'So have you called him?'

'Called who?'

'Have you called the guy who knows the woman?'

A pause.

'Sorry, Mum. I've gotta go. My battery's really low.'

Or I'll say: 'You do realise, don't you, that the second
month's rent is due in less than two weeks?'

'What?'

'Eddie, Dad and I aren't lending you any more money.
You've got to be able to pay that rent yourself.'

'Mum,' a small sigh, 'look, I've been to talk to someone
who's going to let us play one night.'

'How does that help?'

'For money. Duh.'

'But play what?'

'A gig, yeah? There's this place where they let unsigned
bands do a bit of—'

'But you haven't got a band.'

'What do you think I've been doing all day today?!'

'I have no idea. What have you been doing?'

'I went to Tufnell Park to see this guy who knows a
drummer.'

'Ed, sweetheart, this band stuff, it's all a bit unreal isn't it?'

'Thanks a lot.'

'No, sorry, wrong word. But it's your hobby, OK? Get as many bands together as you like in your spare time, but you also need a job.'

Total silence.

'Eddie?'

'Sorry, Mum. I'm going to have to go.'

'But we need to talk about this.'

'My battery's really weak.'

The fourth time this happened, Becca was in the room. I put the phone back in its cradle with a little noise of exasperation.

'What?' Becca said.

'Oh, nothing. It's just . . . why doesn't that boy ever charge his phone?'

'He does.'

'Then why does he always say his battery's about to run out when I'm talking to him?'

Becca smiled. 'Mum. You are so gullible.'

'What?'

'Why d'you think he says it?'

'I honestly don't know.'

'He doesn't want to talk to you, that's why. He knows you're going to ask him a load of difficult questions, so – oh my gosh, how convenient – suddenly my battery's going!'

When we left Ed at his flat with eight bin bags of possessions and an old duvet, I don't know what I felt. He stood in the middle of the brown-carpeted, brown-painted sitting room and looked jumpy. His flatmate was on his way. Maybe he wanted us gone.

I hugged him. Already he smelled of other people's houses. 'If it doesn't work out,' I said, 'you can always come home.'

'It had better bloody work out,' his father said, as we drove home with an empty car. 'We've lent him a fortune. I don't want it all collapsing before he's paid us back.'

'Oh come on, you know what I meant,' I said a little sharply. 'I just don't want him to get sad and lonely and be too proud to say so, that's all.'

His father breathed out hard.

'What?'

'Nothing.'

'What? Please tell me what you're thinking.'

'Oh, I just think it's time for you to stop mollycoddling these kids, that's all,' he said. 'But I don't suppose that's what you want to hear right now, is it?'

It wasn't, and we drove the rest of the way in silence. When we got home, I felt like a very old person, fragile and slow. It wasn't that I was missing Ed. More that my heart needed to find a way of adjusting to one less person in the house.

But when, at supper that night, I denied Jack barbeque

sauce on a really lovely piece of fresh halibut, he said, 'I hope you're not going to turn horrible now that Eddie's gone.'

'What's that supposed to mean?'

'I mean not letting us have stuff because you're so upset and all that.'

I laughed. 'I'm not upset about Eddie.'

'Like hell,' Becca said.

I gave her a steady look. 'I really am not,' I told her.

'Anyway,' Jack said, smearing mayonnaise on his fish instead, 'you needn't worry. He'll be back.'

'You think so?'

'Sure,' Becca agreed. 'He'll never pay the rent.'

'Really?' I glanced at their father. 'What makes you so certain about that?'

'The thing you've got to understand about Ed,' Becca said, 'is he has no interest in money. He just doesn't care about it.'

'Yeah,' Jack said, 'Eddie's an artist. He's above all that stuff.'

'So basically,' Becca explained, 'once he's eaten all those groceries you bought him and run out of credit on his phone and spent all the rent money on drugs, he'll be home.'

Jack's Place

It's 7 p.m. on a school night and Jack's not home.

'OK,' I say, when he finally slams the door behind him and drops his bag at his feet, 'this had better be good.'

He looks at me. His face is sweaty and his tie undone.

'Where have you been all this time?'

He shrugs. 'Just me and my friends, yeah? We played some football, didn't we?'

I think about this. 'In the dark?'

He glances at the window. 'It wasn't dark when we started.' Except he doesn't say 'started', but 'star-ed'. When he's getting ready for a fight, Jack loses his Ts. And most of his Gs.

He walks into the kitchen – a mistake because it gives me a view of his back.

'What's that all over your trousers?'

'What?' He pulls at the fabric, trying to see.

'Kind of grey stuff – all over your bum.'

He turns on the tap, fills a glass of water, glugs it down, then refills it. He thinks for a long moment. 'Anti-climb paint,' he says at last.

'Right.' I pull out a kitchen chair and lay a sheet of newspaper on it. 'Sit down. You'd better tell me where you've really been.'

He could refuse to sit, but he doesn't; he comes and he sits. He has the same studiedly casual face on that he always wears when he's about to be interrogated. He sips at the glass of water.

'Where have you really been?'

He takes a breath. 'Look, Mum, I'm not trying to be funny or anything, but you wouldn't understand.'

'What wouldn't I understand?'

'Just . . . me and my friends. We do things. Not everything a fifteen-year-old boy does, he has to tell his mum.'

'I think when it involves coming home two hours late on a school night with anti-climb paint all over his clothes, then maybe he does.'

Jack scowls.

'I don't even know if that will wash off,' I say.

'Sorry.'

'But that's not important. What wall did you climb? Seriously, Jack, if you've been doing something dangerous, you'd better tell me now.'

He looks straight at me. 'Why?'

'Because . . .' I struggle for a moment, 'because Dad and I will find out anyway.'

'How will you find out?'

'Never mind that,' I say, knowing already how weak I sound. 'Just take it from me, we will.'

Jack takes another sip of water and gives me a long look. He knows that, for the moment, he has won.

'You're such an idiot,' his father tells me later, after Jack has been further interrogated, revealed nothing and been grounded for the weekend. 'Can't you think more carefully before you threaten these kids with something, unless you're prepared to carry it out?'

'But I was prepared—'

'Yes, but to tell him that we can find out. Ludicrous. We can't and he knows it. I'm not trying to get at you, but don't you see? You played right into his hands.'

I'm silent a moment. 'What do you think he's been doing?'

'I don't know.'

'Are you worried?'

'I don't know.'

The next day, Jack and I are driving somewhere. The bad mood between us has, temporarily at least, dissolved.

'Mum? Can I ask you something?'

'Of course.'

'Well, if a bunch of boys, yeah, who're all such good friends, yeah, if they discover a place where they really enjoy going, which might involve climbing one or two walls – quite high walls, but not dangerously high, yeah? Well, what harm is that doing anyone?'

I slow down at the traffic lights and sneak a look at him. 'What sort of a place?'

He looks straight ahead. 'Just a place. A place that doesn't belong to anyone.'

'Jack, everywhere in London belongs to someone.'

He flicks a look at me. 'Not this place. This place is just, like, waste ground. No one cares about it.'

'You may think that, but it probably belongs to some borough and a council will be responsible for its upkeep and—'

294

He makes a noise of annoyance. 'OK, but if they don't know and it's not hurting anyone, then really what's the problem?'

'Jack,' I say softly, 'I can't have you going to places like that and climbing high walls and—'

'Forget it,' he says.

'What?'

'I don't want to talk about it.'

'You started it.'

'I've changed my mind.'

'Just tell me where the place is.'

He regards me with dark eyes. 'You? You're the last person on this earth I'd tell.'

And in my head, I hear his father's voice: Congratulations. Just when he might have been about to tell you, you started telling him off. You had your chance, woman, and you blew it.

Jack's Party

When Jack came home two inexplicable hours late from school and with anti-climb paint all over his trousers, he was grounded for the whole of the coming weekend. This was especially upsetting for him as there was a party on Saturday night that he was hoping to go to.

'How about you let me go to the party and I make up for

it by letting you ground me for any night you like next weekend?' he asked brightly at supper on Thursday night. His father made a wry face. It's not the first time Jack's tried to direct his own punishments.

'Sorry, boy,' he said, 'but it just doesn't work like that. You're grounded this weekend and that's that.'

'But it's Rowan's party!'

'Tough.'

'But I've been looking forward to it!'

'Then you should think twice before you stay out late after school climbing high walls, shouldn't you?'

Jack got up from the table so abruptly that his chair fell over. 'Honestly! None of my friends have this trouble with their parents. You guys are like some fucking olden days people!'

'You mean Victorian,' Becca said helpfully.

'Pick up your chair,' Victorian Mother said.

'The meal's not over,' said Victorian Father. 'Sit down, please.'

Jack tutted. 'I'm getting some water.'

'There's water on the table.'

'I'm getting some other water,' he said, going to the tap.

Becca chuckled. 'Actually,' she said, 'I don't see what the big deal is. Can't he go to the party and have some other kind of punishment?'

Her father sighed. 'Won't you guys ever grasp the concept

of punishment? You do a bad thing, you pay by going without something. And it hurts. End of story.'

'Well, congratulations, you're hurting two people,' Jack said.

'Two?'

'Rowan won't get to see me and she didn't even do anything wrong!' He blushed and Becca chuckled again.

Later that night, while we were watching TV, he texted me from his room. 'Y r u being so unfair 2 me?'

I held my phone out to his father. 'What shall I say?'

'Don't enter into any sort of dialogue with him,' he said. 'I think we spend far too much time negotiating with these children.'

I put the phone down. It dinged again.

'I need 2 talk 2 u about this relly stupid punisment.'

'He can't even spell,' I laughed. I texted back: 'Sorry not budging xx'

'I'm not sure why you're adding the kisses,' his father muttered.

'I always add kisses.'

He said nothing.

'What's wrong with kisses?'

'The child's in disgrace. He's hassling us about this punish-ment, and you're texting him kisses.'

That was Thursday. Now it's Saturday night. In the past two days, Jack seems to have simmered down and accepted his fate. At seven o'clock he puts on a clean shirt.

'You look nice,' I tell him. 'It's really nice when you bother to wear clean clothes.'

At 7.30 he tells me he's just popping down the High Road to take a DVD back to Blockbuster.

'OK,' I say, 'but straight there and back.'

'I'll be ten minutes, maybe fifteen.'

At 7.55 he's still not back. 'He's probably loitering,' I tell his father, who calls his mobile. It's on voicemail.

I text him. 'Where r u??'

Worryingly, he texts straight back: 'Sorree Mum.'

I call him again and he answers. 'Sorry, Mum. I just can't do this to Rowan. I'll be home by midnight.'

For a second I'm speechless. 'He's gone to the party,' I mouth to his father, whose face crumples.

'Jack,' I say, 'you turn around this minute and come back home or—'

'Careful,' his father hisses. 'Careful what you threaten.'

'Jack, I want you home right now, please.'

'Sorry, Mum, but that's just not happening.' He hangs up. My heart's pounding.

'It's simple. He comes home, or we ground him for two further weekends,' his father says and he sits down at the kitchen table with his head in his hands.

I dial again. 'Jack? Either you come home right now or—'

He hangs up again. So I text: 'Home now or 2 more weeks grounding. U decide.'

I don't add any kisses.

In fact, Jack comes home just after 10. We are both sitting in the kitchen, empty wine glasses in front of us. He walks past us, opens the back door and sits gloomily on the step, chin in hands, staring out into the garden. It's a warm night, balmy for November. The dog comes over. He pushes him away.

We get up and put our glasses by the sink.

'Lock the door when you come up, please, Jack,' his father says. He doesn't turn around. And though I find it really hard to walk away, we go to bed.

Eddie's Job 2

Becca spends quite a lot of time round at Eddie's flat. Sometimes she drops in on her way back from school and by the time she finally gets home, she's pale and exhausted and snappy.

'I don't think I want you going there on a school night,' I tell her after this has gone on for a couple of weeks, '5.30 is too late to be getting home in the winter. You've got no energy left for homework.'

My daughter strikes a dramatic, persecuted pose. 'So-rree. Didn't realise I had to apply for a fucking visa just to see my own brother.'

'Don't be silly, of course you don't. I just don't think you can do it during the week, that's all.'

She narrows her eyes. 'What exactly are you worried about?'

'I'm worried about your energy levels, I suppose.'

She glares. 'Like hell.'

'What?'

'Stop lying to me, Mum. I have a right to know what you're accusing me of.'

'I'm not accusing you of anything,' I shout after her as she stomps upstairs.

'Oh God,' I tell her father later. 'I've just thought of something. Do you think Becca's going there to smoke?'

'Did she seem stoned when she got home?'

'Not at all. Or at least . . .' I think of her drained face, 'I don't think so. I suppose I didn't look that hard.'

Her father thinks about this. We've both recently had huge concerns about the casual way in which both Eddie and Jack smoke 'draw', but as far as we know, Becca's never really been into it.

'Look,' their father puts his hand on my shoulder and gives it a squeeze, 'we can't stop her wanting to see her brother, and she's sixteen, she's in the sixth form, we can't stop her smoking if she really wants to. But we can absolutely stop her going there on a school night and that simply has to become the rule from now on.'

Later that evening, Eddie phones. 'What's all this about you accusing me of running some fucking drugs den?'

'Hey, darling, how are you?'

'I'm fucking pissed off that you and Dad think all I do is fucking well blaze.'

'I don't think that at all.'

'Oh yes you do. Becca says she's not allowed to come and see me any more because I'm giving her drugs.'

'What rubbish. Of course she's allowed. Just not on a school night, that's all. *Are* you giving her drugs?'

He sighs. 'I think what you and Dad have got to realise, Mum, is that we're not babies any more. We do have lives of our own, you know.'

'Fine, but Becca's still at school and we're still responsible for her and while we are, we'll make the rules. And speaking of lives of our own, how's the job going?'

Ed's been doing shifts at a wine bar – a job he got, in the end, not through his much talked-up flatmate Andy, but through a friend of a friend of mine.

'Not very well, actually.'

'Meaning?'

'I don't think they like me.'

'Why wouldn't they like you?'

'I don't know, they're just so fucking fussy.'

'Fussy about what?'

'What time we turn up, that kind of thing.'

I take a breath. 'You were late to work?'

'Only a couple of times. For fuck's sake. I really don't see why it has to be so—'

301

'Oh, Ed.'

'What's "Oh Ed" supposed to mean?'

'Welcome to the wonderful world of work, that's all.'

Later Becca comes to our bedroom. 'I'm sorry I shouted at you,' she says, sneaking onto the end of our bed.

'You didn't shout,' I say. 'Not really.'

'Well, I'm sorry I was rude.'

'OK,' her father puts down his book, 'what do you want?'

'Come here, sweetie,' I hold out my arms and she comes. I kiss her neck and breathe in the smell of her hair for a moment, before I look at her face. 'Are you OK?'

'Mmm.'

'But?'

She bites her lip. 'It's not exactly that I miss Eddie, because I see him and all that. It's just, well, I didn't know he'd be gone quite so soon.'

'Oh, Becs.'

'We've grown up our whole lives together,' she says and her lip is wobbling. 'I just never imagined living in this house without him, that's all.'

Her father pulls her to him. 'It's OK for you,' he says. 'Think of your mother and me. We've got to go through this not once but three times.'

Even though there are tears on her cheeks, Becca giggles. 'Not three times,' she corrects him. 'Twice. Cos Mum's gonna keep her little darling cutie Jack here forever, knitting him sweaters and feeding him boiled eggs and soldiers.'

'You're right,' her father concedes. 'I forgot about that.'

Becca's Coat

Now that Becca's in the sixth form and no longer has to wear school uniform, a deal about clothes has been hammered out. She buys most of them out of her allowance, but anything that qualifies as a necessity – shoes, coat, rucksack and so on – we'll pay for. They've got to be sensible, though. I'll only shell out for stuff that's practical and well-fitting and suitable for all weathers.

For ages now Becca's been desperate for a military-style coat. I say that shouldn't be a problem. As long as it fits and it's warm, I'll pay for it. 'It won't be waterproof,' she warns me, gazing out of the window with a mournful look on her face.

'That's OK, as long as it's warm.'

Most of all though, she wants the genuine thing. No high-street copies for our Becca. She wants vintage. If possible she wants to get it from an actual military shop, with appropriate bullet holes.

I'm not keen. 'They're made for great big six-foot men,' I tell her as, in a dingy dive in Covent Garden, she tries on some grey monster that makes her look like an extremely height-challenged extra from *War and Peace: The Remake*.

She eyes herself in the mirror. 'Maybe they do a smaller size?' she says hopefully. 'I mean, you get some quite short men in the army, don't you?'

'Do you?'

'Napoleon – duh brain!' She pulls the collar up and shakes her hair out and I have to admit that she looks quite fetching. 'If I do it up, look.' She struggles to get her small fingers around the massive gilt buttons.

'Look, sweetheart,' I say, 'can't we at least try H&M?'

She rolls her eyes. 'Mum! That rubbish chain-store is not going to have the coat I want. And anyway they all have frogging. I don't want frogging.'

'What exactly is wrong with frogging?'

'Oh – you wouldn't get it.'

We try eight more shops. In All Saints there's a coat that briefly appeals but it's very thin material and costs £120. Even Becca admits that's a no-no. Like Napoleon from Moscow, we go home coatless.

Friday afternoon, I'm in town for an appointment and find myself in Topshop. Hundreds of coats, many of them military. There's a navy one which has Becca's name written all over it. I phone to see if she's home yet.

'What's it like?' she asks me.

'Well, it's navy and warm, not too long—'

'Is it military?'

'Very military.'

'Has it got frogging?' Her voice is suspicious.

'Not a frog in sight.'

She sighs. 'It sounds quite nice. But I just don't trust you, Mum. There's bound to be some horrible little chavvy detail you haven't noticed.'

I don't buy the coat. And just as well, because back home Becca looks it up on the internet. 'My God, but it's got all this fucking ludicrous stitching round the collar! How could you ever have thought I'd like that?'

A couple of days later, I have an idea: 'Laurence Corner!'

'Laurence what?'

'It's only the biggest military outfitter in London. It's where people went when I was a teenager.'

Becca looks worried. But I google it and show her. 'It seriously is where you'll find your coat,' I tell her and I dial the number. No reply. It rings and rings. 'Oh well, we'll just have to go there.'

It's a rainy Saturday afternoon when we set off for Laurence Corner. Becca is quietly hopeful. 'All I want, yeah, is one a bit like that grey one we tried, only smaller and a bit less stiff.'

We drive down Hampstead Road towards Euston. 'It's really weird,' Becca says. 'I've been down this road on the bus so many times and I've never ever seen any military place.'

'Just you wait,' I tell her – but even as I speak those words,

I see it, on the left. Laurence Corner. Utterly dark and boarded up. 'Oh no,' I say.

'We're too late!' shouts Becca. 'It's closed down.'

'But – it was there a few months ago. I know it was.'

We park in a side street and look at each other. 'No wonder they didn't answer the phone,' I say.

Becca giggles. 'There's probably this little phone, like, in the middle of the room, and it's been ringing and ringing – my crazy mum trying to get through.'

We drive home, coatless again. In the car, Becca's quiet. 'Thanks anyway. For taking me, I mean.'

'That's OK. I'm so sorry it's gone.'

'Well, I was thinking, I might go and look at the one in Topshop anyway. You can't always tell on a website. The stitching might not be as bad as I thought. It might be just about OK, you know?'

Jack's Friends

It's a measure of how hard we're finding it to trust Jack at the moment that the nicer he is, the more I worry.

So when, on a cold and crisp Saturday morning, he's up by 9.30 and has not only put all his school clothes in the wash, but also emptied his bedroom bin, brought every used glass in his room down and is busy unloading the dishwasher,

I feel seriously tense. 'Hey, honey,' I say nonchalantly, 'you're up very early.'

He looks at me. He has on two layers of hoodies, a scarf and a beanie. Looming over the small white dishwasher he looks ready for some kind of urgent action. 'I just didn't want to waste the day, you know?' he says, avoiding my eyes.

'So where're you going?'

'Just out. Me and Chad. We might do some Christmas shopping.'

'Christmas shopping?' Jack's Christmas shopping normally consists of borrowing a fiver from me on Christmas Eve to buy a bunch of chocolate bars from Costcutter.

'Yeah, probably. Anyway, I thought I'd do something to help you first.'

'Thanks. But haven't you got any homework?'

He rolls his eyes. 'It's almost the end of term, Mum. They haven't set us any. By the way, I thought I'd take the dog out with me. Give him some exercise.'

'That's nice,' I say, but a bit uncertainly, because when did Jack ever in his life offer to walk the dog? I try to picture Jack out Christmas shopping with the dog trotting along in tow. No, I can't do it.

I start sorting the washing. Jack's phone goes. He answers it with one eye on me. 'But look,' he says, 'I set an alarm, see? . . . You said— OK, but how much coursework do you have to do? . . . ' Jack tuts . . . 'But I thought we had an arrangement, man?'

He catches me listening, a bundle of towels in my hands, and holds the phone away from his ear. 'Look, Mum, do you think you can give me a bit of privacy?'

When I don't move, he shakes his head and walks out of the kitchen and into the sitting room, clicking the door shut. I drop the washing and put my ear to the door. And no, I don't feel ashamed. Recently, Jack has lied to us about just about everything. Any respect I might have for his privacy is overridden by a burning need to know what he's up to. Unfortunately I can only catch:

'Oh, but man . . . But you said . . . Yeah, I know she did but . . . Oh no, that's just not happening. I can't get hold of her now. I don't have a number . . . Fuck's sake, I told you I didn't.'

He returns and I throw myself at the washing. 'What?' he says.

'What?' I say.

He laughs. 'Something about the way you're looking at me, Mum. It's really freaking me out.'

I pull out a chair and sit down. 'Look, Jack, I'm sorry but I have to say it. I'm worried. Can't you just tell me what you're planning?'

His face goes hard. 'Planning?'

'You sound like you're up to something, that's all.'

He sighs and picks at his nails. 'Why can't you ever trust me, Mum?'

'Why? Because you often lie, that's why. Because it's only a matter of weeks since you were stealing money from us. Because when you say you'll be home by a certain time—'

'It's not my fault that London Transport—'

'Look, darling, I don't want to know personal stuff. But if you could just give me a rough idea of what you're doing today?'

He looks at me with the big baby eyes that don't seem to have caught up with the rest of his now largely man-shaped body.

'OK,' he says very slowly. 'The dog and I are gonna show up at Chad's. Then we're gonna hook up with Alex, but that's only if he gets his coursework done, and we're all gonna head off to Camden and buy some Christmas presents and stuff. Then after that I'm meetin' up with three more friends and we might come back here for a bit. Is that OK?'

'Sounds great,' I tell him brightly, even though I still don't believe a word of it.

And so he leaves. And about four hours later, he's back, with the dog, a carrier bag full of what looks a lot like Christmas shopping, and three friends. All three of them are female, blonde and, as Jack himself might say, buff. Jack introduces them – Anna, Flo and Lucy – and they sit at the kitchen table chatting and laughing and fiddling with their mobile phones while Jack does something I've never seen him do in his life before. He makes a pot of tea.

Eddie's Plans

I call Eddie to talk about Christmas.

'I'm a little bit tied up right now,' he says, sounding very much as if I've woken him up. 'Can you give me a call back in about forty-five minutes?'

'OK, darling,' I say, feeling somehow messed around. How come Ed always seems to have the power to make people jump around him? 'But it will have to be at least an hour and a half as I've got to take Becs to the doctor's.'

I wait for him to reply but realise he's already hung up. I sigh. Becca – who's sitting at the bottom of the stairs very slowly threading new, fat, glittery laces through her old Converses – glances up. 'What?'

'I don't think he was even awake.'

She smiles to herself as if it's hilarious that I might expect my son to be awake at half-past ten in the morning. She sucks and then twizzles the end of the lace to make it go through the hole. 'Hmm, let me see. He usually gets up around two or two-thirty. Then he has a cigarette. Then he—'

'OK, thanks, I don't need you to take me through his life-wasting schedule. But he's impossible. I still don't even know if he's coming over on Christmas Eve or not.'

Becca gives me a bored look: 'Why d'you need to know?'

'I'm just trying to organise a really nice family supper, that's all. I think Grandma might come over and we'll have champagne and—'

'I don't think he'll want to come.' The way she says it – blunt and final, implying she's somehow party to his life and intentions in a way that I never will be – annoys me. Wrongly, I know, because it's Eddie I'm annoyed with.

'Well, he should want to.'

'Why?'

'Because we're his family. Because Christmas is a family time. Because . . . because I have presents for him!'

Becca smiles as if I've said something funny again.

Two hours later, I try Ed again. No answer. An hour after that I finally get him. 'Hey, Mum.' I hear him suck on a cigarette.

'Hi, darling, you OK?'

'Not really.'

'What's wrong?'

'Well, the rent's due on Tuesday, right? And the point is, I just don't have any fucking money right now. And I really don't know how I'm supposed to fucking well find it, that's all.'

'But what's happened to all the money you've been earning?'

'Well, obviously, I've got some left. But I owe Andy a bit from last month.'

311

'Last month?'

'Yeah. He had to lend me, just for the fucking rent. And I don't know, I suppose I've just got through it. Bar work doesn't pay very much you know.'

'Eddie,' I say, 'this is serious.'

'Of course it's fucking serious! That's what I'm trying to tell you if only you'd actually bother to listen!'

'We're not lending him money,' his father says when I tell him about this. 'Absolutely not. Not again. He's made no effort to pay back what he already owes us. Anyway, bar work was always a lazy option. He's just going to have to get a real job if he wants to cover his rent.'

Later I call Ed again. 'You're going to have to get another job,' I tell him. 'It shouldn't be that hard. Lots of places are taking on extra people over Christmas.'

'God, you talk as if it's so easy. I'd like to see you get a job.'

'I have a job!'

'I mean another one. As well as your day job.'

For a quick second his insane logic almost floors me. 'Eddie,' I say slowly, 'I don't need another job because the one I have pays well enough. Yours does not. Therefore you need more work. Now, about Christmas.'

'What about it?'

'Will you come on Christmas Eve?'

He sighs. 'I doubt it.'

'Why not?'

'I've got plans.'

'What plans?'

'I don't know yet. Maybe I'll get a job or something.'

'On Christmas Eve? You're going to go and work as a reindeer?'

And, to his credit, Eddie laughs. A loud, uncomplicated laugh that takes me straight back to a little baby-haired boy in brown jumbo-cord dungarees. A little boy who insisted each Christmas Eve on putting out a mince pie and a glass of lemonade for Santa 'and a carrot for his reindeer'. A little boy who didn't quite know whether to be excited or frightened by the idea that a man might actually be about to climb down the chimney, and who always vowed to stay awake and see it, but who (like every other child in the land) was always out for the count by the time we crept in and laid his stocking at the end of his bed.

Night

It begins with Jack, who's due home by midnight latest. As usual (especially when his father's away) he rings me at 11.20 to start negotiations. 'Look, I know what we said, yeah? But Luke says I can sleep over at his and—'

Quickly I weigh up the pros (I can go to sleep) against the cons (does Luke's mum even know about this?). 'OK,' I say, 'as long as I can get hold of her to check she really doesn't mind.'

I dial the number. No answer. I try it again. Still no answer. I call Jack back. 'Darling, look, I can't get any reply, she may even be asleep. I'm sorry but you'll have to come home as planned.'

Jack sounds on the verge of tears. 'Oh, God! You wouldn't believe how shit my evening's been! And now this. Can't you just at least try her again?'

'No, it's way too late. And I want you to set off right now. We agreed midnight and even if you get straight on a bus you're unlikely to make it.'

At five to midnight, waiting in the hall (yes, as usual) I phone to see where he is. No reply. I try again. Straight to voicemail. Now (yes, as usual) I'm a bit worried. Ten minutes later – still no sign – I try him again. He answers with a little sob. 'Jack! Are you OK?'

'I just – just – got smacked in the face by about ten rudes.'

'What? Are you hurt? Where are you?'

'It's OK. I think they've gone. Oh, Mum, they hit me about eight times in the fa-ace.'

I pace the hall. 'Right, come straight home now. Can you get home? Do you need me to come out and get you?'

Standing here in my black satin nightie, furry boots and an old pilled cardigan, I realise this isn't really an option. But then, listening to the voice of your child who has just been beaten up is not much of an option either.

But five minutes later, he's at the door, his face not bleeding but definitely bruised. And he's shaking. 'You're in shock,' I tell him and I touch his head. He shrugs me off. 'I'm OK, Mum, honestly. I'm just so fucking annoyed. They wanted my phone. I mean, what right do they have?'

I make him hot chocolate and he drinks it. He tells me exactly what happened. Attempted robbery, though Jack (understandably? stupidly?) did lash out when cornered. 'We should really tell the police,' I say, but without much conviction.

He shakes his head. 'No way am I staying up and giving statements and all that shit.'

We both go to bed. What feels like seconds, but is in fact at least an hour later, I'm woken by a whimper. 'Mu-um?'

Becca is standing in our bedroom rubbing her eyes. 'I need some painkillers.'

'Are you OK?'

'Got this awful, like, pain in my head.'

I stumble out of bed and to the bathroom, get her the Nurofen. She goes and I fall back into sleep. For about an hour.

At first the ringing is just in my dream but it gets slowly louder and louder – my mobile. 'Ed!' The bedside clock says 3.30 a.m.

'I'm terribly sorry, Mum.'

'Are you OK?'

'I got locked out of the flat and I've nowhere to sleep.

315

I've been walking around but it's so fucking freezing out here.'

'But – where are you?'

'At the end of the road.'

By the time I get downstairs his shape looms in the glass of the door. 'I'm so sorry,' he says again, his cheeks raw with cold. I tell him the bed's made up, squeeze his arm, say goodnight.

It's 3.47 a.m. Sleep. But at seven the dog barks at the milkman and I realise that's it. I give up, get up, put some washing on, make coffee. When Jack comes down at ten, I ask him how his face is and get a gruff, non-committal reply. When Becca shuffles in, I offer her coffee and eggs but she scowls at me and takes her cereal back to bed.

Eddie is all sunshine, chatting to me about this and that. I think how much I miss having him around. It's only when I'm making our second round of toast that the obvious question occurs to me.

'But hold on, if you were locked out, why didn't you just call Andy or one of your other flatmates?'

He looks up from the vegetable drawer of the fridge where he knows Jack hides the Nutella. 'At three fucking thirty in the morning?' he says with the wide, sweet eyes of a seven-year-old child. 'It wouldn't exactly have been very considerate to wake them up, would it?'

Jack's new Rucksack

Jack's godmother gave him a new rucksack from Topshop for Christmas. Exactly what he needed: his current school one has never really recovered from a strawberry drinking yoghurt. But she also (kindly? stupidly?) handed him the receipt. 'Do change it if it's not right,' she said. 'I mean it. I won't be at all offended.' Jack thanked her, but said not only did he love it but it was actually the exact one he'd wanted.

'Really lucky,' I told him later, 'that she managed to pick something you genuinely liked.'

'She didn't,' he said, 'and I don't. I really hate it. It's shit.'

'Well, congratulations in that case for behaving so maturely,' his father said, surprised.

'If you want to change it, you'd better do it soon though,' I told him. 'You probably only get twenty-eight days. Do you want me to look after the receipt for you?'

He gave me a filthy look. 'I'm not a toddler,' he said.

Now, two Saturdays into the New Year, I hear Becca and Jack shouting at each other. 'She's had my fucking receipt,' moans Jack, 'the one I need to change my rucksack.'

Becca stomps into the kitchen and starts peeling a carrot. 'I have not. Tell him, Mum! What the fuck would I want with his pathetic little receipt?'

'I know I put it in a certain place and now it's gone.'

'Where did you put it?' I ask him with a sigh, resisting the obvious response which is: I knew this would happen.

'On the floor,' says Jack as if it's the obvious place. Over at the sink, Becca laughs and, peeler still in hand, bites into the carrot.

'I only put it there for a second,' he adds, 'while I tidied my desk.' He looks at me and bites his thumb.

'Come on,' I say, 'let's go and look.'

Jack's room is even worse than it was a few days ago. His bed – a mattress on the floor ever since he rejected its base – is indistinguishable from the rest. Piles and piles of clothes and plates.

'This room is disgusting,' I tell him. 'I suggest you tidy it up right now and I bet you anything you find the receipt.'

Jack's eyes light up. 'How much?'

'What?'

'How much do you bet me?'

'I didn't mean literally. I meant I am sure you'll find it.'

He looks disappointed. 'I just really need some cash.'

I give him a long look. 'Tidy up,' I tell him again, 'and I think you'll find your receipt.'

Half an hour later he comes down grinning, arms full of dirty clothes and towels which he flings by the washing machine. He waves the receipt. 'I'm going up town.'

'So where was it?'

'Oh,' he says, as though it was nothing. 'In my jeans pocket.'

'Hmm. What do you say?'

'Thanks, Mum. Sorry, Mum.'

He goes off to Oxford Street with rucksack and receipt. A couple of hours later he returns – in an even worse mood than before. Becca regards him with curiosity. 'What's the matter? Wouldn't they change it?'

He looks furious. 'Not for what I fucking well wanted. You need the fucking card apparently.'

'Card? What card?' I'm confused.

'The card it was originally bought with, of course!' he snaps. 'The Visa card or whatever the fuck it was.'

'Hold on,' I say, struggling to work out what he means. 'No you don't. Louise checked when she bought it that you could definitely swap it. That's why she gave you the receipt.'

Jack throws himself into a chair. The dog jumps up and skitters backwards. 'You don't understand! I didn't want to swap it for anything in that moronic shop!'

Now Becca looks interested. 'What did you want to swap it for?'

'For money, duh brain. And they said they wouldn't swap it for money unless I had the card.'

Now Becca starts to laugh. 'You went up to the till and actually asked to swap it for cash?'

'Yeah, so what?'

'So – but what happened? I mean, where's the rucksack?'
I ask him.

'I sold it,' he says.

'You what??!'

'I went up to this person, right, who was lookin' at all the
rucksacks and said did they want to buy a brand-new one
cheap? And they did, so I sold it.'

'How much for?' asks Becca, open-mouthed.

He shrugs and looks away. 'A tenner.'

'A tenner?' she echoes in disbelief. 'But it cost about thirty
quid, didn't it?'

'Oh, Jack,' I say, dismayed.

'What? I told you I fucking needed cash,' he says. And his
voice is hard, but his face is miserable as he drops a crumpled ten-pound note and the original receipt on the crumb-
strewn kitchen table.

Jack's Good Time

Just four days ago, on Saturday night, Jack had four boys to
sleep over in his room. Four is the maximum he can fit in
there and even then they have to be arranged like a tin of
sleeping-bagged sardines on his floor. And now it's Wednesday
evening and I'm in the bath when he shuffles in and slumps
down by the door. 'Hi, Mum.'

'Hello, Jack.'

'I just wondered if you and Dad had any plans for the weekend?'

I shut my eyes and smile. 'Plans? No, we don't have any plans. Absolutely my favourite kind of weekend – no plans. Why?'

'Because I'm thinking of having a gathering.'

I open my eyes. 'You just had a gathering!'

He looks wounded. 'When?'

'Saturday night? Four boys to sleep over, remember?'

He scowls. 'That wasn't a gathering, Mum. That was a sleepover.'

The bath's too hot. I turn on the cold tap. 'Well, whatever it was, it was people to stay and it was just four days ago and so the answer is a categorical No.'

He smacks his forehead with a disbelieving hand. 'Christ, Mum! You're just so fucking against the idea of me having any kind of a good time, aren't you?'

This makes me laugh. 'You think that's why Dad and I said Yes to the Saturday night sleepover even though we were tired and didn't especially want four boys to stay?'

'But, for God's sake, how did it affect you?'

'It always affects us having several extra people in the house overnight.'

'But why?!'

'Because we're responsible for them, that's why.'

'But no one expects you to be responsible.'

'You may not. But we do. Adults do. If something happened to any of them, their parents would rightly expect us to deal with it.'

'But what the fuck kind of thing's going to happen?'

'If someone needed to be driven to Casualty for instance.'

Another disbelieving look from Jack – and I realise we've gone a bit off message now. 'My God, Mum, that is so like you. I arrange one simple sleepover and suddenly everyone's being rushed to ER!'

I smile. 'ER's American. And that's not the point.'

'So what is the point?'

'The point is, I think it's a tiny bit over the top, asking to have a party this weekend when you already had so many people over on Saturday.'

'Not a party! I never said a Party, man! I said a Gathering.'

The bath's too cold now. I turn on the hot. 'Party, gathering, what on earth's the difference?'

'There's a massive difference! A gathering's just a few people cotchin', yeah? A party's where you trash the house.'

'I hope not.'

'You know the one at New Year? The one where Eddie was there as well.'

'What about it?'

'Well, the parents were away and didn't know it was happening, right? And the house just got totally trashed.'

'Jack, that's terrible.'

He looks slyly pleased. 'Only idiots have a party in their own house.'

'I hope you didn't damage anything?'

'Of course I didn't! Except it wasn't exactly my problem either.'

I try to take this in. 'And how bad was it?'

'Put it this way – by the end, some rooms you had to slide through them rather than walk.'

'That's awful,' I say as he shrugs and stares at the floor as I stand up to wash. 'Hearing stuff like that,' I tell him, 'doesn't exactly fill me with confidence, you know. And anyway what about your coursework?'

'What about it?'

'I thought you had Geography coursework to do this weekend?'

'That won't take long. The teacher doesn't want us to do too much.'

I sit down in the bath again. 'OK, but Dad also wanted you to do some extra maths.'

'Fuck's sake! Why?'

'Because your maths mock result was a bit worrying.'

'Mum. I told you! The mocks don't mean anything. Everyone goes up a grade for the real thing. All the teachers say so.'

I step out of the bath. He covers his eyes. 'They only say

it, darling boy, because they count on people doing some work between the mocks and GCSEs.'

'I'm going to. But I don't see why it has to start this weekend.'

'It has to start sometime,' I say, grabbing my towel.

'Oh!' – Jack peeps between his fingers to see if I'm draped. 'You guys, you are just so over the top about stuff like work. I don't see how any of this affects you!'

I sit on the edge of the bath and look at him. 'It affects us because we love you very much and we want you to fulfil your potential.'

He thinks for a moment. 'But what if my potential is having a good time?'

Granny's birthday

On the Monday before my mum's birthday, I corner Becca and Jack:

'Remember, it's Granny's birthday this Saturday and she's coming here for a special tea. I'm telling you now because I don't want any excuses. You have to be here.'

Jack sighs: 'How long will it take?'

'It'll take as long as it takes! It'll take as long as you'd like it to take when you're old and you live alone and really look forward to a birthday tea with the people you love.'

He sighs again.

'All I'm asking,' I say, more softly, 'is that you sit and pretend to drink a little cup of tea and eat a little bit of cake. Is that really so hard?'

'I'm going out that night.'

'We have tea at tea-time.'

'But how am I supposed to get her anything when you don't give me any pocket money?'

'You get pocket money. You're just getting a little less than usual because you're still paying us back for the two lost Oyster cards, the money you borrowed for Christmas and all the fines you've run up at Blockbuster because you can't be bothered to take things back on time.'

He scowls: 'All the same, I don't see how I can be expected to buy her some great big present.'

'You know she doesn't expect something big,' I tell him. 'Anything, however small, will do. Or you could make her something – even just a card. She'd love that. Come on, Jack, you know it's the thought that counts.'

'I'm probably going shopping after school on Friday,' Becca says. 'I'll get her something then.'

'Don't feel you've got to spend too much, darling,' I tell her, because my daughter has just recently – finally! – begun to realise that giving can be more fun than receiving.

'I suppose I could bake her some biscuits,' says Jack, who quite enjoys Food Tech at school, even though all he ever seems to make are endless variations on Kentucky Fried Chicken.

'That's a great idea,' I tell him. 'Why don't you write down what ingredients you need and I'll get them in time for the weekend.'

'Um, yuh, well, we've probably got everything,' he mutters, already lost in the paper, looking to see what time the match is on.

'All the same,' I say, 'can you check and let me know?'

When he's gone, Becca looks at me. 'Sorry, Mum, but did I just hear that right? You're going out to buy the little baby-waby his ingwedients? So he can make a plate of his nasty flat burnt biscuits for Granny?'

'It's just – I really, really want him to make some effort,' I tell her, 'for his own sake more than anything. He and Eddie are getting worse and worse about other people's birthdays. It's just embarrassing.'

'So you want a repeat of Christmas,' she says, 'when I was out there madly texting him from all these shops because we'd agreed to get something for people together and then he left me to do the work?!'

'OK, what do you think I should do?'

'Make him get his own fucking ingredients. And if he won't, let him take the consequences.'

'But there won't be any. That's exactly the problem. He'd be quite happy just to sit there and give her nothing.'

She shrugs. 'Don't get him anything for his own birthday, then. Let him see how it feels.'

She's right, of course. But only someone who isn't a parent could say that.

Meanwhile I call Eddie, tell him he's got to be here on Saturday. 'It depends what I'm doing,' he says, yawning, 'I'll try, but I can't tell you definitely right now.'

'That's not good enough,' I tell him. 'It's Granny's birthday.'

'Mum, all I'm saying is I really want to come, but I might still be asleep or something, OK? What is this obsession of yours of always wanting everyone to commit to everything in advance?'

In the end, this is what happens: Becca goes shopping on Friday and comes back with a new top, some sparkly gloves and the latest *NME*. 'Oh my God,' she claps her hand over her mouth, 'I totally forgot about Granny!' So she nips out after Saturday lunch and, in the nick of time, gets her a plant. A perfectly nice plant.

Jack, pushed, and given money by me, does actually go out and buy the ingredients, but then lies on the sofa all morning watching repeats of *Friends* and claiming he feels too sick to cook. At tea, though, he charms his grandmother utterly by telling her how much he loves her and promising to go round and mow her lawn for her. She looks absurdly happy.

Eddie is a no-show.

Jack's School Coat

The school's policy on uniform is very clear. Coats must be black. They must not have any kind of logo or pattern. Same with shoes. They must be black. They must not be trainers. Black trainers that look a bit like shoes won't do. Same with jumpers. They must be black and V-necked. They must not be hoodies.

I catch Jack going to school in trainers. 'Ah, yeah, but you see it's PE and it takes me so long to get changed, I end up missing the beginning of the next period, so I'm just saving time, innit?'

I catch him going to school in a grey hoodie. 'They never ever say anything when it's under your blazer,' he assures me sweetly. 'In fact I think they actually sort of understand that kids need to keep warm when it's randomly freezing outside.'

I catch him going to school in a big puffa jacket with a huge great Puma logo leaping across the back. Where did he get it? I know that I would never in a million years buy him such a thing to wear to school. This time he scowls, ready for a fight. 'Josh lent it to me. I'm just wearin' it till he grows into it.'

'Does Josh's mum know you've got it?'

He shrugs. 'Dunno. I've been wearing it for weeks.'

'But – I haven't seen you in it.'

He grins. 'I keep it under another coat in the hall and put it on just before I go out the door, innit?'

'But it's not uniform,' I tell him. 'Surely there's no way the teachers will let you wear something with a logo like that?'

'They've never said anything.'

'But why not?'

'I s'pose they're too busy telling me off about other things,' he says, without a trace of irony. 'I've already got done for so many things this term. It's going to take ages before they get around to tackling me about my coat.'

A week later, though, the teachers do get around to it. Jack is hauled into the office and told he can't wear it any more. He needs a new school coat, and fast.

'But what happened to the one you had before?'

'Grew out of that ages ago. You think I'm some little baby. I'm bigger than Dad.'

'It's just – you've only got about a month of winter left and then it's warmer and then sixth form and you're out of uniform for good.'

He looks at me kindly. 'The best thing, yeah, is if you can buy me a really good coat. But with just a very small logo on it. They won't notice that.'

'Not worth the risk,' I tell him. 'No logo means no logo. That's what we're going to get.'

Which is how, two days later, I find myself in the place I

detest most in the world – Oxford Street – at the very worst possible time – Saturday afternoon.

We go into Gap. 'I don't like Gap,' Jack warns me. 'Gap is for neeks.' Straightaway we find a nice black slightly waterproof coat for a fairly reasonable forty pounds. Jack shudders and steps away.

'Look, can't you just wear something that's not ideal if it keeps you warm till April?'

'If I wear that, I'll be mugged. If you want me to be mugged, then fine.'

We go into Top Man. He declares everything rubbish. I reluctantly agree with him.

In Foot Locker, though, his eyes light up. Throbbing music, lights that make your teeth ache. Enough Nike ticks to make your eyes go funny. Jack snatches up a puffa-type jacket.

'This for instance! Look how tiny the logo is.'

I look. 'It's not tiny. It's just black.'

'Yeah,' he soothes. 'A black logo on a black background. How could they possibly say anything about that?'

Exhausted, I check the price label. 'Seventy pounds. No way!'

'But Mum, it'd be such good value, cos I'd wear it all the time. For weekends as well as school, I mean.'

It takes me a moment to come to my senses, to remember why we're here. 'What am I saying? Forget the price. I don't care what it costs. It's not school uniform!'

A spiky-haired assistant in a shiny black-and-white striped shirt sidles up and glances at the coat Jack's still touching.

'Look,' he says, 'I shouldn't really be saying this, but that's well overpriced. You're only paying for the logo, man. Go down the road to Top Shop or Gap. You'll get a decent winter coat for half the money.'

I look at my youngest son and I start to laugh. For once, in fact for the first time in ages, he really can't think of anything to say.

Becca and My Clothes

When Becca was little, she was a tomboy. The only doll she ever agreed to be bought was Shaving Ken – a boyfriend of Barbie's, who came complete with evening shadow and razor. Becca loved him. Aged five or six, she'd sit in the bath and sing to herself while she lathered him up. No one else was allowed to touch him. I don't know which instinct Shaving Ken was appealing to, but it certainly wasn't a maternal one.

Naturally, she refused to wear dresses. There was a brief phase when I got away with squeezing her into pink stripy dungarees, but it didn't last. As soon as she twigged that pink was for girls, the offending garment was scrunched right to the back of her chest of drawers. From then on, she wore mainly camouflage. Sometimes with the addition of baseball cap and utility belt and compass and water bottle. And the boy thing continued right into her teens. Even the fifteen-year-old Becca was pretty much an exact sartorial carbon copy of her brothers.

And then she changed. Something happened inside her. A softening, a relaxing, a separating from the boys. It was fascinating to see. Suddenly babies were 'cute'. Suddenly her eyes were ringed with kohl. Suddenly she was furious if there wasn't enough hot water left for a nice long shower. And now in the last month or so, having always previously mocked my occasional enjoyment of glossy magazines, I notice that she goes out of her way to snaffle them.

'Becca, have you seen that *Vogue* that was on the table in the hall?'

A pause. 'Well, yeah. It's in my room.'

'Can I have it, please?

'Um, I haven't quite finished going through it yet. There's some bare sick clothes in there!'

Inevitably, she also has her eye on my wardrobe. 'Mu-um? Those stretchy grey trousers of yours, the ones with the buttons down the side—'

'Mmm, what about them?'

'Well, it's just that I think they'd look really good on me.'

I look at her. She's concentrating on twisting a long strand of hair around a biro.

'You think they would look good? Or you think they do look good?'

She chuckles and releases the hair. 'I didn't exactly try them on! What I mean is, I don't want you to think I go poking around in your wardrobe when you're out.'

I smile. That is exactly what I think.

'It's just, they were in the utility room drying, right? And I happened to be in there in just my underwear, so I kind of, you know, slipped them on.'

'I'm sorry, but they're my best trousers. Otherwise I might consider giving them to you.'

'But you might get sick of them soon, right?'

'If I do, you'll be the first to know,' I promise her.

Later, we're lying together on my bed watching TV. Or half-watching, because Becca may be coming my way but she doesn't yet see the point of *Grand Designs*. 'How long before the fucking rain starts?'

'I don't think there's going to be any rain this time,' I tell her.

'Ah, because they've got the roof on, right? It's only good if it rains before they get the roof on.'

Suddenly she looks at me and gasps.

'What? What is it?'

'Oh my God, I'm sorry, but it's just – you look so old!'

'Thanks a lot.' I relax again.

'I don't want to be rude or anything but there are just so many lines around your eyes. A whole network of fucking lines! Oh my God, I'm sorry, but close up it's disgusting.'

'I'm middle-aged,' I tell her. 'Of course I have wrinkles.'

'You're cool with that?'

'I'm trying to be. It doesn't help being told I'm disgusting.'

'Sorry.' Becca snuggles against me as the rain finally hits Kevin. 'I didn't mean it. You know something I was remembering the other day?'

'What were you remembering?'

'That when you used to come and pick us up at primary school I was so proud of you because you were the prettiest mum in the playground.'

'Seriously?'

'Everyone thought so. Girls in my class used to draw pictures of you in art because you were pretty. They'd do this stick figure with all this hair!'

I laugh and she sighs. 'I love you, Mum,' she says.

I kiss her head. 'I love you too, you funny girl.'

'But you know,' she leans up on her elbow and looks at me carefully. 'The only thing you ought to consider is this. If something, like say those trousers, actually looks OK on me, a seventeen-year-old – then should someone of your age really be wearing them?'

Becca Cooks Lunch

It's Saturday and Becca wants me to take her shopping. But I have a bit of work to do. So I tell her that what would really

334

help is if she could cook lunch for everyone. That way, I can get my work done and we'll be free to go straight after.

The old Becca of a year or so ago would have scowled at this suggestion, slumped down in her chair, pleading some kind of sudden illness, before growling that, if that was how I felt, she'd rather not fucking well go shopping after all. But the new Becca – current Becca, a Becca I find myself liking more and more each day – jumps at the suggestion.

'Sure. You go and work. I'll have lunch ready for one o'clock.' I go upstairs smiling. Life with teenagers. Who says things can't change?

Sitting upstairs, I begin to smell onions frying. I hear Jack's voice, then Becca's, then Jack's, then an almighty yowl (Becca). I decide I won't go down. They need to learn to sort these things out themselves. A moment later, the sound of a brief scuffle in the hall. Becca's voice raised in frustration. Jack laughing. Then all quiet again. I get on with my work.

Just after one, Becca calls us all down. Pink-cheeked, large apron slipping off her little shoulders, kitchen full of steam as the spaghetti boils like crazy. The sauce looks quite promising though.

'I put olives in it,' Becca says, poking at it with a wooden spoon.

'It smells really good,' says her father, planting a kiss on her head. She wriggles free.

'Yeah, well, it's no thanks to your moronic son,' she says. 'You really would think, wouldn't you, that if I'm cooking lunch he'd at least be prepared to lay the table? Instead he just stands there burping and farting.'

Jack laughs loudly and stupidly.

'Come on,' I tell him. 'Lay the table please.' Slowly, he goes to get the mats out.

Their father gets a beer and sits down. 'Now perhaps you'll understand how your mother and I feel,' he tells Becca, 'when we do all the work and none of you lot lift a finger.'

'None of us!' Becca glares at him as she drains the spaghetti. 'Here I am slaving away and you STILL bracket me in with those boys!'

Her father and I exchange a glance. It's just one lunch, after all. But you're not really allowed to say things like that to Becca.

We all sit and eat. I tell Becca the sauce is great. Then Jack announces that he's lost his front-door key.

'Again?' His father pushes back his chair to make his point. 'You've lost it again?'

Jack frowns. 'Dunno. I mean it could be at Jacey's. I just don't know.'

'But Jack, Jack, darling,' his father says, despair etched on his face, 'we only just got a new one cut.'

'Is Jacey a boy or a girl?' I ask him. My son's face darkens.

'What the hell's that got to do with it?' he snaps.

'Hey,' says his father, 'don't talk to your mother like that. You're the one in the wrong here.'

Jack twirls spaghetti on his fork. 'I don't exactly see what I've done wrong.'

'You've lost your key! That's what you've done.'

He shrugs. 'I can't see how it was my fault. If you're going to go blaming—'

'Excuse me,' says Becca, 'but I just cooked a really nice meal for everyone. Do we really have to ruin it by talking about Jack's key? Can't we have a proper conversation?'

'She's right,' I say. 'Let's eat lunch and we'll deal with Jack afterwards.'

'Deal with me! Why do I always have to be dealt with? Why is it always me who gets talked about like that?'

'Because it's always you who loses things!' his father says. 'It's always you who causes us the effort and expense of replacing the countless things you can't be bothered to look after properly!'

'So, Mum,' Becca says brightly, 'what I'm thinking is we'll go and look in Office first, right? The boots I want have these slightly pointy toes but not too much of a heel.'

'The thing is, yeah?' says Jack, 'I don't really see how it's my fault if something just slips out of my pocket.'

'It's your complete lack of remorse,' his father says, 'your refusal to take responsibility!'

'Please!' Becca wails, 'I just can't stand it. After all the effort I put into cooking!'

'This spaghetti is fucking well undercooked anyway,' says Jack. 'Look at it. You didn't put enough water in.'

Becca looks at him, pushes her plate to one side and lays her small, dark head down on the table.

Jack's iPod

Two weeks or so ago, Jack lost his iPod. Or, he didn't exactly lose it, he was mugged and it was stolen. Or:

'Not quite mugged, right? But I was walking down this quite dark road in Finsbury Park and suddenly this big man kind of stumbled against me and he had a flick-knife and so obviously I handed it over.'

'I think I'd call that mugged,' his father said.

Jack has lost things before. Many times. He's also been mugged before. But the word 'knife' got my attention. 'You're serious? He really had a knife and he threatened you with it?'

Jack nodded enthusiastically. 'I saw the blade of it gleaming right there in the street light.'

Becca scowled. 'I thought you said the road was dark?'

'Yeah,' Jack spoke slowly as if he was talking to a toddler, 'dark. As in: night-time. But, duh, there's always street lights.'

338

'But, darling,' I said, 'what on earth were you doing on a dark side street in the first place?'

'I never said it was a side street,' snapped Jack.

'You know you're so much safer on the main road.'

'It makes no difference,' said my six-foot baby, who seems to be a target for every thieving psychopath this side of Archway. 'They get you anywhere. Basically, if they want to get you, they're gonna get you.'

'Sure. But at least on a main road there are people around.'

'Not people who would help a boy like me!'

'Maybe that's because you dress like a mugger,' observed his father, eyeing his son's double layer of mud-brown hoodies.

'Why don't you ask him what he was doing in Finsbury Park in the first place?' growled his sister.

Jack turned to her: 'Just shut up. Just you keep out of it.'

'What were you doing, as a matter of interest?' his father asked.

'None of your business. Never you mind.'

'So how old was this person? Was he black or white? And no, Becca, I'm not being racist. We need a description. We should tell the police.'

'There's no fucking point,' Jack said. 'No one will find him. I didn't even get a proper look at him.'

'Come on, black or white?'

Jack shook his head. 'I just don't know.'

And Becca shot him another narrow-eyed look.

Now, more than two weeks later, he comes home with good news.

'That guy who stole my iPod, yeah? Well, some kids at school in the year above, right, they were out in the same area and suddenly there he is, attacking them! Same man, same knife and everything. And they decide not to stand for it so they rush him and bang him, right? And they find all this stuff on him and apparently one of the things is my iPod, so it looks I'm almost certainly going to get it back!'

All three of us stare at him, struggling to make sense of the story. 'How did they know he was the same man?' his father wants to know.

'Duh!' says Jack. 'Because he looked exactly the same!'

'I thought you never got a look at him?'

Jack bites his lip. 'I saw just enough to know.'

'And these people, these friends of yours, you're saying they beat the man up?'

'Look, Mum,' my son explains in a softer tone, 'it was perfectly fair, right? They only did to him what he tried to do to them.'

'That doesn't make it right,' says his father.

Jack makes a spluttery sound. 'You're saying they should have let him bang them?'

'Has anyone reported all this to the police?'

'There's no fucking point, man! All I care is that I might get my iPod back.'

340

Becca laughs, and her brother turns to her. 'What?'

She widens her eyes. 'What?' she says.

Later, I find Jack alone in the sitting room. I turn off the TV and sit down next to him: 'But honey, there's one thing I still want to know.'

'Look, I only didn't want to give Dad a description because I didn't want him starting up the whole fucking police thing—'

'What were you doing in Finsbury Park? None of your friends live there.'

Jack takes a breath. 'One of them does.'

He looks at his feet and I wait.

'Come on, Jack, you've got to tell me.'

'I haven't got to tell you. It might be none of your business. It might be something to do with – a friend.'

'A friend who's a girl?' I say, beginning to understand.

'Mum!'

'Sorry. Sorry. I'll shut up.'

Careful not to look at him, I walk over to the window, pull down the blinds.

Going Out

I'm rushing to get ready for an important work dinner. The cab's coming in half an hour, I'm nervous because I have to make a speech, and I still haven't decided what to wear.

Meanwhile Becca's sprawled on our bed, instructing me on the subject of the menopause:

'It really is ironic,' she sighs with some satisfaction, 'that just as I'm getting all fertile, your ovaries are literally shrivelling up and dying.'

I pull on my knickers, search around in the drawer for a strapless bra. 'Very ironic,' I agree, trying to decide whether the bra will give me too much of a cleavage. 'But I'm not sure ovaries actually die, do they?'

'Oh, yeah,' she eyes me thoughtfully as I struggle into the bra, 'I'm pretty sure they do.'

'OK,' I glance down to check my breasts don't look too augmented.

'You're OK with that?' She sounds astonished.

'With this bra?'

'No, dead ovaries!'

'Sorry,' I tell her as I look for my good opaque tights. 'My mind's not really on my ovaries right now.'

At that moment, Eddie – yes, Eddie, who has recently been making himself conspicuous by his presence – comes in and plonks himself down. Pulls off his left sock.

'See that? That was your dog. He just attacked me!'

'I really don't know what's the matter with him,' I mutter. 'He's going through a really nippy phase at the moment.'

'He nipped me the other day,' Becca agrees. 'I just went

342

to get some cheese from the fridge and suddenly there he was, nipping away at my bum!' She laughs at the memory.

Eddie scowls. 'This wasn't some little nip. This was him getting my whole fucking foot in his mouth and not letting go. Seriously, he could've severed an artery or something!'

Becca smiles at me and I smile back. How many times just recently have we both wanted to bite Eddie?

'I don't see what's so fucking funny. That dog's dangerous. If I wanted to, I could probably get him put down.'

Now Becca sits up. 'Ed! That dog was your childhood dog. He grew up with you, like a brother. You even took him for walks back in the days when you weren't such a selfish person. And now suddenly you want to kill him? How can you be so fucking harsh about everything?'

'She's right,' I say, pulling my red stretchy dress over my head and making a mental note that I must check my speech is in my bag before I go.

Jack enters, closely followed by his father.

'He wants to smoke!' says his father. 'He's got eight friends coming round for a little party—'

'Not a party!' wails Jack as usual. 'A gathering! And it's not me smoking, just them.'

'Eight people coming round and now he's saying that there's no point unless they can smoke.'

'Only outside,' groans Jack. 'You've no idea how weird you are. Every parent I know allows smoking in the garden.'

'Darling,' I say, as I flick powder over my nose, 'we just don't think fifteen-year-olds should be smoking.'

'But you did allow it once!' says Jack. 'That time back in the summer when I had a little party, remember?'

'Did we?' I blink at myself, think how tired I look. Why can I never keep track of what we have and haven't allowed Jack?

'He's right, you know. You guys are cracked,' says Eddie. 'Every single fucking parent I know is cool with kids smoking.'

'You make me look like such a neek!' wails Jack, and he slams out of the room.

His father looks at me. 'It would really help me if just occasionally you expressed an opinion on this kind of thing.'

'But I just did!'

'No, you wavered. And straightaway he feels you're on his side.'

'OK,' I say and I march to the top of the stairs. 'Jack? Is it true that one time we allowed smoking outside?'

He appears in the hall. 'Just in the garden, yeah!'

'OK, then they can do that tonight. But just this once, do you understand? And it doesn't mean I approve.'

He grins. 'Thanks so much, Mum.'

'You what??!!' says his father when he hears what I just allowed. 'You just said Yes? You could at least have made some kind of a deal!'

Becca and Eddie are laughing. I don't care. I take a breath. 'I have to go,' I say as I grab my speech, my bag and run down to get my coat. Just as I'm leaving, Becca appears at the top of the stairs.

'Good luck, Mum. With the speech, yeah? I think you look great, by the way. Not old at all. Just really, really buff.'

Jack and the Sugar

Jack loves puddings. Any pudding, but especially Sainsbury's chocolate mousse. He'll force me to give him money to go down the High Road and buy a whole stash of them – twelve in one go. I say 'force' but of course it's my decision too. I don't know why but I find it really hard to refuse my youngest son treat food. And I've told him not to eat them all at once, but I have to admit he gets through them fast.

Becca, who is, and always has been, a singularly wholesome eater, says her brother's sugar habit is 'disgusting'.

'Come on,' I say. 'We all like sweet things now and then.'

'Now and then? This is total sugar overload 24/7.'

I tell her she's overreacting, but quietly I think about this. He never puts on weight and his teeth are fine. But still, is he having too much?

Meanwhile, his father, fed up with yet another bout of his son's bolshy behaviour, comes to find me. 'I seriously do think you need to look at his diet. Have you seen how many of those mousse things he gets through?'

'But he's her 'ickle baby and she gets high on buying him desserts,' snarls Becca. 'Their relationship is seriously warped when it comes to food issues.'

I look at them both, father and daughter, with their mutual love of spicy, savoury foods, sharp flavours, not to mention pickled gherkins. 'He's always been thin,' I tell them, 'and he's growing at an unbelievable rate. As long as he eats plenty of healthy things as well, I can't believe the chocolate stuff matters.'

'Does KFC count as plenty of healthy things?' asks Becca.

'Are you his mum?' I ask her, a little sharply.

'No, but I'm the one who has to put up with his sugar-induced frenzies. You've no idea how hard it is to live with someone who leaves his pants all over the bathroom floor.'

'I'm not sure excess sugar ever stopped a man picking up his pants,' I tell her. 'I'll have a word with him about that.'

'No puddings?!' My baby gazes at me with open-mouthed dismay when I tell him about the new policy.

'Not *no* puddings,' I tell him, 'just different ones. I'm worried about how many chemicals and additives you're eating.'

'What am I allowed then?'

I think for a moment: 'A banana is always nice. With maybe a bit of yoghurt on top.'

Becca laughs loudly at her brother's face.

Meanwhile, Jack's world is about to crumble still further because, when he tells us his plans to go to a party tonight, we remind him he has an eleven o'clock curfew – a punishment held over from last weekend when he came home an hour later than agreed.

His face falls. 'But – you can't do that!'

'Of course we can,' I tell him. 'It was the punishment. It was settled last Sunday.'

'But – if I'd remembered you were going to do that, I'd have gone out later last night.'

I shrug.

'So why didn't you remind me? It was your job to remind me and you failed. You can't just inflict it out of the blue tonight.'

'It's not at all out of the blue,' says his father. 'As your mother just pointed out, we all agreed this last weekend.'

An hour later, he finds me alone and launches another attack. I'm trying to read through some stuff for work and I tell him so. I tell him there's no point in haranguing me as nothing will make me change my mind.

'All right, all right,' he says. 'I get the message. I'm going. You don't need to act like I'm some kind of terrorist.'

'Thanks,' I say, but the forlorn, retreating shape of him – party-less and pudding-less – somehow breaks my heart.

Two hours later I go shopping and come back with a slice

of vanilla cheesecake. 'To prove I don't think you're a terrorist,' I tell him as I unwrap it and put it on a plate. He beams at me.

'You bought him cheesecake?!' splutters his father when he sees the box.

'Only really good cheesecake,' I explain. 'Organic. From the market. I bought it for him because I felt bad that he thought I thought he was a terrorist.'

I smile at Jack who is tucking in.

'She wouldn't give cheesecake to a terrorist,' he says with a satisfied little sigh as he licks his fork.

'She so would,' says Becca. 'I can just see it. "Here, although you blew up that plane, I know you didn't mean it and I know you're really, really sorry. Have some nice vanilla cheesecake."'

Jack's breakfast

Friday morning and Jack's down early for breakfast. I ask him if he slept well. 'Not really.' I ask him if he'd like some eggs. He shrugs. 'Don't really care.'

'All right, but would you like some?'

Another shrug: 'S'up to you.'

'I'll do you some eggs.'

He gives me a softer look. 'Thanks, actually that'd be very nice, Mother dear.'

As I walk past, I grab his head and kiss it even though he doesn't want me to. It smells of recently washed, still-damp male teenager, with a greenish undertone of hair gel. Then I bend to get a pan out of the cupboard and my eyes fall on his legs. 'Are those your black jeans you're wearing?'

He looks at his legs then he looks at me. Blinks. The eyes of an angel. 'It's Friday,' he says.

'What, and there's a new rule that you can wear jeans at school on Friday?'

He smiles. 'Just I'm going out straight from school, that's all, so it's easier.'

I light the gas and break two eggs into the pan. 'I can't possibly approve of you wearing jeans to school.'

He smiles. 'Don't worry, Mum. I swear I'll get away with it. I've done it the last three Fridays.'

'But that's not the point!'

'For God's sake! What's it to you?'

'It's – I'll tell you what it is to me. It's the fact that just the other day the school sent another piece of paper round, detailing what you are and aren't allowed to wear and asking for parents' co-operation. And jeans were definitely not on the list.'

Jack sighs. 'I've only got a few weeks of uniform left.'

'All the more reason to abide by the rules.'

I put his eggs on the table and he grabs his knife and fork. 'You just don't get it, do you?' he says, as he half cuts, half tears at the toast.

Hungry, I think.

'Don't get what?'

'Oh, it's just like Becca says, that's all.'

'What does Becca say?'

'You and Dad – the whole problem with you two – is you have no sense of perspective.'

'What's that got to do with you breaking school uniform rules?'

He doesn't answer that. His mouth is full. 'By the way, Mum, is it just me or is Eddie sleeping here more and more?'

I glance at the stairs. 'Is he here now?'

'Well, his door's closed and there's bare snoring coming out, so if it's not him, maybe we need to worry that a burglar crashed out in there.'

I think about this. Eddie is a month behind with rent on his flat and jobless once again. His father and I have made it clear we don't intend to help him this time. 'Is he moving back home?' Jack asks me now.

'I don't know,' I say slowly. 'He certainly hasn't talked to Dad and me about it.'

Jack mops up egg yolk and laughs to himself. 'That's not how he'd do it. The way Ed would do it is he'd just slowly move back in and then one day when you tackled him about it, he'd look all innocent and pretend he'd been here all along.'

'Like you wearing jeans to school?'

'Not quite.'

'Yeah, well, Ed and Dad and I need to have a proper discussion.'

Jack grins. 'He'll do anything to avoid that. He knows he's not going to win that.'

Becca bursts in, her face covered in turquoise glitter. 'Mum,' she says, 'is it true that Ed's moving back in?'

'Not as far as I know but I'm going to talk to him. What's that stuff all over your face?'

'Because if he is, you need to tell him not to use that fucking awful deodorant.'

Jack nods. 'That Lynx. It makes me want to vomit. By the way, Becca why do you look like an alien out of *Doctor Who*?'

Becca turns to look in the mirror. 'Shit. My eye shadow's gone everywhere. Give me some kitchen towel, quick!'

'Please,' I say, as I hand her the roll.

'Mum, I'm already running late!'

I clear Jack's plate and ask him if he'd like some cereal.

'Go on then.'

'Granola?'

'I'll be all right, thanks.'

'You mean you don't want cereal?'

'No, I mean I don't want the fucking granola. Give me the Golden Nuggets.'

'Say please,' mutters his sister, as she rubs at her face.

'Thanks a lot,' says Jack, as I put the packet in front of him. 'Hey, you're a good bitch.'

'Jack!!'

'I mean it,' he pats my hand. 'You'll make someone a very good wife one day.'

Eddie's Shirt

For the last couple of months, I've been very busy at work. Early starts and late meetings and stuff to do in the evenings at home. Though the children's father has always been a 50-50 parent around the house, his methods are idiosyn-cratic. So, he'll do a load of washing, but forget to hang it up.

'This shirt!' says Ed, thrusting it in his father's face. 'It bare stinks! I can't possibly put it on.'

'Don't be such a baby,' says his father, who's not exactly famed for his olfactory sensitivity. 'Nothing wrong with it at all.'

'It smells of – yuk – of dead rodents!'

'You're nineteen years old,' says his father. 'You're not even officially living here. Maybe it's time to do less sniffing and more job-hunting.'

'I'm afraid it does need to go back in the wash,' I say, although reluctant to ally myself to Ed's supreme fastidious-ness.

It's not just the washing though. He orders a supermarket delivery and gets all the wrong things. 'We always buy juice, not juice *drinks*,' I tell him. 'If it says "juice drink", it means it contains added sugar. And when will you learn that no one ever eats those Petits Filous yoghurts?'

'They do eat them. I eat them.'

'Then why are there a dozen of them well past their sell-by date at the back of the fridge?'

'We don't eat them,' Becca confirms.

He does cook very well – all three children agree his meals are far better than mine – and he puts stuff in the dishwasher. But he never ever wipes down the counters. A few days into his regime and you can deduce the menus for the last week from the cauliflower leaves, the sprays of flour, the smears of Bolognese sauce across the worktops.

'So what? No one ever gets ill in this house. Show me a person I've poisoned by not wiping the counters.'

'Maybe we get mentally ill,' suggests his daughter. 'Maybe it's the germs from the kitchen counter that make your elder son into such a retard.'

Anyway, Becca doesn't need to worry because now at last my deadline is over. I've even negotiated to work from home two days a week for a while. I tell the kids I'm taking over all the household chores and this afternoon I'm doing a great big shop at the supermarket.

'Coke!' says Jack. 'Can you make sure you get some Coke?'

'And pickled gherkins,' says Becca. 'A great big jar of pickled gherkins. And chocolate soy milk.'

'Coke and gherkins and soy milk. Who's going to help me? Will you come and help me, Ed?'

Eddie stares at me as if I just suggested he set fire to his best guitar. 'But – what about the other two?'

'They're going to school.'

'But – I don't live here.'

Becca laughs loudly.

'Look,' I say, 'whether you think you live here or not, for the past month or so you've eaten a good many meals here, slept here several times a week, had your clothes washed, some of them twice – in fact, I'd say you were very much a part of the family. So come on Eddie, pull your weight.'

'It's just – I don't know what I'm doing yet today,' he mutters, glancing at the place on his wrist where his watch used to be.

'It's OK,' I say. 'If we go at about eleven, we'll be back well before lunch.'

'Make sure she gets some Coke,' says Jack again.

Ed shakes his head. 'I've got to call someone,' he says, and he somehow manoeuvres himself through the door and out of the room. I sigh a long sigh. Becca looks at me with her careful, adult face.

'I can help you,' she says, 'after school, if you like.'

Later, when the other two have gone, Ed comes to find me. 'I really do think it's a bit much. Dad can't even wash

354

my shirt so it smells clean, and yet still you guys expect me to slave for you.'

I look at my elder son. His strong, fit body. His even, expectant face. I remember myself at that age, the chores I did without a second thought. 'I don't call giving your mother a hand at the supermarket slaving,' I say coolly.

He shrugs. 'I'm trying to earn a living, like Dad told me to,' he says, and his face is deadly serious, 'get this band off the ground. You've no idea how hard it is, getting hold of people.'

'Why is it so hard?'

He continues to look at me and his eyes are frank and blue: 'Well, for a start, no one seems to get up till about 11.30.'

Weekend Away

When the children were little, my parents-in-law would sometimes have them for the whole weekend, so we could go away together. We loved those weekends – romantic, relaxing, replenishing. Now, though, the parents are old, and the kids a whole lot more horrible and – just when we most hunger to get away from them – we daren't leave them alone for five minutes. My brother has always been really generous with his barn in Herefordshire, and in the old days we'd regularly borrow it for the weekend. But last time we suggested that, Becca's face morphed into something from *Psycho*:

'You really think it's fair,' she gasped, 'to ask a person who might have parties to go to, to spend three days in the Middle of Nowhere?'

Finally, about six months ago – with all three kids swearing we could trust them – we went there alone. We returned to find several bottles of good wine gone, the back door unlocked and the key lost, and a stranger asleep on the sofa. We resigned ourselves to never going anywhere again.

But now we have an idea: Hannah, a friend of a friend, is between houses and needs somewhere to stay. We tell her she can move in here rent-free – if she doesn't mind looking after house and kids for a weekend.

'Or not exactly look after them,' we reassure her. 'Just text us to say they're safely home, and make sure they don't have people round.'

Jack tells us this is really mean.

'When we've been away a few times and you've proved yourself trustworthy,' his father says, 'then maybe we'll be able to relax the rule.'

'Most people's parents trust them in advance,' he mutters.

'And look what happened when we did exactly that,' I remind him.

By Thursday, their father and I are quite excited about our weekend away. Then Becca comes and flops on the sofa next to me and takes my hand. 'I know you'll think this is a bit strange,' she whispers, 'But . . . I'd really love to come too.'

I stare at her.

'I haven't been to the country in ages and it would be bare relaxing.'

'But – it will be all green and there'll be nothing to do.'

'I want to do some sketching. For my coursework. Are you saying you don't want me with you?'

When I tell her father, his face wobbles.

'I'm afraid I just didn't have the heart to say No.'

He sighs. 'I suppose we should be grateful one of them finally wants to come.'

On Friday morning, Jack bounds into the kitchen. 'I was thinking, right? If you and Dad go off and leave me here with Hannah, I'm not going to have the self-discipline to get any revision done. But if I come with you and bring a friend, we could go for long walks and get our heads all calm and then we'd feel like revising really hard.'

Now I'm shocked. 'You want to come too?!'

'Me and Luke. We could get a train Saturday morning, yeah? One night here and one night there.'

'I don't know how Becca will feel about that.'

'She said she's cool with it.'

Stunned, but hopeful, we pack up car and dog, and drive to the country. It's raining, but Becca seems happy. But when on Saturday, she hears that Jack and Luke are on their way, her mood turns:

'There is no fucking way I am sharing a room with those two stinking freaks.'

'But – he said you were cool with it!'

'No way! You can put me on a train to London right now unless I'm allowed to sleep in the study!'

Her father looks tired. 'Great. So Jack lied.'

'You can sleep in the study,' I tell Becca.

At lunchtime, I collect Jack and Luke from the station. Jack has one tiny rucksack. I ask him where his revision books are?

'Oh. I forgot them.'

'But you promised you were going to revise!'

'I never promised.'

'You did! It was the whole basis on which we agreed to let you come!'

'Sorry, but I'm very forgetful, you see.'

And that's just the beginning. Soon the weekend is no different at all from our London hell – except that now we're all crammed into one small space. While it rains, then hails, then snows. We have one fairly romantic dinner alone at the pub. Jack and Luke watch TV, then disappear for three hours. Becca lies reading on a mattress in the study, scowling every time I have to step over her. And at one point, their father drops to his knees and almost weeps.

Hannah tells us she had a lovely, peaceful weekend.

Jack's Pockets

Jack comes home and says he's lost his phone.

'Oh, Jack! How did you lose it?'

'Never mind how. I just lost it, innit?'

'Jack,' says his father, 'you are not Afro-Caribbean.'

'Seriously, darling,' I say, 'how did you lose it? I mean, where?'

'Hey, it wasn't the man who took your iPod was it?' Becca chips in. 'The bad guy with the flick-knife who lurks down dark alleyways near Finsbury Park tube?'

Jack scowls at her. 'Shut up!' He drops his long body into a chair and sighs. 'How do I know how I lost it? I guess it must have just dropped out of my pocket or something.'

I look at his father and he looks at me and we don't say anything.

'I don't know what I'm going to do without a phone,' our son continues, 'I mean my whole social life is just going to fucking well crumble.'

'Oh,' says Becca, 'I'm sure Lauren and Anje and Lizzie will still find a way to get hold of you.'

'He really does need a phone,' I tell his father later. 'It's not exactly that I think he deserves a replacement – he is so careless with his possessions – it's more that if he doesn't have a phone, then I've no way at all of keeping track of him.'

'And he'd really relish that,' his father agrees. 'Do you believe him, by the way, about it dropping out of his pocket?'

'I don't know. I suppose with Jack anything's possible. But I just really need to be able to get hold of him, that's all.'

Reluctantly, his father buys Jack a phone on eBay. The last one was on contract and we paid for that – bigger bills than we ever wanted. At least this one will be pay-as-you-go, so he can foot the bill himself.

When his father tells him the new phone's arriving tomorrow, Jack beams. 'Hey, thanks a lot Dad. I really, really appreciate this. I'll do everything in my power not to lose this one, OK?'

His father smiles. 'Accidents happen. We know that. At least you were sorry. But please try and be a bit more careful in future.'

Meanwhile Jack asks me if he can borrow my phone.

'Just for tonight. The new one arrives tomorrow and it's just I really don't think I can get by without one for tonight.'

I hesitate. 'But it's six o'clock already. Can't you just phone all your friends from here and then go out? You've got to be back by eleven, remember.'

Jack takes a step back and regards me as if green slime is issuing from my head. 'You don't understand! Me and my friends, we don't plan in advance. We all make up our arrangements as we go along.'

'Well, can't you make an exception, just for tonight?'

'It's not like that! I mean, stuff just happens.'

I take a breath. 'All right, you can have it, but please, please don't lose it.'

He gazes at me, wide-eyed. 'What the hell do you mean don't lose it? Why the fuck am I gonna lose it?'

Next morning, he comes in to return my phone, which he thankfully didn't lose. But he has a confession to make: he seems to have lost the thirty pounds (two fives and a twenty) we gave him to put on his Oyster card.

His father rolls his eyes in despair. 'You've lost it? How could you possibly lose it? What exactly is the matter with you, Jack?'

Jack shrugs. 'I'm really, really sorry, OK? It's like – I thought, I got to be extra careful with this, so I tucked it in the waistband of my trousers, yeah? And it must've just worked its way out.'

Again, I look at his father and his father looks at me.

When he's gone: 'Do you believe him?' I say.

His father sighs a long sigh. 'I can't bear it. I really do want to trust him, but—'

'The waistband.'

'Exactly.'

We're just starting a long, depressing talk about what's the best way to challenge Jack about this, when Becca comes back from a trip to the High Road. 'Hey guys, look what I just found lying on the pavement practically outside our front door!'

She's waving a twenty and two five-pound notes. 'It was just lying there, in the street. What do you think, there was no purse or anything, so is it OK to keep it? Please don't tell me I've got to take it to the police or something idiotic like that.' She stops a moment and looks at our faces. 'What? What is it? What's so fucking funny?'

Becca's Car

Becca's learning to drive. It was absolutely the only thing she wanted for her seventeenth birthday: driving lessons. 'So I can, like, drive myself to school and never ever have to wait for a bus ever again.'

Although we don't want to discourage her from learning such a useful skill, her father and I point out that, a) school is not so far away that you could really justify driving; b) that even if she learns, we can't possibly afford to buy her a car; and c) even if we did, we couldn't afford to insure it.

At this, she looks surprised. 'But why would it be expensive to insure someone like me?'

'You're a teenager. You're a liability,' her father explains, giving her hair an affectionate tug.

'But it's not like I go round getting drunk or stoned or breaking things like Ed. Or losing things, like Jack does.'

'Will I be expensive to insure?' Jack asks.

'I don't know what they think about people who can't even hold onto an Oyster card for a month,' his father says.

Jack shrugs. 'Anyway, all my friends get the bus. And I wouldn't want to not be able to drink and that.'

'You're not even sixteen,' I tell him, 'and you're talking like some binge-drinking 35-year-old.'

'Cars aren't that expensive,' says Becca, 'not second-hand ones. There are loads on eBay. I want a green one.'

'You mean something like a Prius?' asks her father, his eyes lighting up.

'Nah. Green! You know, apple-green. That would be sick!'

'You mean it would look like sick,' says Ed.

Unlike Becca, Eddie has never expressed even the smallest desire to learn to drive. And secretly, I suppose I'm with him. If I were a London teenager now, I don't think driving would be high on my list. But still there's something about our Becca's determination that I like. Nothing scares our Becca. I love her undiluted, kick-ass energy – the way she seems so ready to take on the world.

Meanwhile, something occurs to Jack: 'If you learn to drive, yeah, and you drive to school, well then you could give me a lift.'

Becca eyes him sharply, clearly weighing up the pros and cons of offering such a service. 'I could probably drive you,' she says slowly, glancing over at us, 'but you'd have to be ready to leave exactly when I wanted. And you realise you couldn't bring any of your fucking bowls of cereal in my nice clean car?'

Jack thinks about this for a moment. 'What about eggs?'

'No eggs!' snaps Becca. 'Don't you get it? My car's gonna be clean. I'm not having any shit left in it by anyone.'

'That's rich,' says her father, 'Little Miss chuck the lolly wrapper on the floor.'

'It's different when it's your own car,' replies his daughter without a trace of irony.

When her provisional driving licence arrives in the post, she brings it in to show me. 'Sick, yeah?'

'Very sick,' I agree.

And she continues to look at cars on eBay, telling me she's already started saving. But when the day of her first lesson arrives and the instructor – a nice, bearded man called Derek – pulls up outside, she stands in the hall in her coat, biting her lip and looking pale.

'Are you OK?' I ask her.

'Just, you know, what if I can't do it?'

'You'll be fine,' I tell her. 'Just don't expect too much from your first lesson. It's a whole new skill. You're not going to get it immediately.'

She goes out meekly. I see her bend her small head to talk to Derek. Then she gets in the passenger seat and, a couple of moments later, they drive off. My girl. I watch till she disappears around the corner.

Two hours later, the car reappears. At first I can't tell who's at the wheel. Or at least, the woman at the wheel looks a little bit like my Becca.

'Don't let her see you watching,' says her father, as the car pulls slowly up to the kerb and stops and I recognise the driver's tense, pale face.

'Wow,' I tell her father, 'it's her.'

He laughs softly but says nothing as his daughter gets out and bends to say goodbye to Derek. And it would be over-doing it to say I am holding back tears. But there's something so intensely incredible about seeing my girl drive up and park outside our house, when the image that is still lodged tight in my heart is of a fierce-eyed, black-haired toddler in a navy-blue terry-towelling Babygro.

becca and Jack

Maybe because she was still a baby herself when Jack was born, Becca and her younger brother have always had a special relationship. They've shared double buggies, bunk beds and sometimes (to Becca's fury) bedtimes. When they were little, Becca knew when Jack was hungry and she knew when he needed to do a poo. For a while she was also the only one who spoke his gobbledegook language, so she became his interpreter – telling us what he wanted, telling us what he meant, smoothing his way through the world.

And not much has changed. The two bicker constantly, but are pretty inseparable. Jack makes Becca laugh and Becca makes Jack lazy – she'll still do anything for him and he knows it. But just like an old married couple, they have their ups and downs. One moment, Becca will be trudging happily up to Jack's room with chocolate milk and biscuits. The next, she'll emerge screaming, hair flying, doors slamming.

'You son is, like, totally fucking disgusting!'

'What's he done?'

'Oh, only gobbing on the carpet and grinding it in with his shoe.'

'He really did that?'

'You think I'm lying? Don't worry. I know he only wants to get a reaction out of me, so I'm gonna do my best not to react.'

'Hey, well done for being so mature.'

Becca doesn't always manage not to react, though. I come down on a Saturday to find them attempting to cook lunch together in a not especially mature way. Jack has put too much spaghetti in the pan and then tried to take some out and fling it in the sink. He's also poured half a carton of cream into his sister's special healthy tuna and tomato sauce. And Becca's definitely reacting.

'How the fuck could you do that? You say you want me to cook you some lunch and now you're fucking it up and it's bare disgusting!'

Jack just laughs and lets out a burp.

'Mum!' Becca lets the wooden spoon drop back into the pan, spraying tomato sauce over the cooker. 'Did you hear that?'

'Jack, stop acting like a two-year-old.'

'Punish him!'

'I've long given up trying to punish you two.'

'Us two?!' wails Becca. 'Us two?! I love that. You act as if I've done something too, when I'm completely innocent.'

'OK,' I say, remembering how I loathed it when my own mum used to make out that my siblings and I were all as bad as each other, 'I didn't mean that, but really, darling, what am I supposed to do?'

'Fine him! Make him pay! Remember the other day, Dad said it was 50p for a burp and a pound for a fart?'

'Really?!' I burst out laughing and Jack eyes me with delight.

'Thanks a lot,' says Becca, stirring her sauce like a maniac. 'Your baby's wind-breaking is hilarious. You are so totally undermining me, Mum.'

'She's right you know,' her father tells me later. 'Jack's never going to grow up if you let him think you find this loutish behaviour funny.'

'I don't normally find it funny. It was just,' – I giggle again – 'the idea of the monetary value of a fart!'

Still, I go and find Becca and apologise. Luckily, she's already forgiven me. 'Maybe I did overreact a little bit,' she acknowledges with a sigh. 'It's just, you two together, you can be so maddening.' She smiles to herself.

'What?'

'Nothing. Just – that boy is so funny. Do you know, the other day he came to ask me where the dressing-up chest was.'

'What, the old dressing-up chest? The one we got rid of years ago?'

'Yeah, well you should tell him that. He was going to a fancy-dress party and he seemed to think his old Early Learning Centre pirate gear would still be there. He also seemed to have forgotten that he's, like, six-foot tall!'

'And the other night – get this – I found him wandering around on the landing at about midnight. And I asked him what was the matter and he said, "Becs, I can't sleep, can you give me some books?"'

'But he never reads.'

She chuckles. 'I know! He said it like he was asking for some kind of medicine or something. But you know what, you're just the same.'

'The same as Jack?'

'Yeah. Sometimes I think it's like me and Eddie and Dad, we're the grown-ups running the place. And you and Jack, it's like you've just been born or you don't know anything. You're just these two dumb little babies starting life all over again each day, right from scratch.'

Last Words

Except that there are no last words where teenagers are concerned – or not for parents anyway. All you really have is the comfort of knowing that life is fluid, that tricky phases pass (thank God) and other, differently tricky ones begin. And as teenagers turn into adults, maybe the balance of relationships and of power shifts. But the burning, wake-you-up-in-the-night sense of responsibility never fades – something my own mother illustrated for me perfectly the other day when, giving me a lift, she demanded to know if I'd done my seat-belt up.

Reading back over these weekly despatches now, I'm struck by the fact that both everything and nothing has changed. Eddie has left home. Kind of. For the moment. Probably. But most of his stuff is still here and he popped back just the other night for a bath, a meal and to sleep in his 'old bed' and see his cat.

And despite, apparently, being such a smoulderingly independent young man, he still makes a fuss about towels. The

369

problem was temporarily solved when I bought him a couple of horrible threadbare ones from a charity shop, and at least he thanked me. But what will happen in the future? Will he have to spend the rest of his life avoiding situations that might involve soft towels? Sweet, strange, impossible, baffling Eddie – who once asked for 'ordinary triangles of cheese' at a party because someone had the temerity to serve a hunk of cheddar instead of his beloved Dairylea. I love him so much.

Becca has changed. The angry, explosive girl we were all living with a few months ago has somehow swapped places with a person who is tender, careful, wise and (occasionally) vulnerable. Yes, she can still be unspeakably rude, and yes, her new pickiness about food drives us all insane, but there's a new uncertainty there – a wobbliness, bordering now and then on anxiety – which I'm keeping an eye on. She has always had so much of her father's no-nonsense intelligence, his sharpness and humour, but just recently I've been startled to discover how much of me seems to be in there too.

More than anything, though, my daughter is absolutely herself. Quite often these days, I see flashes of softness, of warmth and generosity and responsibility, all of which hint at the young woman she's on the edge of turning into. Becca and I hug each other easily and often. And when we do, she doesn't see that sometimes my eyes are full of tears.

And Jack. Oh Jack. As a sweet, placid third baby, you could

plonk Jack in a corner of any room and put something in his hand and he'd be happy. Holding a toy, or mouthing a piece of carrot, he'd eye the family chaos with an air of gurgling content. Even a year ago, Jack was still pretty much that same child – easygoing, friendly, careful to demand only whatever he was likely to get – but a few months and a big dose of hormones erased all that.

These days Jack (who, by the way, has still not lost his watch, but has recently mislaid an iPod, his science folder, a set of house keys and *two* pairs of school trousers) is a force to be reckoned with. I have this sense of my Jack out there in London, learning to survive in a city which isn't always kind to teenage boys. Some days, with his uneasy combination of fury and vulnerability, Jack breaks my heart. His father and I haven't quite yet worked out how to help him turn into a man. And maybe we can't help him do it. Maybe all we can do is stand back and watch and hope. Because along with the responsibility, parenthood also brings its own special sense of helplessness – something I'm still struggling to come to terms with.

The other day, Jack asked me if I ever wished I'd never had kids. I thought about it. 'I can see why you might ask that,' I told him truthfully, 'but the funny and wonderful thing is, I don't think anyone ever regrets becoming a parent. It's like, you have a baby and something in you just changes.'

He scowled as if he didn't believe me.

'It's like the bit of you that used to look out only for your-self kind of shrinks to make room for someone else. Someone you care about even more than that self.'

'I think I'd hate that,' said Jack.

'No, the funny thing is, this makes you happier than you ever thought possible. Well, happier and sadder actually.'

'You mean how you cried so much when Eddie was born?' said Becca, who'd been listening carefully to this.

'Did I cry?'

'You said you did. You said that when you realised how much you loved him and how you couldn't bear for anything to ever happen to him and all that, you just burst into tears and Dad had to comfort you.'

An image floated back to me. Eddie, wrapped in a white baby blanket, asleep on our vast bed. Eddie, eyes and fists tight shut, smaller even than the pillow.

'That's true. I did. I wanted to be Eddie's mum, but a part of me almost couldn't stand the responsibility – the full-time, full-on loving feeling of it. It was exactly the same feeling I have now about all three of you. It never stops, the love feeling. I can't stop thinking and caring about you. Even when I'm away from you, you're so completely in my mind.'

'But that sounds like such fucking hard work,' sighed Jack who always (still!) looks for an easy way. 'What I don't see is why you and Dad didn't just have one child? I think when

I'm older I might just have one, then I'll get some time for my own life too.'

'But that's just it,' I said, 'they're not separate. Your child – your children – they *are* your life and anything else you want to do or be sits alongside them. And that's fine too. It's hard to explain, but it just doesn't feel like any sort of sacrifice.'

'I'm going to have at least five kids,' Becca said. 'I want three girls and two boys.'

'That's only because you like thinking up names,' said Jack. 'Why not have cats instead?'

'It is not! What a rubbish thing to say!'

'Anyway, you could never look after five. If you can't even take the dog out for one single fucking walk . . .'

'And you couldn't look after even one single child. The idea of you as anyone's dad just makes me want to burst out laughing!'

But it was me who was laughing. Because I was about to say something else, but I realised there was no point. You don't get many windows for serious talking with teenagers and this one had passed.

What I was going to say was this:

Having children is an optimistic act. Isn't it really the most optimistic thing a person can do – make another person and try to love them enough and keep them safe, then send them out into the world, to live and love and maybe make children of their own? It's an act of hope, it really is. And hope might be a flimsy thing, but in the end isn't it all we have? That, and our love.

Postscript

When, almost exactly two years ago, I sat down to write the first 'Living with Teenagers' column for *The Guardian*, I had only one real intention: to be as direct and truthful as I could bear. To tell it like it is – or like it seemed to be, back then, for us anyway. Did I feel bad about not telling our children? Not really. I imagined I might write half a dozen (completely anonymous) columns and then call it a day. By the time they found out, it would all be over and, anyway, we'd have moved on. And one day they'd see the funny side – wouldn't they?

But two years – and more than a hundred columns and a book – later, I admit I feel a bit differently. Yes, the writing slowly stopped being a chore and became a comfort, a delight, a reliable way of letting off steam. I laughed so much as I remembered heated conversations, apparently intractable situations, tearful arguments we'd had. The great and wonderful thing was that nothing ever seemed half as bad in the recollection. Writing it all down gave me persepctive, restored my calm, made me count my blessings.

Of course, honest as they claimed to be, the columns didn't really tell the whole truth. How could they? I was as selective as all authors always are. I had total control over what I chose and chose not to reveal. I did try very hard to be as tough on myself as I was on the rest of the family, but I'm not sure I always managed it. Certainly, I could never claim I'd drawn a clear-eyed portrait of my three teenagers. It's naturally skewed and incomplete, forever viewed through a mother's frazzled, hectic, subjective and – I hope – passionately loving eye.

Still, the columns do fairly truthfully reflect the arc of our lives over two years. The changes in our children – and in our relationships with them – have been, to us, miraculous. And, reading back over the columns now, I can see the clues scattered here and there, the small beginnings of all those changes. All three of them have grown up so much – in blissful and graceful and unexpected ways. It just goes to prove right what I suspected at the beginning: that teenagerhood isn't so very different to toddlerhood. Just like the Terrible Twos, the Terrible Fifteens/Sixteens/Seventeens do pass. Just hold on in there. They will pass for you. They almost have for us.

But as, over those two years, our teenagers bloomed and matured and softened and became so much more vulnerable, so the column began to feel less like some kind of benign, semi-comic revenge and more like a betrayal. Many people wrote in to thank me – I'd saved their lives, restored their sanity, made them feel so much less alone. And thank you so much, your messages of solidarity have meant a great deal to me. But others were outraged. What kind of a mother did I think I was? Did I really have so little control over my kids? And, anyway, how could I do this to them?

And I didn't really have answers to those questions. The truth is, I could – and still can – see both sides, and it isn't always a good feeling. Was I wrong to write about my kids? I do so hope not, but it's hard to know for sure. Have I got any better at dealing with them? Well, today, after the scenes we had at breakfast, I'd say no. But ask me tomorrow and I'll probably give you a whole dfferent answer. Do I feel like a good enough parent? Are you crazy? Hardly ever! Can I live with that? Hmm. Well, I'm doing my best.

There was only one thing I'd always been clear on: if ever the kids found out, I would stop. Immediately. Completely. No questions asked. There was no way I would (or could) continue writing with them knowing what I was doing. And in the end, of course, they did find out. On a Sunday lunchtime they confronted me: their friends were insisting this so-called column couldn't possibly be about anyone but them . . . so, was it? I glanced at their father, blushed – and confessed. And they weren't impressed. The next few days were tough and I deserved it.

And so to my kids: Eddie, Becca, Jack. Those aren't their

real names, of course, and their real selves are so much sweeter and more complex and more unique than I could ever possibly begin to convey to you on the page. They've dealt with all of this so heroically, with such characteristic good sense and good heart and good humour. But I'd like to take a last opportunity to beg their forgiveness and to say that I really hope that one day they'll pick up this book and read these accounts of their delectable teenage selves – frozen in a time that by then will seem so painfully long ago – and laugh. I also hope they'll see what I know is true: that they were observed and written about with nothing but love, love, love.

February 2009